INTRODUCING LIBERATIVE THEOLOGIES

Introducing Liberative Theologies

Miguel A. De La Torre
editor

Maryknoll, New York 10545

Founded in 1970, Orbis Books endeavors to publish works that enlighten the mind, nourish the spirit, and challenge the conscience. The publishing arm of the Maryknoll Fathers and Brothers, Orbis seeks to explore the global dimensions of the Christian faith and mission, to invite dialogue with diverse cultures and religious traditions, and to serve the cause of reconciliation and peace. The books published reflect the views of their authors and do not represent the official position of the Maryknoll Society. To learn more about Maryknoll and Orbis Books, please visit our website at www.maryknollsociety.org.

Published by Orbis Books, Box 302, Maryknoll, NY 10545-0302.
Manufactured in the United States of America

Library of Congress Cataloging-in-Publication Data

Introducing liberative theologies / Miguel A. De La Torre, editor.
pages cm
Includes bibliographical references and index.
ISBN 978-1-62698-140-9 (pbk.)
1. Liberation theology. I. De La Torre, Miguel A., editor.
BT83.57.I59 2015
230'.0464—dc23

2015009995

To the memory of one of the forerunners of Latin American liberation theology and my intellectual mentor

"As always, it is the humble, the shoeless, the needy, the fishermen who band together shoulder to shoulder to fight injustice and make the Gospel fly with its silver wings aflame! Truth is revealed more clearly to the poor and the sufferers! A piece of bread and a glass of water never deceive!"

—José Julian Martí

Contents

Part II: The U.S. Racial, Ethnic, and Class Context

Preface

I was at first hesitant when Orbis Books approached me to write an introductory text on liberation theology. A few decades ago the task would have seemed relatively easier; one could simply look at the conversation occurring in Latin America, mainly among Catholics, and discuss the contributions they were making to the overall theological discourse. But much has changed since then; specifically, liberation theology began to manifest itself among different types of communities. Some believe that liberation theology began in Latin America and then spread to North America, and from there to the rest of the world; but such an assertion is erroneous. If we claim that liberation theology is rooted in how the oppressed theologically reflect on the liberative actions in which they are engaged, then a liberative movement has always existed among the disenfranchised. The question is not which came first or which manifestation of the theology influenced whom; but rather, how do different manifestations of liberative theologies coexist and strengthen one another?

Another misconception is that liberation theology was a 1960s theological fad, leaving many to wonder if what we called liberation theology was still valid in the new millennium. Gustavo Gutiérrez, who is often credited for being among the first to articulate a Latin American liberation theology, said it best during the 1996 convention of the American Academy of Religion in New Orleans: While all theologies are born to die, a theological voice from the margins will always exist. Latin American liberation theology of the 1960s through 1980s was important and true for those suffering under the brutal U.S.-backed military dictatorships of that era. But today Latin America, like the rest of the world, exists under vastly different circumstances. What was known as liberation theology a few decades ago must radically change to be relevant for those suffering under more sophisticated global structures of oppression.

All too often we codify theologies as representations of eternal truths. What we call Scholasticism, Lutheranism, or Calvinism (just to name a few) tells us more about those engaged in these theological conversations of the past than it tells us about God. All theologies serve an important purpose within a brief moment in time before they are destined to die. And let the dead bury the dead.

The danger is found when the spiritual descendants of some past theological discourse attempt to immortalize the conversations of some distant era, feverishly trying to make it applicable to their vastly different present-day context. Whatever God may be, God is not static. How we come to understand God and God's message must change to match the new forces of prevailing death-dealing theologies and ideologies.

Each generation has the responsibility to find a word from God within the chaos of its own time. This is not to reject or dismiss the work done in the past by some of the earlier liberationist thinkers; but it is to build on their work, and, when needed, change or update their thought so as to adequately respond to the challenges faced today. Those committed to liberationist theologies are less interested with constructing eternal truths than they are with interpreting the signs of the times so that a justice-based message can be fashioned, aware that said message may very well be temporal, developed by, for, and with those suffering oppression today. The goal of liberative theologies is not the creation and proclamation of ethereal abstract concepts to tickle the fancy of a small group of academics who remain disconnected from the flesh-and-blood reality of those among the least of the least. Rather, the goal is to change the structures by engaging in praxis, action; moving humanity toward a more justice-based existence. This is not to dismiss the importance of rigorous academic scholarship, but it is to place the focus on proclaiming good news to the poor, freeing those captive to political and economic structures of oppression, raising the consciousness of those who refuse to see, bringing liberation to the oppressed, and proclaiming God's good favor for humanity.

This textbook explores how theologies considered liberative are globally manifested today. To engage in liberative theologies is be concerned with forging a justice-based social order interested with the liberation, understood as salvation, of those who are denied humanity and those whose humanity is lost as they pursue power and privilege at the expense of the disenfranchised. Our goal is to expose the reader to liberative theological concepts from the perspective of marginalized communities through the presentations of those residing within the communities of faith from which they write. To do theology from the margins of power forces the reader to move beyond a traditional understanding of the faith, one that masks how those privileged by the religious tradition present their faith to the Euro-American audience. Rather, it shows how the vast majority of believers who exist on the underside of power and privilege interpret the same faith for daily survival. To do theology from the margins becomes a life-affirming venture that is liberating for the oppressed as well as for the readers of this textbook—whose consciousness, we hope, will also be raised.

My hesitation in writing an introduction to liberative theology was based on concerns about faithfully capturing the contexts from which different liberative theological perspectives arose. To write an introduction to liberative theologies with integrity requires a matrix of voices from different marginalized communities. And even while such a methodology falls short of perfection (can any one individual truly represent an entire people-group?), the alternative of simply having one voice limited by a particular social context speak for all would have proven much more problematic. To that end, I agreed to spearhead this project as an editor rather than an author. In other words, space was created to bring together different voices (grant you, due to space limitation, not all voices) from different communities to discuss their perspectives from within their particular contexts.

Additionally, it was not my desire simply to create an anthology of essays that may or may not necessarily be interconnected. Hence, each participant of this project was given specific instructions. All the chapters follow the same format so that the entire book can appear as a unified work. Each chapter is structured to cover (1) the basic tenets of liberative theology within their particular group, specifically the theology's historical development; (2) why a need for liberation exists, paying close attention to the specific social structures responsible for oppression and the particular issues and questions with which their particular group wrestles; and (3) some of the main themes and methodologies employed by their particular group, paying close attention to leading scholars and figures and possible future trends. In addition, study questions, glossaries, sidebars, and textboxes fleshing out the theology were added to each chapter. It is our hope that the reader is exposed to the richness and diversity of liberative theological thought and gains a sufficient working knowledge to conduct further exploration.

One of the important themes of liberationist thought is the communal nature of conducting theology. Moving away from the typical ivory-tower approach of ethereal abstractions divorced from the everyday experiences of the least among us, this was a project conducted *en conjunto*, that is, a project done not in isolation but as a conversation with our respective communities. In a very real way, my task was simply to bring these voices together; therefore, I am deeply indebted to my colleagues who not only agreed to participate in this project but who just as importantly adhered to a strict timeline and willingly rewrote sections I targeted without any hesitation. It is always a pleasure to work with colleagues such as these.

Introduction

Miguel A. De La Torre

Theology is the English translation of the Greek word *theologia* (θεολογία), derived from two words: *theos* (θεός), which means God, and *logia* (λογία), which connotes "the study of" or "the branch of knowledge concerning." Although theology can be and normatively is defined as the study of God, where the subject God becomes the object of what is being studied, such a definition—unfortunately—is extremely limited. To assume God can objectively be fully known or understood is problematic (if not blasphemous). What we can know is how God is understood by different cultures, and more importantly, by different groups within the same culture.

Perhaps what we really must be asking is: *who* is doing the studying of God? In reality, theology has less to do with God than with how a particular group of people, limited by geography, epoch, historical experiences, and identity, constructs the branch of knowledge concerning the metaphysical—that which is beyond their finite minds. We know who God is based on how the concept of God is created by a particular segment of a culture or society. Hence, to understand who God is, it becomes crucial if not essential to focus on those with the social power and capital to determine who is God for the rest of society. To assert therefore that any particular understanding of God is both universal and complete becomes highly problematical, if not the source of oppression. Whatever theology is, it is but a contextualized perspective. All too often, people-groups have fused and confused their constructed theological perspectives with absolute truth, asserting that their particular understanding of God is true and universal for all people during all times. This type of certainty is the source of so much of the world's past and present marginalization.

Perhaps a better definition for theology should be the study of people-groups' understanding of God (or lack thereof), thus highlighting those constructing the knowledge of God as the subject of the word "theology." If the focus is placed on those "doing the studying," we could expect that however they (or we) define God is true only for that particular group, and we can expect said definition of God to differ from how other groups, separated by geography, identity, and time, might understand God. This is not to say that

God is a relative concept, but that no one group can fully capture the knowledge of God. The biblical text reminds us that "For as high as the heavens are from the earth; so too are my [God's] ways higher than your ways, and my thoughts higher than your thoughts" (Isa. 55:9). Even those who claim theological truth because they received some holy writ or revelation directly from God can in reality claim, with any integrity, only that their interpretation of said scripture or revelation remains subjective to the limitations of their particular context and influenced by the components of said context. Nevertheless, history has shown that those who control the instruments of societal power are usually able to claim a monopoly on theological truth to the detriment of everyone else, particularly the disenfranchised.

Ideologies and social structures are shaped and formed by individuals, who are in turn shaped and formed by these same ideologies and social structures. Like everyone else, those engaged in theological discourse are born into a society where the dialectical relation between the person and the community informs one's religious beliefs and one's character—in short, one's identity. For this reason, the sociohistorical context of any people profoundly contributes to the construction of their understanding of God and of their theology. This becomes dangerous whenever any one group has the cultural, economic, social, political, and linguistic capital to make their limited perspective universal for everyone else. This is further complicated when they can name their limited perspective as true and label those that diverge from what they established as normative as wrong, evil, or Satanic. Rivers of blood have flowed throughout history (think of the witch trials, the Inquisition, genocides, the Crusades, or the religious wars of the past and present) because of the power of one group to make their subjective understanding of God normative for everyone else. Their construction of their theological perspectives and interpretations have more often than not provided license to decimate "heretics," who refused to accept the theology they constructed. Humanity has experienced and continues to experience the greatest human rights violations by the hands of those claiming faithfulness to whatever their theology happens to be.

This historical dilemma leads us to begin this introduction by asking not if God exists, and if so, who is God, but instead by focusing on those who are studying God. How a wealthy Hindu businessman of the 1600s living in China understands God(s) will be radically different from that of a poor undocumented Latina living today in East Los Angeles. Context, more so than doctrines, tenets, rituals, or practices, is a crucial aspect of understanding who is God (at least for those trying to understand God). But not all contexts are the same; hence, the usage of the plural in the title of this book—"theologies" as oppose to the singular "theology." There is not one true theology, but a multiplicity of theologies true within many different shades of contexts. If there is such a thing as "ultimate truth," then the closest that can be achieved is through discourse among different contexts; for by hearing the other's truth, I can discover the weaknesses and inconsistencies existing within my own version of truth. Books such as this one are crucial as we wrestle with one another in our joint effort across different identities to study God—to do theology.

Our station and status within society determine the God we have come to define. While all understandings of God are valid to those doing the constructing, not all understandings are liberating. In fact, more often than not, understandings of God impose rules, restrictions, regulations, and restraints on vast segments of humanity. With this in mind, we will begin with an unapologetic methodology for studying God, for doing theology. As liberative thinkers, we will construct our subjective theological perspectives from a particular segment of society, specifically the margins of society. Furthermore, we possess the audacity to claim that to conceptualize theology from and in solidarity with the margins of society comes closer to a clear and true understanding of God over and against those who construct their theology from a position of power and privilege.

Through the ages, the sole interpreters of reality have been the political and economic elites. The perspectives of the dominant culture (within a particular society or the global Eurocentric culture) have been and continue to be the norms by which the rest of society is judged for being theologically sound or heretical. The power to make one's subjective theology objectively normative contains the hidden agenda of creating theological interpretations and justifications that protect the self-interest of those whom society privileges, those who usually have the power to construct the theology in the first place. Consequently, which theological "truths" are chosen or discarded becomes an act that establishes power relationships.

Choosing one theological precept over another justifies those who will eventually benefit from whichever was chosen to be theological truth. Once members of the dominant culture recognize the theological precepts that support their lifestyle, claims of absolutism can be made. Legitimizing the dominant culture's theological perspectives advances their power within the social structures as moral "truths" and justifies their particular social context as ordained by God. The theology advocated by the dominant culture legitimizes power—specifically, who has it, and how it is to be used. And those who object to these theological concepts are not only opposing the power relationships created by the dominant culture but more seriously are seen as contesting the very authority of God. As such, they are defined as "evil" for questioning and challenging God and country.

To do theological analysis from the margins of society, that is, to study God from the context of the disenfranchised, makes the role of power paramount in the development of any theological discourse. The quest for any theological "truth" by those who are marginalized becomes a response to the use, misuse, and abuse of power rather than adherence to religious traditions, issues of doctrines, church teachings, tenets, or spiritual rituals or practices. We begin our liberative theological quest with those who experience massive, ever-present oppression, while remaining cognizant that not all who are marginalized have similar experiences. The world's oppressed are not some monolithic group.

Because all theologies are contextual (including Eurocentric theologies) the theological reflections of one disenfranchised group cannot simply be exported into a different social location as if it were some sort of commodity. And while different societal constructs create different forms of oppression, liberative theology begins with the existential location of the poor, the oppressed, the dispossessed, the marginalized, the outcast, and the disenfranchised. To engage in liberative theology is to begin with, and from, the perspective of those whom society has cast away, the so-called (no)bodies of history, cognizant that God makes a preferential option for the poor and oppressed over and against the pharaohs of this world.

Wherever there is oppression, there too exists resistance, a cry for liberation uttered from the depths of the inhuman condition in which the vast majority of the world's population are forced to exist. At times, this resistance takes form in the language of faith, becoming a theological understanding of and a call for liberation from death-dealing social structures. Theologies of liberation are spiritual responses to unexamined social structures responsible for oppressing a marginalized majority so that a privileged powerful minority can live abundant lives. Any liberative theology is deeply concerned with fostering life, as opposed to the prevalent theologies of death that remain complicit with social, political, and economic structures responsible for disenfranchisement, dispossession, disempowerment, and destitution.

A preferential option is made for theologies that celebrate life; it rejects those theologies, along with those who study them, that instead bring or are complicit with death (literal death as well as spiritual death). We currently live in a world where, according to the United Nations Food and Agriculture Organization, 850 million people, or about 12.5 percent of the global population, experienced hunger or were malnourished between 2010 and 2012. By 2010, of the roughly seven billion inhabitants of the earth, about 1.75 billion in 104 countries, consisting of about one-third of their population, lived in multidimensional poverty. This world in which we live operates on global economic policies that produce much of the marginalization experienced by the least among us.

The globalization of the economy, coupled with the military strength held by a few nations (specifically the United States), ensures and maintains a continual flow of cheap labor and raw materials to a privileged minority of the world's population. Not surprisingly, the rich become fewer yet wealthier, while the poor continue to add to their numbers while they slip into greater poverty. Ironically, those who benefit from these arrangements have constructed theologies that either justify or ignore the global structures responsible for much of the misery experienced by the "least of these." Underdevelopment at the global periphery is the by-product of the development of European centers. The gluttonous consumption of the world's resources by the dominant culture within First World nations is not only theologically indefensible but also the root cause of much of the present global political instability.

Global oppression and marginalization are real. The question asked by liberative theologians standing in solidarity with the world's wretched is not if there is a God, but what is the character of this God we profess exists in the face of these global oppressive structures? What word does this God have for the world's disenfranchised? And is this word a static noun or a verb? What we need to ask is if a theological response to the decimation of so many of the planet's inhabitants exists. What does a religious response uttered from the depths of inhuman conditions look like? Those of us who identify as liberation theologians argue that ignoring the world's oppressed is a modern form of idolatry, privileging materialism over and against humanity. Resistance to the powers and principalities of this world responsible for so much global misery becomes foundational to what will eventually be termed liberation theology.

Any religious, spiritual, or faith-based discourse (not necessarily Christian) that seeks dismantlement of oppressive global social structures responsible for causing much poverty and oppression can be called liberative. It is important to note that I make a subtle difference between liberation theology and liberative theologies. Liberation theology is rooted within Christian faith (originally Catholic), while liberative theologies need not be Christian. Liberative theologies can be found among Muslims, Hindus, Buddhists, or even humanists. Whatever liberation finally looks like can only be determined by the local people who are living under oppressive structures.

To engage in liberative theologies is to seriously consider the social, political, and economic contexts of the disenfranchised. From the margins of power and privilege, a fuller, more comprehensive understanding of the prevailing social structures can be ascertained. Not because those on the margins are more astute but because they know what it means to be a marginalized person attempting to survive within a social context designed to benefit the privileged few at their expense.

Liberative theologies are based on praxis, an action, that informs theology, rather than the reverse, theology informing action. The focus of liberative theologies is praxis oriented, moving away from orthodoxy (correct *doctrine*) toward orthopraxis (correct *actions*), which is a necessity if the goal is to bring about salvation, understood as liberation. Like liberation theology, liberative theologies make a preferential option for the oppressed; however, in doing so, they may—but not necessarily—be centered on Christian thought and beliefs. The theological task is not to reverse roles between those who are oppressed and those who are privileged by the present institutionalized structures, nor to share the role of privileged at the expense of some other newer group; but, rather, to dismantle the very structures responsible for causing injustices. Justice-based praxis, engaged in transforming society, brings individuals closer to understanding the spiritual.

Any theology constructed within the dominant culture may critique and demand reform of the social structures that privilege that culture's race, ethnicity, gender, orientation, class, and/or physical ability; but seldom does a call emerge to dismantle these very same social structures. The theology of the dominant culture may appear sympathetic to the plight of the marginalized, and may even call for charity as an appropriate response; nevertheless, seldom will a proactive call be made that might threaten that culture's privileged place within society. History has taught us that those holding unequal power seldom willingly give up said power for the sake of the powerless. However, unless the power and privilege of the few are dismantled, the marginalized (as well as those who benefit from their marginalization) can never achieve their full humanity.

Obviously, no liberative theology exists on which all marginalized groups agree. Nor does a neat dichotomy exist between those who are oppressed and their oppressors. The reality is that within different marginalized groups, structures of oppression also exist based on skin pigmentation (who is closer to the white ideal), gender, physical ability, sexual identity, and class. At other times, marginalized groups are pitted against one another for limited resources. Any intellectual resistance against injustice must include a concerted effort to eliminate the abuses of all oppressed groups, even when the disenfranchised participate in the oppression of those groups they see as other. Although it is obvious that differences, particularly in cultural expressions, exist among numerous marginalized groups, a shared common history of disenfranchisement and the common problems of such a history create an opportunity to work together to dismantle oppressive structures that affect all who live on the periphery of power and privilege. And while equal access to the socioeconomic resources of our society is desirable, the marginalized must stand vigilant of the danger of simply surmounting the present existing structures that cause oppression. Not until separate marginalized groups begin to accompany one another in the work of theological reflection that is based on praxis (understood here as the dismantling of oppressive structures) can the hold of the dominant culture upon the normative and legitimate definition of theology be challenged. This introductory text is an attempt to begin this conversation among different marginalized groups in the hope that we all can learn how to accompany one another in the struggle for a more just society.

Contributors

Jorge A. Aquino is Associate Professor of Theology and Religious Studies at the University of San Francisco, in California. A member of the university's Latin American Studies faculty, Aquino teaches on liberation theologies, Latin American religious history, religious social movements, and critical race studies. He has served as president of the Academy of Catholic Hispanic Theologians of the United States (2014–2015). He also served as cochair of the "Religion in Latin America and the Caribbean Group" of the American Academy of Religion (2007–2011).

Sophia Rose Arjana holds a B.A. in Pacific Island Studies, M.A. in Art History, M.T.S. in Theology and Ethics, and Ph.D. in Religion. She is a scholar of Islam and comparative religion and has published books and journal articles on Orientalism and race, postcolonial liturgy in Islam, and Shi'a pilgrimage and shrine architecture. Dr. Arjana's first monograph, *Muslims in the Western Imagination*, was published in 2015. Her forthcoming book examines the great variety of Islamic pilgrimages, from *hajj* to shared Hindu-Muslim sites, and will be published by in 2016.

Sharon V. Betcher is an independent scholar, writer, "crip philosopher," and farmer living on Whidbey Island, Washington. She is the author of *Spirit and the Politics of Disablement* (Fortress, 2007) and *Spirit and the Obligation of Social Flesh: A Secular Theology for Global Cities* (Fordham University Press, 2014), as well as of multiple theological essays in diverse collections. Her constructive theological contributions are worked through the critical lenses of ecological, postcolonial, gender, and disability studies theory.

Rebecca A. Chabot is a social ethicist who focuses on the ethics of professional club soccer where soccer is understood as a religion. She is an ardent FC Bayern München fan and serves as the Bayern editor for GSO Football. She has a B.A. in theology from Creighton University, an M.Div. from Boston College School of Theology and Ministry, and is a proud Minnesotan who spent a year as a full-time volunteer with the St. Joseph Worker Program.

Hugo Córdova Quero holds a Ph.D. in interdisciplinary studies in religion, ethnicity, and migration (2009) and an M.A. in systematic theology and critical theories (feminist, queer, and postcolonial) (2003), both from the

Graduate Theological Union in Berkeley, California. Currently he is an Adjunct Faculty member at Starr King School for the Ministry (SKSM) at the Graduate Theological Union and Researcher at the program on multiculturalism, migration, and inequality in Latin America, Center for Advanced Studies at the National University of Córdoba/CONICET, in Córdoba, Argentina. Additionally, he is member of EQARS and editor of the journal *Religión e Incidencia Pública.*

Miguel A. De La Torre is a scholar-activist and ordained minister. Since obtaining his doctorate in 1999, he has published over thirty books, five of which have won national awards. He presently serves as Professor of Social Ethics and Latino/a Studies at Iliff School of Theology in Denver, Colorado. He was elected the 2012 president of the Society of Christian Ethics. Additionally, he is the editor of the *Journal of Race, Ethnicity, and Religion* (www.raceandreligion.com), and serves as executive officer for the Society of Race, Ethnicity and Religion.

Rodolfo J. Hernández-Díaz teaches at the Iliff School of Theology in Denver, Colorado. He serves on the steering committee of the Latina/o Religion, Culture, and Society Group and the Latina/o Critical and Comparative Studies Group of the American Academy of Religion. He has published a number of essays on Hispanic liberative theology. His current research focuses on the intersection of political economy ethics and marginalized communities.

Travis T. Judkins is a doctoral learner and Kingdom Diversity Scholar at Southeastem Baptist Theological Seminary in Wake Forest, North Carolina. He holds a Master of Divinity (2013), concentrating in the area of Hebrew Bible/Old Testament, from Shaw University Divinity School. His academic research focuses on biblical interpretation as a catalyst to speak to issues of inequality: race, class, and gender; postcolonial theory; African American liberative theologies; and interreligous dialogue. Judkins is a noted preacher-scholar and ordained Baptist minister with more than ten years of pastoral experience and a former adjunct instructor of Religion and Humanities at Halifax Community College in Weldon, North Carolina. He currently serves as an adjunct instructor in the Department of Religion and Philosophy at Shaw University, Raleigh, North Carolina.

Grace Ji-Sun Kim is Visiting Researcher at Georgetown University. She is the author of six books, *Theological Reflections on "Gangnam Style"* (co-written with Joseph Cheah); *Reimagining with Christian Doctrines* (co-edited with Jenny Daggers); *Contemplations from the Heart*; *Colonialism, Han and the Transformative Spirit*; *The Holy Spirit, Chi, and the Other*; and *The Grace of*

Sophia. She is a co-editor with Joseph Cheah of the Palgrave Macmillan book series Asian Christianity in Diaspora. Kim serves on the American Academy of Religion's Research Grants Jury Committee and is also a co-chair of AAR's steering committee for the Women of Color Scholarship, Teaching and Activism Group. She sits on the editorial board of the *Journal for Religion and Popular Culture.*

Cheryl A. Kirk-Duggan is Professor of Religion and Director of Women's Studies at Shaw University Divinity School (Raleigh, NC). She is the 2009 and 2011 recipient of the Shaw University Excellence in Research Award, is author and editor of over twenty books and numerous articles, and is an ordained elder in the Christian Methodist Episcopal Church. She is the 2011 YWCA Academy of Women Honoree in Education, a 2011 Black Religious Scholars Group Honoree, and a 2012 Womanist Legend Awardee. Her research and teaching are interdisciplinary, liberationist, theoretical, and practical. Her recent co-authored work with Marlon Hall is *Wake Up! Hip Hop, Christianity, and the Black Church.*

Sarah A. Neeley is an ethicist whose work focuses on economic justice with a particular interest in criminalization laws and unaccompanied homeless women. She uses ethnographic methods and Christology to suggest kinship as a way of addressing homelessness in the United States.

Joseph Ogbonnaya is a priest of Awgu Catholic diocese, Nigeria, and Assistant Professor of Theology at Marquette University in Milwaukee, Wisconsin. He is the author of *Lonergan, Social Transformation and Sustainable Human Development* (2013) and *African Catholicism and Hermeneutics of Culture: Essays in the Light of African Synod II* (2014), and co-editor of *The Church as Salt and Light* (2011).

Joerg Rieger is Wendland-Cook Professor of Constructive Theology at Perkins School of Theology, Southern Methodist University, Dallas, Texas. Known for his prolific and visionary writing, his most recent books include *Religion, Theology, and Class* (2013), *Occupy Religion: Theology of the Multitude* (2012), *Grace under Pressure* (2011), *Globalization and Theology* (2010), *No Rising Tide: Theology, Economics, and the Future* (2009), and *Christ and Empire* (2007). Rieger is on the steering committee of Jobs with Justice in North Texas and is co-founder of the Workers' Rights Board in the Dallas area.

Andrea Smith is Associate Professor of Ethnic Studies and Media and Cultural Studies at the University of California Riverside. She is the co-editor of *Theorizing Native Studies* and author of *Native Americans and the Christian Right.*

Jonathan Y. Tan is the Archbishop Paul J. Hallinan Professor of Catholic Studies at Case Western Reserve University, Cleveland, Ohio. He holds a Ph.D. from The Catholic University of America and is the author of *Introducing Asian American Theologies* (Orbis Books, 2008) and *Christian Mission among the Peoples of Asia* (Orbis Books, 2014). He writes on issues in Asian and Asian American Christianity, World Christianity, and mission studies.

Part I

The Global Context

1

Latin American Liberative Theologies

Jorge A. Aquino

No one ever invited me to the funeral of liberation theology—and I think I've done a thing or two to deserve such an invitation.
— Gustavo Gutiérrez, *La Opción por los Pobres Hoy*

The philosophers have only interpreted the world, in various ways; the point is to change it.
— Karl Marx, *Theses on Feuerbach*

Liberating Theology and Society in the Americas

If we wish to speak of the roots of *liberative theologies,* we must begin in Latin America in the 1960s, when Christianity awoke to the cry of the poor and fashioned what Peruvian theologian Gustavo Gutiérrez called *a theology of liberation.* The liberation theology that emerged from Latin America in the years following was no mere rearranging of deck chairs atop the great vessel of Christian dogma. It proposed a *revolution* in the life of Roman Catholicism, as ancient Judeo-Christian ideas of social justice merged with a broad front of progressive Third World social movements that arose after World War II. Its ideas were engaged throughout world Christianity, inspiring Protestant theologies of liberation as well as proposals for liberative religious thought from Judaism, Islam, and even nontheistic religions such as Buddhism.

Liberation theology arose not just out of "revolutionary" ideas but out of what theologians would call a *kairos:* a propitious moment when God's will for history seemed to be manifesting itself with a particularly inescapable force. For many, Christianity was opening itself to what Gutiérrez called "an evermore worldly world," and the great awakening of the poor and marginalized peoples of the world was a true *sign of the times.* Liberation theology's principal contribution to Christian thought and praxis was the *preferential option for the poor,* a proposal that the churches orient all their work around the needs of the poorest and most vulnerable in society, because in the deepest

Option for the poor: a policy, adopted after 1968, by which the Latin American Catholic Church would orient its pastoral planning and activities, and its theological reflections, from the standpoint of the poorest and most vulnerable in society.

Decolonial social movements: any number of political or militarized/guerrilla movements seeking an end to foreign control over the internal economic, political, and cultural affairs of one's own country. Typically, one thinks of decolonial movements as living in antagonism with the established capitalist societies of the industrialized world—most often Europe and the United States.

Ecclesial Base Communities: Known by their Spanish acronym CEB (*Comunidades Eclesiales de Base*), base communities were units of Catholic parishes throughout the Americas where Christian formation, Bible study, political organizing, and antipoverty activism merged under the influence of liberation theology.

reading of Christian tradition this represents the clearest sense of God's will for history.

The preferential option for the poor has been a point on the compass of the Latin American church since 1968. It is rooted in the social-justice discourse of the Hebrew Bible and in the teachings of Jesus of Nazareth. But its modern emergence in liberation theology's option for the poor has a historical trajectory that includes (1) the modernization of Roman Catholic social teaching, culminating in the reforms of the Second Vatican Council (1962–1965); (2) the deep turn to the world one sees in Christian lay culture and social movements; and (3) the ideological influence of Latin America's decolonial movements, from the nineteenth-century independence struggles to the Cuban Revolution of 1959 to today's antiglobalization movements.

This global merging of passions for modernization, activism, and decolonization brought about a massive turning of the Christian gaze from transcendent mysteries in the unknowable heavens to very concrete questions of politics, economics, and the ethics of social relations. In Latin America, that turn was concretized by tens of thousands of Christian Ecclesial Base Communities (CEBs, after the Spanish acronym, *Comunidades Eclesiales de Base*) that sprang up throughout the Americas starting in the late 1950s.

These communities became centers of Christian formation and Bible study, but the primary contribution of the base communities to the edification of Christianity was in matters of social and economic development in the many areas where CEBs were active. Literacy efforts and Bible study together unlocked both the truth about an oppressive social reality *and* the realization that God's will for the poor was not for them to accept their poverty passively but to fight it.

Because *liberation theology* names both a theological perspective *and* the base communities that practiced it, liberation theology ought to be presented more as a religious and theological social movement than as some laundry list of perspectives on God, Christ, the church, the human person, and salvation. To that end, this chapter will consider the perspective of Catholic and Christian theologies of liberation by reviewing three developments that define late-modern Christianity:

1. Modernity, secularization, and liberation. This section discusses the five-hundred-year unfolding of modernization in the West and in Latin America that secularized Christianity and made possible the activist worldview out of which liberation theology emerged. I treat this shift largely according to the way Gustavo Gutiérrez framed the modern condition of theological work in his classic book *A Theology of Liberation.*
2. The *kairos* of Latin American liberation theology. This section traces the history of liberation theology as a movement in the Catholic churches of Latin America.
3. The emergence of liberation theology in a larger liberative matrix. This section presents a genealogy of liberative theologies growing elsewhere in the Americas in filial relation to what is called "Latin American liberation theology." Some of those developments arise as critiques of the "limits" of Latin American liberation theology as a liberative project—particularly its sexism and homophobia.

Modernity, Secularization, and Liberation

One of the central innovations that Latin American liberation theology contributes to global Christianity is its interest in the *historical* dimension of salvation. Not only are God's saving actions historical, but human historical action—especially historical projects undertaken as part of a socially outgoing Christian work of love—has salvific value and power. Liberation theology's attempt to historicize salvation opens up two profound questions: (1) What were the historical conditions out of which liberation theology itself could arise as a social movement? (2) What does the historicity of liberation theology's emergence say about the historicity of salvation in general?

Latin American religious historians understand the emergence of liberation theology not in terms of a theological evolution but in terms of Catholic-Christian cultures forged amid the struggles of imperial hegemonic politics. In Europe and the Americas these struggles resulted in a series of historical Christendoms. At the very least, the term "Christendom" refers to a merging of Christianity with secular politics in certain nations such that they can properly be called "Christian" societies. In a society oriented

Christendom: a merging of Christianity with secular politics in such a way that those societies can properly be called "Christian" societies. A more negative definition understands Christendom as the ideological cooptation of Christian ideas in a way that transforms the faith into a weapon of empire.

to Christendom, matters of faith and matters of state are commingled in such a way that it is sometimes difficult to distinguish which interests—those of religious institutions or secular ones—predominate.

But Christendom can also be understood more negatively, as the wholesale ideological cooptation of Christian ideas in a way that transforms the faith more into a brutal weapon of empire than the "good news" for the poor and dispossessed that Jesus proclaimed. The Spanish who began colonizing the New World after 1492 brought with them a particularly exclusionary form of Christendom: a militant, crusading, Catholic nationalism forged over eight centuries of antagonism with Muslim occupiers. King Ferdinand and Queen Isabella unified four historical Spanish-Christian kingdoms in part by outlawing after 1492 the religions and citizenship of non-Catholics, particularly Jews and Muslims.

Their militant Catholic nationalism meant that too many of the earliest Spanish-American theologies ignored the ethical abuses of the faith as it was proclaimed by missionary priests, conquistadors, and other Spanish nobles in the New World. Many of the earliest racial projects of the Spanish New World took root in the context of debates over the intelligence, morality, and religious capacity of New World peoples. Spanish theological debates about the Indians warped European natural law philosophy into a rationale that justified war against and enslavement of the "inferior" Indians, who were thought to be "slaves by nature." Strangely, such positions were held to be compatible with a gospel whose central proclamation seemed to demand that people love their enemies as much as they would love members of their own family.

As Indian slaves were being consumed in their infernal crucible of "cruel and horrible servitude," a vocal minority of Spanish Christians stood up and spoke out for their well-being as a matter of vital evangelical interest. Antonio de Montesinos, scandalized at the wholesale destruction of Taínos in Hispaniola, challenged the viceroy and the nobles of the early colony to consider how they could call themselves "Christian" in the face of the exploitation and destruction they were inflicting on the Indies. According to his famous 1511 sermon in Santo Domingo, he said, "You all are in mortal sin; in it you live and in it you will die because of the cruelty and tyranny with which you use these innocent peoples. . . . Are these not men? Do they not have rational souls? Are you not obliged to love them as you love yourselves?"

Montesinos's indictment of Spanish-Christian genocide cited a precept at the very heart of the gospel—to "love your enemies and pray for those who persecute you" (Matt. 5:44)—in defense of a Christian politics of justice toward the New World peoples.

Likewise, Bartolomé de Las Casas inveighed against the violence accompanying Spanish evangelization. "What will the Indians think of our religion, which those wicked tyrants claim they are teaching by subjugating the Indians through massacres and force of war before the gospel is preached to them?" He developed a manual for peaceable evangelization and pioneered new missionary settlements, later adopted by the Jesuits in South America, that placed Indians more in control of their self-governance and economic productivity. Las Casas's ideas of reading the gospel, his embryonic notions of a culturally sensitive faith, and his missionary models became powerful seeds for the reflections of latter-day liberation theologians. They informed institutions like the *Comunidades Eclesiales de Base* (ecclesial base communities), which would organize much of the material life of those inspired by the theology of liberation.

These episodes in the long history of liberationist Christianity in the Americas became part of the focus of liberation theologians and historians in the 1990s. This impulse prompted the substantial historical project of CEHILA—the *Comisión de Estudio de Historia de la Iglesia en Latinoamérica* (Study Commission on the History of the Church in Latin America)—which produced a major multivolume history of Latin American Christianity. That project was much more than a compilation of theological concepts and debates. It sought to reinterpret historical Christianity on the basis of the relations between the practice of the faith and what Enrique Dussel, the project's main protagonist, called the "practical-productive relationships" that organize the life of individuals in the political economy of each moment in that history.

Theology and the life of the church would be reconsidered in terms of liberation theology's option for the poor by a historical method that interpreted the praxis of the church in terms of how it was responding to Jesus's demand to help "the least" in society (Matt. 25:40). Dussel speaks of the work of constructing categories that allow for a reinterpretation of the church's history "from the standpoint of the poor, from the oppressed." In 1990, Leonardo Boff and Virgilio Elizondo published an edition of the Catholic journal *Concilium* that drew together reflections toward a liberationist reconstruction of the history of the Americas in light of an imperial Spanish Christendom and the genocidal violence against the Indians, New World women, and African slaves. The volume, *1492: The Voice of the Victims*, proved a sobering antidote to the soporific triumphalism otherwise marking the celebrations of Columbus's quincentenary in 1992. One of the most important historical revisionings was Gustavo Gutiérrez's reading of the life and writing of Las Casas, who "saw in the Indian, in this 'other,' this one-different-from-the-Westerner, the poor one of the Gospel, and ultimately Christ himself."

This is to emphasize that liberation theology concerns itself with history, not only thinking of salvation as a historical project but also thinking at length about the historical conditions out of which religious movements and counter-movements emerge. Dussel's work frames theology and religious life as refracted by the practical-productive condition of societies beset by every kind of conflict—a widely shared gesture among liberation theologians. For scholars such as Dussel, Gutiérrez, and Ignacio Ellacuría, the question of the historicity of salvation would be joined in creative ways with the question of the historicity of social movements such as liberation theology.

The *Kairos* of Latin American Liberation Theology

If liberation theology is considered as a social movement rather than just a set of ideas floating in space, then what were the conditions out of which such a movement emerged? One fact shines some light on the question: In at least two places in the world, Latin America and North America, social movements that identified themselves as practitioners of a "liberation theology" made similar recourse to scriptural authority, developed similar pastoral and theological methodologies, became politically active mass movements, and contested state power and hegemonic class relations in their respective societies out of a Christian vision of a social option for the poor, the marginalized, the oppressed, and the excluded.

Those movements, respectively, were "Latin American liberation theology," and "black liberation theology" as practiced by Afro-descended Christians in the United States during the age of the great civil rights (1954–1965) and black power (1965–1980) movements. It is important to emphasize that both movements emerged *mutually incommunicado,* mostly unaware of the presence of the other, at least at the beginning. Later collaborations would emerge through joint scholarship and dialogue at international theological conferences. The point is not that this sibling theological journey was a coincidence. Rather, when it came to the state of things in the world ca. 1968, the time was ripe—as one might say, with sensitivity to the meaning of the ancient biblical Greek word ***kairos*** (καιρός): The world was ready for a revolution or a series of revolutions. The saga of *Los '68,* "The '68s," as the late Mexican novelist Carlos Fuentes recalls the time, unwound a dense braid of antisystemic struggles all over the world involving students, workers, peasants, women, ethno-racial minorities, environmental, antiwar, and human-rights activists, and poor people of all conditions.

***Kairos*:** from the Greek, often used to mean a propitious moment when God's will for history seems to be manifesting with a particularly inescapable force.

Christians were active in all these movements, both explicitly in their identities as Christians and as "anonymous Christian" laypersons. The concatenation of mass social movements in *Los '68* had been building for more than a generation, inspired by postwar decolonization movements in Africa, Asia, and the Black Caribbean, by radical social movements (antiracist, feminist, gay liberation) everywhere, as well as by more radical projects such as the Cuban and Nicaraguan revolutions and a variety of other Latin American guerrilla movements battling U.S.-backed national security states. All of these can be fruitfully categorized as "antisystemic" movements, according to Immanuel Wallerstein's grammar of the modern capitalist world system, which shared disdain for "both the hegemony of the United States and the collusion in this hegemony by the Soviet Union."

This effervescence of antisystemic movements corresponds to a deeply rooted "structured crisis" unfolding in the world system very slowly over the last half century. Considered theologically, the upwelling of antisystemic movements, particularly in the "world revolution of 1968," as Wallerstein calls it, and more recently with Occupy Wall Street, has the shape of a *kairos.* The word has its strongest Christian biblical resonance in Mark 1:15, which quotes Jesus's inaugural message in his first public talk: "The time is fulfilled, and the Kingdom of God has come near; repent and believe in the good news." The idea of chronological time fulfilled in such a way that the eschatological reign of God is breaking into history is the root of modern Catholic theologies of the **signs of the times**, which in turn inform liberation theology's idea of the relationship between historical social movements and salvation.

Signs of the times: signs of particularly powerful events or trends in human history that seem to manifest God's will in a particular way (cf. *kairos*).

For the bishops at the Second Vatican Council, the troubles of the age cried out for evangelical intervention by conscientious, service-oriented Catholics who could ably read the signs of God's presence in their own times. The church "has always had the duty of scrutinizing the signs of the times and of interpreting them in the light of the Gospel," so as to respond to "the

Second Vatican Council (or Vatican II): a major modernizing reform of the Roman Catholic Church (1962–1965) that reimagined Catholicism as a "church of the people," rather than a church of power, called for the replacement of Latin in the Catholic Mass with vernacular languages, and refocused the pastoral work of Catholicism in the activism of laypersons. It was a major development in the advent of liberation theology.

Secularization: a historical process in which the intramural interests of a religion become externalized and interlaced with the nonreligious cultures and thought frames of the society in which the religion is embedded.

Eschatological reign of God: refers to the heavenly kingdom that Jesus proclaims in the Gospels and that God would install at the end of human history (*eschatological* = of or referring to the end times). Liberation theology understands the reign to be partially present in human initiatives for social justice and mutual solidarity.

perennial questions" afflicting the human race, the church held in *Gaudium et spes,* the pastoral constitution adopted at Vatican II.

For Gustavo Gutiérrez, much of this ferment is driven by the desperate "irruption of the poor," a phenomenon that he described as the "new presence" in history of a constituency that had previously been almost invisible. For Gutiérrez, this was perhaps the most important of the signs of the times in which liberation theology emerged. But this emergence was also due to other factors; Gutiérrez marked a matrix of social, cultural, economic, and political developments, unfolding over half a millennium, that marked the emergence of the modern world and the profound secularization of Christianity that modernity wrought.

In his classic *A Theology of Liberation* (1971), Gutiérrez describes three historical forms theological reflection took. In antiquity, the church of Christendom was oriented to the otherworldliness of the reign of God and the supremacy of the earthly mission of the church as the indispensable portal to the hereafter. Theology aimed at the cultivation of spiritual *wisdom*, considering first questions around the formation of the nascent faith, and interpreting scripture in the service of contemplation, often in monastic settings. In the Middle Ages, however, as the doctrine of the faith congealed in a more uniform fashion, theology began a slow evolution into its guise as a *rational science*, substantially in dialogue with the auxiliary science of Aristotelian philosophy. There it developed authoritative and systematic expressions of orthodox Christian faith to feed the teaching office of the Roman Catholic Church and to campaign against doctrinal error. But as modernity began to unfold, in the centuries after the "discovery" of the Americas, a series of deep shifts in the epistemological condition of Europe and the Americas took place, leading theology to reshape its approach yet again. While they would continue to seek edification through spiritual wisdom, as well as systematic, rational inquiry, theologians in the late modernity of the twentieth century would open new themes and approaches, remaking theology as the "critical reflection on Christian praxis in the light of the Word." This is the type of approach liberation theology takes.

Gutiérrez explains this shift in terms of deep cultural and social processes in a long-historical reading of the Christendoms of Europe and the Americas. He described a new stress on "the existential and active aspects of the Christian life," which re-envisioned the old idea of *Christian charity* as a posture of "active presence in history" marked by commitments and relationships with others, as well as a "total human response to God." This total response is registered in the field of Christian spirituality, which moves from the inner-directed, contemplative spirituality of the Middle Ages to a more activist, service-oriented spirituality, particularly after the advent of the Ignatian spirituality of the Jesuit order. A new sense of the "anthropological aspects of revelation" became evident: a sense of the Word of God as a promise to the world and as a call to human beings to make peace in their mutual relations.

This modern, relational, socially directed spirit in Christianity naturally called out for reflection on the church itself as a ***locus theologicus*** (meaning a site of theological investigation). The self-reflective, critical turn in Christian thinking, especially evident in Catholicism, bolstered the call at Vatican II for theological contemplation of the signs of the times.

Locus theologicus: a site, theme, or problem calling out for theological reflection.

"It must not be forgotten that the signs of the times are not only a call to intellectual analysis," Gutiérrez wrote. "They are above all a call to pastoral activity, to commitment, and to service." Gutiérrez spoke of developments in modern philosophy, such as Maurice Blondel's idea of "critical reflection on action" as a developmental work of self-transcendence, which seem to make a direct contribution to the notion of theology as critical reflection on Christian praxis.

But perhaps more vital was the contribution of Marxist thought, its historical materialism, its notion of capitalist inequality as manifesting class conflict and struggle, and its political option for the proletariat. Because of its critical confrontations with Marxism, Gutiérrez wrote, "theological thought, searching for its own sources, has begun to reflect on the meaning of the transformation of this world and human action in history." All these contributions to the work of theological reason mark a sharp turn from medieval reflection on transcendent mysteries to consideration of sociohistorical life as the *locus salvificus par excellence*, the Ground Zero of salvation, and of humankind more and more as "the agent of its own destiny."

The maturation of social praxis that develops out of this great awakening leads to an increasing radicalization of the energy and options for change from below, from the underside of history. This, in turn, draws attention to the question of the salvific dimension of human action in history, focusing unprecedented reflection on the *secular* role human beings play in the construction of the reign of God. "Social praxis is gradually becoming more of the arena itself in which Christians work out—along with others—both their destiny as humans and their life of faith in the Lord of history," Gutiérrez wrote. "Participation in the process of liberation is an obligatory and privileged *locus* for Christian life and reflection." Gutiérrez frames this long-historical process of secularization in the ambit of his remarkable theology of history, which seeks to understand, simply, "What relation is there between salvation and the historical process of human liberation?"

His answer struggles to distinguish the different roles human beings play vis-à-vis God in the construction of the reign, which is being built by humans in history but is also believed to be coming in its fullness at the end of historical time. In the Catholicism of antiquity, rooted as it was in the politics of the late Roman Empire, human praxis was viewed as all but irrelevant to the Christian work of salvation. As modernity unfolds, however, a "New Christendom" emerges that envisions the work of the church in more secular terms. The "integral humanism" of twentieth-century French philosopher Jacques Maritain was a critical step. The "profane Christendom" he imagined was edified by Christians who, inspired by the gospel, fought for a secularized version of God's reign in historical projects promoting human rights, democratic governance, human development, and social fraternity.

In Europe, and up to a point in Latin America, the activism of this new Christian humanism shows respect for ecclesiastical authority, and—perhaps as a consequence—circumspection or hostility before proposals for more radical or revolutionary transformations of society. As the Second Vatican Council drew near, Gutiérrez observes, the church was seen to have two missions: "evangelization and the inspiration of the temporal sphere." For much of the twentieth century, "the Church is not responsible for constructing the world." That work would belong to lay Christians, as opposed to ordained priests, nuns, or their bishops. Laypeople on their own initiative, operating under Christian principles, will work in the secular world as crypto-representatives of the values, and sometimes the interests, of the church. However, they will do so with a deep respect for "the autonomy of temporal society."

This division of labor, in which the institutional church plays a role of advocacy while the laity inserts itself into the world in the manner of this New Christendom, was known as the "distinction of the planes" model; it became a crucial approach shaping the perspective of Vatican II. Gutiérrez observes that the model seems to strike "a difficult balance between the unity of God's plan and the distinction between Church and world." However, as the crisis of underdevelopment grew more sharply in Latin America in the 1960s, the distinction-of-the-planes model came under stress and finally fell apart, particularly around the commitments of lay apostolic groups. Feeling compelled to take ever-more-radical positions on poverty and national-security states, such groups forced the institutional church into difficult choices that always threatened to pull the church hierarchy toward "a political radicalization incompatible with an official position of the church which postulated a certain asepsis in temporal affairs."

Salvation history: theological or biblical accounts of divine interventions or communications in which God seems to act in a way to save human beings.

The failure of this model opened the way for a new sense of salvation history that was unique to liberation theology. The idea of a boundary between the supposedly graced activism of the institutional church and the profane activism of its laypeople proved artificial. More and more the gospel was read to signal "one call to salvation" in which humans discern their vocation to encounter God beyond the old "temporal-spiritual and profane-sacred antitheses." As Gutiérrez put it, "There is only one human destiny, irreversibly assumed by Christ, the Lord of history. His redemptive work embraces all the dimensions of existence and brings them to their fullness. The history of salvation is the very heart of human history."

In this vision of things, social justice work becomes a valuable contribution to the building up of the reign of God. Liberation becomes a sign of the indwelling and in-breaking of the reign into human history. Liberation theology's perspective on history, bringing the *kairos* of salvation history more clearly into theological register with the *chronos* of secular history, arises as a great epistemological awakening, inspiring new liberating approaches to the challenges of poverty, oppression, war, and exclusion.

First-Generation Liberation Theology

In an early appreciation of Gutiérrez's work, Leonardo Boff praised his contributions to liberation theology as a work of "universal theological significance." His "new way of doing theology," as critical reflection on Christian praxis in the light of the Word of God, was nothing less than an "epistemological break" of world-historical importance. What are the major themes and theology of liberation theology?

God of Life, Lord of History. Liberation theology's interest in the mundane, in what Gutiérrez called "an entirely worldly world," is rooted in the materiality of God's promises to human beings in history: that God is a God of life, and the promise of salvation is delivered through the medium of love, the love of God for humankind (John 3:16), as well as love of human beings for God and for one another (Matt. 22:34-40; cf. Luke 10:25-37). The Christian God is a God of life, and love is God's first principle.

God's love is infinite and infinitely gratuitous. John the Evangelist's observation that God's love was great enough to surrender God's son to the violence of human history suggests God's love is the warrant of the divine promise of salvation. But liberation theology goes deeper, reading Jesus's life as a practical demonstration of the power divine love has to save the world. The identification of God as a God of life is revealed in the praxis of the historical Jesus of Nazareth, before coming to the question of Jesus's identity as the Christ of faith. The question of Jesus's praxis drives the Christologies produced in the ambit of liberation theology.

For Jon Sobrino, the historical Jesus is the beginning of christological reflection because his orientation to God was grounded in his praxis, which sought nothing less than to augur and mediate the coming of the reign of God. To know God means understanding the project of the reign of God through the historical Jesus. "To know the Christian element of the reign, one must turn to Jesus. But . . . to know Jesus one must turn to the reign of God." For Sobrino, Jesus's miracles and healings merely signaled the coming of the reign. The perception that Jesus himself is the definitive mediator of the reign, however, emerges out of what Sobrino calls Jesus's prophetic "daring," claiming not only that the reign is at hand but that it has come for the poor rather than for the rich. In this sense, there is a sort of dialectic of class conflict and historical struggle built into the sense of the reign as presented in liberation theology. It exists in terms of what Sobrino and other Central American Jesuits called the *anti-reign*; that is, in a conflictual, dialectical relationship with the gravest historical evils coming out of human sinfulness. "Jesus does not appear as mediator . . . on a *tabula rasa,* but amid a reality with which he struggles."

There are many warrants in the New Testament witness to vouch for Jesus's identification with God the Father: the titles with which Jesus was named ("rabbi," "high priest," "suffering servant," "Son of Man," etc.); the intimacy of his son-to-father relationship with God; or the miraculous voucher of Jesus's healings and resurrection. But Sobrino observes that the more sustained gesture, particularly in the Synoptic Gospels, is to express the ultimacy of Jesus in terms of his advocacy and praxis around the coming of the reign of God. In these practices Jesus shows not only his identification with God but also his identity as a human being. Sobrino cites several elements of Jesus's relationship with the reign of God that evince "the totality of the human": (1) Jesus's knowledge and preaching on the reign and the anti-reign; (2) the hope he stirs in others concerning the coming of the reign; and (3) Jesus's praxis performing the coming of the reign—"and his historical celebration of the fact that the Reign has 'already' come."

Epistemology / epistemological: refers to the broad structure of human knowledge as it is held by collectives of people, as their understanding evolves in history.

Divine and Human Agency in Salvation History. The incarnate, praxis-centered focus of Sobrino's Christology is representative of liberation theology's turn to the historical and to the underside of history. Ignacio Ellacuría likewise pivots from an idea of an antagonism between the reign of God and the anti-reign of historical evil to construct a human- and history-centered **soteriology** (or theology of salvation). Ellacuría opened a two-sided analysis of the relationship between historical action and salvation. First, faith requires consideration of the question, How historical are the salvific acts testified to in the scriptures? The other side of the question was, How salvific are historical acts? The second question presupposes faith in the answer to the first question; but Ellacuría's theology was more interested in the second question: How much do human actions in history contribute to salvation in the eschatological reign of God? How do Christians participate in salvation history?

Soteriology: A theology that considers the situation and conditions of human salvation.

The question of the historicity of salvation matters not because liberation theology is a political theology but because it is a "theology of the kingdom of God," a material historical development in which human beings play a decisive and very political role. The salvific power of Christian praxis lies in its historical partnership with God's salvific praxis, which Ellacuría calls *theopraxis*. "Christians, compelled by their faith, and as an objective realization of that faith, seek to make human action correspond as much as possible to God's will." Thus, the key question becomes, What are the ways in which human beings and God intervene differently in history? To approach this question, Ellacuría reinterprets the meaning of divine transcendence. Transcendence is commonly, but badly, understood as God's position away from or above material human history. By contrast, Ellacuría proposes that God transcends within history, and that the divine life is "infra-historical." "When one reaches God historically—which is the same thing as reaching God personally—one does not abandon real history, but rather deepens one's roots," he wrote. While "God can be separated from history . . . history cannot be separated from God."

But this historicization of salvation is itself not particularly new. Ellacuría recognizes it as a driving force in the accounts of Yahweh's Old Testament apparitions, miraculous occasions that nevertheless were precipitated by, or unfolded in relationship with, human initiative and historical action. While there is a world of difference between the history of Israel as narrated in the scriptures and that presented in modern scholarship in the historical sciences, "salvation history depends on events that the historian can prove to be real." If the Old Testament story is rendered in the historical genre, it is not out of an apologetic interest to justify faith in God or to animate faith, but because the historical genre represented the experience the Israelites had of God.

This leads Ellacuría to the startling conclusion that while it is Yahweh who liberates the Israelites, Yahweh could not have succeeded without human action to actually bring about the divine will. So salvation history is a co-creation in which God and humankind play complementary roles. And "history is the fullest place . . . of a transcendence that does not appear mechanically, but only appears when history is made. . . . Only a God who has come down into history can raise it to God. But this happens in the history of a people." This materiality of the project of salvation means that liberation is not just an ethics or a political praxis severable from faith; rather, faith becomes politicized because it is historical: "The so-called politicization of the faith . . . should rather be called the historicization of the faith [because] salvation does not reach its fulfillment if it does not attain that historical . . . and . . . political dimension."

The politicization of salvation history introduces a sharp dimension of historical antagonism into the praxis of the faith, particularly where the option for the poor becomes the basis of prophetic denunciation of wealth, and the oppressive, warlike, and exclusionary practices by which it is often procured. In theological terms, Ellacuría frames this antagonism between the reign and the anti-reign not as a conflict between nature and the supernatural but between sin and grace. While a Marxist way of thinking might understand history as the history of class conflict, Ellacuría understood history as the history of the struggle between grace and sin, between the reign of God and the anti-reign of evil.

His line of thinking opens up a political metaphysics in which salvation is keyed to participation in the liberating constructions of the reign of God. In this sense, human action matters, each intervention contributing in small or large measure to the heavenly or hellish destiny of the human race. "Some actions kill (divine) life, and some actions give (divine) life," Ellacuría writes; "some belong to the kingdom of sin, others to the kingdom of grace." This is because Ellacuría sees an almost seamless nexus between human and divine agency, joined in the material body of history in the work of salvation. In this totality, all things, "each in its own way, have been grafted with the triune life, and refer essentially to that life." The *imago dei*, the image of God, is not an abstract and indifferent divine imprint in the soul, but names the way in which human life is grafted into God's life, a grafting that signals something closer to an identity with God than a relation to God as divine Other. "All created things are a limited way of being God, and the human being, in particular, is a small God because the human being is a relative absolute."

The People of God and the Scandal of Poverty. For liberation theology, poverty is not at all an object of sentimentality or romanticization. It is not the field of the noble or the virtuous. Instead, poverty is a scandal, a slippery slope to early and unjust death for those in its grasp. The widespread, massive poverty that prevails in much of the Americas south of the United States is an "injustice that cries out to the heavens," as the Latin American bishops proclaimed in the path-breaking documents of their Second General Conference, held in 1968 in Medellín, Colombia.

Medellín was a watershed for Latin American Catholicism. The first regional episcopal meeting since the close of the Second Vatican Council, it was heavily influenced by the presence of liberation theologians who served as theological advisors to many of the bishops present. The Medellín bishops saw the roots of poverty in the region's perennial underdevelopment and colonial subjection, but that did not prompt them to embrace the promises of economic development proffered by the United States or Europe. Instead, they aimed critical fire at questions of neocolonialism and dependency in the global economy, an order in which Latin America had always played the role of dependent pauper.

As one measure for increasing evangelization and promoting human development, the bishops encouraged the widespread deployment of Christian base communities, which became centers for Christian formation as well as for social organizing. Base communities used the Bible in a circular praxis that read the events of everyday life against the narratives of scripture. The reading follows a hermeneutical circle based on pastoral methodologies as developed by twentieth-century lay apostolic communities. That method, dubbed the "see-judge-act" methodology, was adopted as authoritative by

Pope John XXIII in his encyclical *Mater et magistra* (*Mother and Teacher*, 1961). In its procedure as John presented it (§236), "one reviews the concrete situation" (*see*); "secondly, one forms a judgment on it" in light of Christian principles (*judge*); and "thirdly, one decides what in the circumstances can and should be done to implement these principles" (*act*).

In base communities, the process then moves from the praxis of life and of the faith into a reflective mode in which that praxis comes under a process of critical analysis. The condition of the present, in all its density, is discussed and deconstructed with whatever tools or sciences are available, not merely with tools coming strictly from the theological sciences. This is described as the socioanalytic mediation. The situation, once analyzed, is then submitted to a process of judgment based on biblical reading and interpretation; this is the hermeneutical mediation. The third step takes the reading into the ambiguous world of responsive and responsible action, in a practical mediation.

The Option for the Poor. The ballast orienting the reading and praxis of the base communities is the option for the poor, which should be understood not only as a pastoral policy and praxis but also as a theological key. Its history involves developments and historical contributions from theology and pastoral experience. Although the option is clearly rooted in Old and New Testament prophetic narratives, including the preaching and praxis of Jesus, its modern provenance owes both to the aforementioned awakening of human agency—Gutiérrez's new presence of the poor swept up in decolonializing activism—and to church policy, which takes a sharper turn toward social teaching starting at the close of the nineteenth century. It was then that the great social encyclicals, starting with Pope Leo XIII's *Rerum novarum* (*Of New Things,* 1891), began to emerge.

From Leo down to Pope John XXIII in the 1960s, the popes begin shaping the embryonic elements of the option for the poor out of their concern for the devastating suffering each saw in the condition of the world's majority of poor persons, especially struggling laborers and those who are entirely excluded from the economy. While poverty was always a pertinent question, however, those popes struck a consistent middle path, criticizing in equal measure the excesses of capitalism and of socialist or communist movements that would contest capitalism. But the idea of a preferential option for the poor took a stronger turn when Pope John XXIII spoke of "the Church of the poor" in a radio address a month before the opening of Vatican II: "Before the underdeveloped countries, that is, before the poverty in the world, the Church is and desires to be a germinal reality and a project, the Church of all and, particularly, the Church of the poor." Gutiérrez notes, however, that the pope's words in favor of a "Church of the poor" had little resonance in the proceedings and documents of the council. "But, yes," Gutiérrez wrote, "they did have a great repercussion among us, in this mostly Christian continent with a high proportion of Catholics—which at the same time has such a poor and marginalized population. A scandal, no?"

Liberative Theology in Action: A Latin American Pope

One important recent development for liberation theology was the election of Cardinal Jorge Mario Bergoglio, the archbishop of Buenos Aires, Argentina, as Pope Francis, the first Latin American and first Jesuit pope. At his election in March 2013, Francis announced that he would place a special accent on the theme of poverty, reaffirming liberation theology's option for the poor. Gustavo Gutiérrez, once investigated and criticized by Vatican officials, is reported to have been received with open arms twice in private audiences with the new pope. His first audience, in September 2013, was to present Francis with the Italian edition of a book on liberation theology that he had coauthored almost a decade earlier with Francis's prefect for the Congregation for the Doctrine of the Faith, Cardinal Gerhard Müller.

Two other developments early in Francis's papacy likewise portended a new lease on life for liberation theology. First was a major interview Francis gave the Italian Jesuit-Catholic cultural magazine, *La Civiltà Cattolica*, speaking of a clean-up of Vatican corruption, a restoration of the authority of the Second Vatican Council, and an invitation to the church to take up simpler forms of spirituality for service in a deeply troubled world. More important was his apostolic exhortation *Evangelii gaudium* (*The Joy of the Gospel*). Dated November 24, 2013, this papal "exhortation" issued a ringing condemnation of an exclusionary global economy that literally "kills." He attacked "trickle-down theories" of the economy, which never deliver the promised goods for society at large. He warned of "a crude and naïve trust" in "the sacralized workings of the prevailing economic system," and of "a globalization of indifference" to the cries of "the excluded." At the root of poverty was "the new idolatry of money." Adopting language strongly resonant with the 1979 message of the Latin American bishops at Puebla, Francis wrote that "each individual Christian and every community is called to be an instrument of God for the liberation and promotion of the poor, and for enabling them to be fully a part of society."

The Medellín bishops took the first steps toward a more radical option for the poor in their denunciation of the impoverishing power of Latin America's neocolonial dependency on the First World. They also offered a richly nuanced idea of poverty in three senses. First was poverty in its ordinary sense: as a lack of vital material goods needed to survive and flourish in a fully human life. This poverty is scandalous. According to the 1968 CELAM (Consejo Episcopal Latinoamericano) document: "The prophets denounced it as contrary to the will of the Lord and, most of the time, as the fruit of injustice and the sin of men" (§14:4a). In the face of material poverty, the church's task is to "denounce the unjust scarcity of the goods of this world and the sin that engenders it."

But the other two senses of poverty have a positive value in Christian faith-discourse. *Spiritual poverty* has to do with "an attitude of opening to God, the disposition of he who hopes for everything from the Lord." Though they might value the things of this world, "they do not fixate on them, recognizing the superior value of the goods of the kingdom." These are "the poor in spirit," whom Jesus beatified in his Sermon on the Mount (Matt. 5:3), "for theirs is the kingdom of heaven." The Medellín bishops urged that we "preach and live according to spiritual poverty, as an attitude of spiritual childhood and opening to the Lord."

The third sense was *evangelical poverty,* "poverty taken up as a commitment, which assumes, voluntarily and for the sake of love, the condition of the needy of this world as a testimony against the evil that poverty represents, and spiritual freedom before earthly goods." This attitude mimics Jesus's praxis, "who 'being rich made himself poor,' " taking up "all the consequences of the sinful condition of human beings" to save humanity. The bishops urged the Latin American "church of the poor" to, in fact, live as a poor church, "committing to material poverty" as a "constant in the history of salvation. All members of the church are called to live in evangelical poverty" (§14:4-6).

The bishops of Medellín began forging their option for the poor in terms of an ideal of human development that was oriented to a horizon of what Gustavo Gutiérrez would call integral liberation, a term that would transfigure the traditional Christian figure of salvation. Gutiérrez described three integral dimensions of liberation in a way that CELAM, in its Third General Conference at Puebla, Mexico, adopted in its concluding document in 1979 (§321-29). According to Gutiérrez, the first step is liberation from all the material conditions that endanger, reduce, and destroy life—socioeconomic oppression and marginalization, which is deemed "contrary to God's will for their life." But a second necessary and coordinate liberation involves cultivation of the spiritual and psychological maturity that liberates a person to love others. This second level involves a practice of Christian love that instills in a person "profound inner freedom in the face of every kind of servitude." These two liberations imply participation in a third: God's divine work of struggling to free the world from the bondage of sinful relations. It is important to underscore that liberation theology understands sin as a relational evil, as a balance sheet of quantifiable moral infractions. Sin names the phenomenon of historical conflicts that break community and loving relations between and among people. Gutiérrez insists that these three levels do not liberate separately but in conjunction—in a word, they are integral—a unified salvation of body and soul.

The option for the poor becomes the pastoral policy of the Latin American church after Puebla in 1979, integrating four basic options: one for the poor, one for the development of youth, one toward the construction of pluralistic societies, and one concerning Christian agency in national and international life. Concerning the poor, the bishops at Puebla stated they "affirm the need for the entire Church to be converted toward a preferential option for the poor, oriented toward their integral liberation" (§1134).

Backlash against Liberation Theology. In many ways Puebla represents a high-water mark in the dissemination and institutionalization of liberation theology in Latin America. It also effectively marks the end of liberation theology's first generation. What followed was a period of trial and tribulation. The anticommunist Pope John Paul II took up a series of disciplinary actions to shut down or coopt the project of liberation theology, with instrumental assistance from Cardinal Joseph Ratzinger, then prefect of the Congregation for the Doctrine of the Faith (CDF), later Pope Benedict XVI. The bulk of their suspicion concerned the imagined induction of Marxist categories, with its supposedly viral atheism, into Christian faith.

In 1983, the CDF published "Ten Observations on the Theology of Gustavo Gutiérrez," citing his supposedly "uncritical acceptance of Marxist interpretation," which gave his theology a dangerous "seductiveness." In general, Ratzinger claimed that Gutiérrez erred by reducing the revelatory mystery of the scriptural faith to "an exclusively political meaning" in which "the struggle for liberation" is substituted for "an encounter with the Lord . . . A concept such as this mounts an attack on the transcendence of revelation and on its normative value, as well as on the specific character of theological faith." And in critiquing liberation theology's conceiving salvation in terms of liberating struggles for social justice, Ratzinger warned that Gutiérrez had assimilated divine agency to secular history in a way that made it seem as though "God becomes history."

In a 1984 article for the general press, Cardinal Ratzinger praised the liberationist image of the church presented in the documents of Medellín and Puebla. But he warned of a receptivity to Marxist thinking and a misleading new Christian universality that liberation theology risked through its assimilation of the Christian faith to an overly political agenda. Marxist influence derails the mystical, transcendent, and spiritual aspects of the faith, Ratzinger wrote, warning ominously that "with the analysis of the phenomenon of liberation theology we are clearly facing a fundamental danger for the faith of the church."

Later that year, Ratzinger published an "Instruction on Certain Aspects of the Theology of Liberation." There he affirmed the centrality to Christianity of the theme of liberation from poverty and the need to reform economic systems to ameliorate the lot of the poor, mainly in terms of Catholic social teaching. However, he condemned "serious deviations" of "some" theologies of liberation, which risk begetting revolutionary responses that would practice a "systematic and deliberate recourse to blind violence." Ratzinger also condemned notions of class conflict, class warfare, or the project for a classless society as "a myth which slows reform and aggravates poverty and injustice" (§XI).

In yet another instruction, "On Christian Freedom and Liberation," published two years later, Ratzinger reemphasized what he characterized as the illusory nature of revolutionary change, which risks promoting "totalitarian regimes," as against the more accessible, piecemeal possibilities presented in projects for reform, which Ratzinger argued should still be "far-reaching" (§78). This instruction, meant to be read in tandem with his 1984 instruction, is less a refutation of liberation theology than a constructive reassertion of modern Catholic social teaching to address liberation theology's more radical claims around the deep sinfulness of socialized poverty.

Alongside these instructions, the Vatican also moved to silence the public speaking and publishing work of many prominent liberation theologians, the most notorious cases being those of Gutiérrez, Leonardo Boff, and the Brazilian eco-feminist theologian Ivone Gebara. Vatican efforts to silence Gutiérrez were all but rebuffed by the Peruvian bishops. Boff was silenced once, in 1985, over his frontal critique of the institutional church in the incendiary *Church: Charism and Power* (1985). Boff left the Catholic priesthood in early 1992 rather than suffer a second silencing over his ecological theology. Gebara, a Brazilian feminist theologian and a Catholic woman religious, was silenced for two years after an interview she gave defending abortion for poor women.

The net effect of these instructions and silencings was to water down the more radical options entertained by liberation theology, particularly those praising projects of more revolutionary transformation, while also coopting the theme of liberation as a core Catholic-Christian value. The institutional church categorically embraced a reformist approach and rejected revolutionary change, without the sort of contextual interpretation that could adequately judge the efficacy or the futility of reformist approaches. In progressive circles in Latin America, this reformist attitude was considered inadequate to confront the extreme violence regularly seen in the region since World War II. For three decades after the mid-1960s, countries throughout the Americas came under the control of military dictatorships, often backed by U.S. aid, weaponry, and training, and oriented by an ideology of national security and anticommunism. In countries such as El Salvador, with its extremely polarized civil conflict (1970–1992), civil war broke out after 1980 precisely because the government's consistent response to demands for reform was corrupt elections, brutal repression of opposition movements, and a recourse to shadowy death squads as violent instruments of repression. As El Salvador's postwar truth-and-reconciliation process showed, that country was hardly the scene for the sort of reformism proposed in the Vatican instructions against liberation theology.

Latin American Liberation Theology in the Matrix of Liberative Theologies

After this period it seemed to many, particularly in the First World, that liberation theology was "dead," a view never entertained seriously among its practitioners, even after the fall of the Berlin Wall. As Gustavo Gutiérrez joked, "I've never been invited to the funeral of liberation theology, and I believe I have done a few things to merit an invitation." In fact, liberation theology is far from dead, at least as an intellectual or theological enterprise. On the other hand, it is less clear that liberation theology retains the same viability and vitality as a social movement as it did in the 1960s and 1970s. Even as liberation theology was coming under attack by the institutional Roman Catholic Church, its hermeneutic and methodology were spreading virally, from Latin America to other regions, particularly Africa and Asia, and from questions of socioeconomic liberation to interrogate challenges to freedom and well-being in gender relations, sexuality, ethno-racial relations, and the global ecosystem.

Inspired by liberation theology, profound liberative theologies have emerged: feminist, queer and sexual theologies, North American Latina/o, black, and womanist theologies, and Third World theologies from Africa, the South Asian region, and Korea, as well as theologies influenced by recent trends in postcolonial criticism. In the last decade, a "next generation" of young liberation theologians has emerged, bringing liberation theology into dialogue with new perspectives in the human sciences, particularly ecology, poststructuralist critical theory, postcolonial criticism, and queer theory. These new works have been joined, more or less, to new social movements throughout the Americas. But it is also clear that as widely disseminated and differentiated as the theology of liberation is today, it does not have the political traction it enjoyed during the years after Vatican II, when the Catholic Church seemed much more disposed to join its spiritual mission to the secular mission of liberation.

Conclusions: Pasts and Futures of Latin American Liberation Theology

As mentioned above, there was a moment after the fall of the Berlin Wall (1989) when liberation theology seemed to have died. Daniel Bell spoke of the "pathos" of liberation theology "after the end of history." Nelson Maldonado-Torres spoke of liberation theology's "search for the lost paradigm." Ivan Petrella urged liberation theology to rediscover new historical projects to take up after the crash of the socialist bloc. Joerg Rieger and Kwok Pui Lan suggested a turn to new forms of antiglobalization struggle, as signified in post-2008 protest movements such as Occupy Wall Street. Marcella Althaus-Reid and Elina Vuola urged liberation theology to overcome its masculinist and heterosexist "limits of liberation."

While all take liberation theology in different directions, each proposal is still centrally concerned with the consuming questions of history that inspired the first reflections on the salvation offered by a God who comes down to earth, assuming the most humbled and debased form the human can take. Here liberation theology always showed its passion for remaining relevant to the human condition. And though laboring with limits, Latin American liberation theology remains an inspiration, a very vital force among the major social movements in Christianity today.

Study Questions

1. Describe why the history of Spanish colonial Christendom in the New World is a particularly informative source for the thinking that would become, in the twentieth century, liberation theology.
2. Describe how liberation theology is a *kairos* moment for the Latin American church. How was its interlacing with secular decolonial movements a *sign of the times*?
3. What is the *option for the poor*? When, why, and by whom was it adopted? What were its biblical and theological roots, as the author describes them?
4. How does Gustavo Gutiérrez understand the relationship between salvation and the historical process of liberation? How does he describe the Christian understanding of that relationship evolving in the history of the church, particularly in modern times?

5. Describe some of the basic dogmatic positions found in liberation theology on *God*, *Christ*, *salvation*, the *church* (the "people of God"), and the *option for the poor*. How did those positions come under critical fire during the papacy of Pope John Paul II?

Suggested Reading

Althaus-Reid, Marcella. *Indecent Theology*. London: Routledge, 2000.

Aquino, Jorge A. "Poverty and Prosperity after the Crash of 2008: Insights from Liberation Theology on Zero-Sum Capitalism at the Twilight of American Exceptionalism." In *Religious and Ethical Perspectives for the Twenty-First Century*. Edited by Paul O. Myhre, 238–60. Winona, MN: Anselm Academic, 2013.

Aquino, María Pilar. *Our Cry for Life: Feminist Theology from Latin America*. Maryknoll, NY: Orbis Books, 1993.

Boff, Leonardo, and Clodovis Boff. *Introducing Liberation Theology*. Maryknoll, NY: Orbis Books, 1987.

CELAM. *The Church in the Present-Day Transformation of Latin America in the Light of the Council*. Edited by Louis Colonnese. Bogota: General Secretariat CELAM, 1970.

Comblin, José. *The Church and the National Security State*. Maryknoll, NY: Orbis Books, 1979.

De La Torre, Miguel A. *Liberation Theology for Armchair Theologians*. Louisville, KY: Westminster/John Knox Press, 2013.

Ellacuría, Ignacio, and Jon Sobrino, eds. *Mysterium Liberationis: Fundamental Concepts of Liberation Theology*. Maryknoll, NY: Orbis Books, 1993.

Gutiérrez, Gustavo. *A Theology of Liberation: History, Politics, and Salvation*. Maryknoll, NY: Orbis Books, 1988.

Hennelly, Alfred T., ed. *Liberation Theology: A Documentary History*. Maryknoll, NY: Orbis Books, 1990.

Petrella, Ivan. *The Future of Liberation Theology: An Argument and Manifesto*. Aldershot, Hants, England; Burlington, VT: Ashgate, 2004.

Tombs, David. *Latin American Liberation Theology*. Boston: Brill Academic Publishers, 2002.

Vuola, Elina. *Limits of Liberation: Feminist Theology and the Ethics of Poverty and Reproduction*. London: Sheffield Academic, 2002.

2

African Liberative Theologies

Joseph Ogbonnaya

Every theology is contextual, emerging from the sociocultural, economic, religious, and historical conditions of its time. The most popular of liberation theologies, Latin American liberation theology, emerged in response to oppression and injustice arising from the socioeconomic and political conditions in Latin America in the 1960s. Foremost were the roles played by transnational corporations in collaboration with corrupt governments and international communities. The inability of Latin American countries to repay the huge sums borrowed from international financial institutions to finance development projects during the economic crash of the late 1960s and early 1970s inflicted hardships that increased poverty and deprivation. These situations were complicated by totalitarian oppression. Latin American liberation theology sought the liberation of the people from such injustices and the promotion of their integral development in the light of the gospel, using predominantly Marxist socioeconomic analysis.

The situation in Africa with regard to liberation theology (especially in tropical sub-Saharan Africa) bears a close resemblance to that of Latin America in many ways. Centuries of slave trade during which Africans were reduced to articles of commerce were followed by centuries of colonialism under various European powers. In this colonial period and after, African communities found themselves distorted by the merging together of previously heterogeneous peoples and the creation of artificial nation-states that seemed almost intended to fail. The neocolonialism that followed the end of the colonial era, during which many African governments worked under the tutelage of their former colonial masters, forced African countries to serve foreign interests.

Still today, many corrupt African leaders selfishly advance their private economic fortunes to the detriment of their fellow citizens, promote group interests, and continue to practice tribalism and nepotism, all of which militate against the national unity of their countries. The predatory practices of transnational corporate organizations seeking to exploit African natural resources only heighten the injustice, deprivation, oppression, violence, and economic mismanagement that all too often characterize the material situation of Africa.

However, in spite of the striking resemblance between Latin American conditions and the African socioeconomic and political conditions mentioned above, Africa has not reacted theologically in the same way. Africans have not formulated a theology that can be called liberation theology in the Latin American sense, although Latin American theology has influenced the formulation of aspects of African liberation theology. Instead of a unified liberation theology in the Latin American sense, African liberative theologies are heavily contextual, dealing with specific cultural issues of African indigenous religions, an African cultural appropriation of Christianity (inculturation theology), the African use of Christianity for political liberation (black/reconstruction theology of South Africa), the reconciliation of peoples for mutual coexistence, especially after political instability has engendered hatred, violence, and war (reconciliation theology), and the developing theology of African women.

Generally, like all theologies of the developing world, African theologies are liberative in that they begin as protests against colonialism and the Eurocentric cultural forms by which the Christian faith was spread by various missionaries, especially to sub-Saharan Africa. They seek liberation from all forms of cultural domination—not only from colonialism, postcolonial oppression, and bad governance, but also from the religious domination that results from presenting the Christian faith in foreign theologies that are mindless of distinct African cultural forms and values through which Africans experience and encounter the risen Christ.

History of African Liberative Theologies

The demand from African nationalists in the 1950s and 1960s for African independence in all aspects of life—social, political, economic, cultural, and religious—gave rise to the first African liberative theologies. Many African leaders who were practicing Christians began to question not only the continuity of expatriate leadership of the church but also foreign theologies that had little or no relevance to African culture and history. For instance, Kenneth Kaunda (a Presbyterian) and Julius Nyerere (a Catholic) began to question why the church in Africa is not more African. At the same time, the emergence of black awareness movements such as that of ***négritude,*** as well as the development of African philosophy through the pioneering work of Placide Temples, resurrected an African appreciation of themselves as distinct peoples. This led to a demand for different forms of Christianity in accordance with African aspirations for cultural authenticity and political liberation.

Négritude movement: The négritude movement of the 1930s and 1940s, a response to the colonial domination that obliterates African history and destroys the African future, awakened a black consciousness that enabled African priests to overcome the invisibility of Africans by helping them begin to formulate a Christian theology that is distinctly African.

The climate was ripe for the emergence of distinctive African ways of being Christian, ways that were quite different from the mission theology of saving souls and the colonial theology of planting churches, theologies that neglected Africa's contexts. There is little wonder, then, that the emergence of distinctly African theology took place in the 1950s and '60s within a cultural rebirth arising from the nationalists' demand for independence from colonialism. This quest for an African theology was first articulated in 1956 with the publication of a book entitled *Des prêtres noirs s'interrogent* (*Some Black Priests Wonder*) by African priests studying abroad.

At the same time, African nationalists and some newly independent African states following the path of the earlier pan-Africanist movement were forming the Organization of African Unity (now the African Union); they aimed primarily at the unity of African peoples as well as cultural affirmation and independence from Eurocentric domination. African Christian leaders were formulating African Christian theologies in the same way Africanization aimed at upholding African dignity, racial equality and independence, solidarity and cultural affirmation. The first meetings of the All African Conference of Churches in Ibadan, Nigeria, and in Accra, Ghana, happened in the same year, 1958, that Kwame Nkrumah called for a meeting of the independent African states at the All Africa People's Congress in Ghana. Another meeting at Kampala, Uganda, in 1963 and in Ibadan, Nigeria, in 1966 led to the formation of the All African Conference of Churches (AFCC). The AFCC is considered the birthplace of African liberative theologies. In other words, African theologies developed at the same time African peoples were emancipating themselves from foreign domination and colonialism. This initial growth of African theologies culminated in the publication in 1966 of *Biblical Revelation and African Beliefs,* edited by K. A. Dickson and Paul Ellingworth.

Because of the tendency (not accepted by all) to think of African theology in evolutionary terms—that is, as constantly changing according to Africa's socioeconomic and political exigencies—some authors think of African theology as progressing from inculturation to liberation to black theologies. These formerly prominent theologies in Africa, proponents of this way of thinking argue, have been surpassed. What are preferable now are reconciliation or reconstruction theologies. It is worth noting, however, that many of these African liberative theologies have existed simultaneously and in parallel, albeit interdependently, reflecting culturally, socioeconomically, politically, and spiritually on African conditions in the light of the gospel.

The Need for Liberation

African liberative theologies aim at restoring the self-esteem of Africans shattered by centuries of denigration and dehumanization; Africans have been made timid before people of other races and nationalities. The **anthropological crisis** (using the terminology of *Africae Munus* of the Second African Synod) that Africans continue to suffer because of subtle forms of cultural imperialism heightened by globalization and totalitarian ideologies makes liberative theologies not only important, urgent, and necessary, but a basic feature without which the theology that is distinctly African does not exist.

Anthropological crisis: The "anthropological crisis" the Africans are undergoing as a result of what the Cameroonian theologian Engelbert Mbveng called "anthropological poverty" is not deprivation of food or other material possessions, but poverty arising from various forms of cultural imperialism, the indigence of being, that is the result of being denied their basic dignity as human beings, "their identity, their dignity, their freedom, their thought, their history, their language, their faith universe, and their basic creativity."

African liberative theologies emphasize the distinctness and worth of Africans and their experiences for articulating the Christian faith and for transmitting this message to new generations of Africans. Their strength is being both African and Christian without dichotomizing African identity, personality, and cultures. They represent the Africanization of Christian faith culturally, socioeconomically, politically, and religiously. For instance, because the colonialism and early Christian missionary activity both denounced African cultures as barbaric and pagan, African theology in much of Africa through inculturation emphasizes a cultural emancipation of the Christian faith from Eurocentric influence.

Throughout Africa, political independence has not brought the much-promised and hoped-for material progress and development, but instead has led to economic backwardness, hardship and deprivation, poverty, disease, and maladministration, especially during the long process of decolonization. With the collapse of the New International Economic Order of the 1970s, the second development decade, and the imposition of the Structural Adjustment Program owing to heavy loans accumulated to finance development projects, Africans yearn for greater economic autonomy and liberation from poverty and want. Some theologians, such as Barnabas Okolo and Jean-Marc Ela, propose an African liberation theology alongside the Latin American model as imperative for Africa. For these theologians, development and globalization, especially neoliberal globalization, must focus on the welfare of the people who are the subjects of development. The poor must be prioritized by theology as God takes the side of those at the margins.

The situation of blacks who suffered under South Africa's apartheid rule is different from that of Africans who regained political independence from other colonial regimes. Consequently, South Africa's quest for liberty is different from that of western and eastern Africa. A theology that addresses the situation of South African blacks must first emphasize racial equality, because they were dominated by white segregationist minority rule. A black theology with an emphasis on black consciousness thus emerged, and black theologians appropriated the Christian faith by reading biblical stories from their particular experience of racial marginalization. Neither inculturation nor liberation theology could address their divergent issues adequately. However, with the dismantling of apartheid and the emergence of black majority democratic rule in South Africa in 1994, as well as the attainment of political independence by all African countries, the emphasis in African theology began to shift from black theology of liberation to a quest for ways of reconstructing Africa in order to benefit from independence much more fruitfully. This shift, called the theology of reconstruction, seeks an end to "the blame game" and advocates that Africans take responsibility for their affairs.

Most, if not all, societies in Africa, like theology in general, are patriarchal. Can one then claim that the interests of women have been adequately represented in the various liberative theologies emerging thus far in Africa? Women theologians confirm that this has not been the case, and they have begun to champion the cause of women who suffer various forms of marginalization both in church and in society. Thus various forms of womanist theologies have emerged in Africa, re-reading and interpreting the scriptures as well as theologizing from women's perspectives.

Method

Methodologically, the various forms of African liberative theologies emphasize "contextualization," that is, the importance of the various circumstances and historical experiences of each people for the appropriation of the Christian faith. Contextualization considers the sociocultural and economico-political, as well as the religious, horizons of people as important for shaping the form the Christian faith takes among them. Contextualization is not anachronistic, seeking to recover the past of the peoples' life and culture, but progressive, attending to the concrete circumstances of the peoples as they are today and their relevance for authentic Christian identity. Contextualization is not just a comparison of African cultures with the Christian faith but also critical analysis of African conditions in the light of Christian faith. Thus, it is dynamic, ongoing, and progressive, and it keeps Christian faith contemporary. It recalls the emphasis of the Second Vatican Council on "reading the signs of the time."

This emphasis on context is the unifying theme for all forms of African liberative theologies. As the last frontier, contextualization as the backdrop of Third World theologies, including African theologies, indicates that the differences among African liberative theologies—Africanization and black theology, African women theology, reconciliation and reconstruction theologies—can easily be resolved in a both/and manner instead of the either/or approach of liberation and inculturation that have been at the heart of the debate thus far. These theologies form part of African liberative theologies, though some theologians tend to dismiss the one(s) they themselves do not emphasize as either irrelevant or surpassed. In other words, inculturation, liberation, black/reconstruction, reconciliation, and theologies of women are also African liberative theologies. One cannot talk of African liberation theology while excluding any of them. They form key aspects of African theology, involving complementary viewpoints regarding the relevance of Christian faith for Africans. Although each has arisen in response to some historical exigency, they all remain in vogue in Africa. This includes the black theology of South Africa despite the end of the apartheid regime.

In no way does contextualization present African theologies as a monolith. On the contrary, the plurality of contexts within which theology is done in Africa indicates not only the complexity of theologies in Africa but the importance of recognizing the variety of contexts in such a way that one is saved from falling into the pit of categorizing Africa in a homogenous, monolithic form. Africa is a diverse continent, and theologies arising from the variety of contexts present the richness of its spiritual reflection. However, this diversity does not rule out sociocultural, economic, political, and religious similarities in African life. While contextualization reveals that doing theology in Africa is no easy task, it also ensures that the human conditions of African people, cultural, social, economic, political, religious, and personal, are given due theological consideration.

Contextualization removes theology from the ivory towers of merely academic theology and situates its dependence on the experience of ordinary African Christians. Contextualization also is cognizant, and therefore respectful, of the distinctness of the variety of human conditions and pays attention to them in their particularity. At the same time, contextualization notes the interrelatedness of the issues the human condition of Africans presents to theology. On account of this, African liberative theologies emphasize different aspects of liberation, depending on the variety of contexts and their peculiarities. These theologies are nuanced in a variety of ways to emphasize the different components, needs, and interests theologians pursue in their contexts.

African liberative theologies are not without influence from theologies from other continents, and they certainly rely on the Christian faith and tradition. As the Christian faith is appropriated by African cultures and situations, these theologies draw from both scripture and tradition to make sense of the faith. Inculturation theologies, both in their moderate forms—applying the adaptation model—and in their radical forms—creatively engaging African cultures—interpret the Christian faith. African liberation theology draws on Latin American liberation theology when it concentrates on the conditions of poverty arising from the structural injustices of the international financial institutions and corporate organizations, globalization, and neocolonialism. Black theology of liberation, which began as a movement for blacks oppressed under the apartheid regime of South Africa, draws from the black theology of the United States, especially from the work of James Cone. These influences in no way override the creativity of African theologies; instead they serve as a springboard for theologizing within African contexts. One can generically speak of African liberative theologies as streams of theology emerging from responses of African Christians to divergent situations in history that deny their self-identity, oppress and marginalize them, and dim their consciousness of who they are as Africans in the light of the gospel.

Let us then examine briefly the various modes of expression of African liberative theologies: inculturation theology, liberation theologies, black and reconstruction theologies, reconciliation and womanist theologies.

African Theology of Inculturation

From Paul VI's 1969 charge to have an African theology, as expressed in his address to the first Pan-African meeting of Roman Catholic bishops at Gaba, Uganda ("Eucharistic Celebration at the Conclusion of the Symposium Organized by the Bishops of Africa," #2), to John Paul II's 1982 exhortation in the course of an apostolic pilgrimage to Nigeria, Benin, Gabon, and Equatorial Guinea ("Address of John Paul II to the Bishops of Nigeria, Lagos, Monday,

February 15, 1982," #3) to African bishops to be responsible for the formulation of African theology, African Christian theology has been dominated by inculturation theology. Inculturation is quite distinct from "adaptation" and "indigenization" contextual models. It involves a dialogue between faith and culture, one whereby the culture and Christian faith mutually influence, benefit, and enrich each other.

Because it is premised on the richness of African cultures and the transformative dynamics of Christian faith, inculturation theology adopts both the wholesome values found in African cultures and gospel values freed of foreign cultural accoutrements. As a liberative theology, inculturation theology liberates African Christianity from various forms of religious and cultural imperialism arising from evangelization methods, including foreign institutional structures that deny the existence of genuine African cultures and civilization. While this theology does not call into doubt that what is inculturated is Jesus Christ, the Christian faith, and its tradition, inculturation theology takes seriously the social, cultural, political, personal, and cultural aspects of African peoples as the important historical contexts within which African peoples religiously experience salvation in Christ.

Inculturation theology holds in tension the universality of gospel values and the particularity of the gospel's expression in diverse cultural contexts. Recalling the westernization agenda of the Christian missionaries in Africa, and its repudiation of African cultures as well as the attendant crisis of identity among Africans, African inculturation theology insists on the transformation of African cultures by the Christian faith as well as the purification of Christian faith of foreign cultural forms, be they Eurocentric, North American, etc.

African inculturation theology pastorally promotes evangelization by making the Christian faith meaningful to the people in the light of the people's cultures and values. By removing the various foreign cultural forms of the Christian faith, inculturation theology creates possibilities for African Christianity to become a way of life, to inform African cultures, and indeed to become part of African cultures in ways that integrate the gospel with African cultures. Since Christ is not encountered in the abstract but through a personal encounter made possible by the religious experience of each person within a particular cultural milieu, African inculturation theology insists that gospel values challenge African cultures. This makes encounter with the risen Christ possible. Through a promotion of the dialogue of the gospel with African cultures, authentic African Christianity will emerge within diverse African cultural milieus. In this way, inculturation theology hopes to contribute to the healing of the anthropological crisis at the heart of Africa's crisis of identity. The gospel of the risen Christ Son of God transforms

African cultures and, by being made relevant to African experiences, it gives new meanings that are redemptive for African anthropological poverty. In this way, African inculturation theology alleviates Africa's crisis of identity with a new identity as redeemed sons and daughters of God in Christ.

There have been advances in the various African christological inculturation theologies. Worthy of note here is the incarnational approach based on the logic of incarnation: that as God became human in human culture, the Christian faith must take flesh in African human cultures and be expressed in such cultures so that the redemption brought by Christ will be actualized in them. This incarnational approach to African Christology is associated with such theologians as Aylward Shorter, Peter Sarpong, Justin S. Ukpong, and Ngindu Mushete. The *logos spermatikos* (seeds of the Word) approach holds that African cultures contain the seed of Christian faith, because Christ pervades all human cultures. This approach is associated with Francis Cardinal Arinze and Efoe-Julien Penokou. The functional analogy approach, which seeks to describe the redemptive role of Jesus in terms analogous to the patterns of African thought, is associated with John S. Pobee, Bénézet Bujo, Charles Nyamiti, and F. Kabasele. For Pobee, Christ is the Greatest Ancestor or Nana of the Akan; for Bujo, Christ is the proto-ancestor, whereas Nyamiti refers to Christ as brother-ancestor. Aylward Shorter uses the African word *nganga*, or witch doctor, medicine man, to refer to Christ analogously as healer. This list is not exhaustive of the varieties of Christologies in Africa as people appropriate the Christian faith to their cultures in the course of encounters with the risen Christ through the scriptures.

Challenges of African Inculturation Theology

In the face of poverty, worsening socioeconomic conditions, political instability and poor governance, the inculturation of Christian faith may appear to be a useless waste of time and resources. The reason for such a position is the difficulty, at times, of grasping the connection between culture and socioeconomic and political development. Also for this reason, some people think African theology is ethnographically reconstructed by the cultural past of the people and cannot therefore engage in the ongoing African condition, one characterized by the dynamics of continuity and change that result from cultural contacts. And again for this reason, some people think African theology is completely different from black theology, which was concerned with the political liberation of South Africans as they suffered under the racist, exclusionary apartheid regime, experiencing deprivation as well as oppression under white minority rule. But theologians in post-apartheid South Africa no longer consider inculturation theology irrelevant. The reconstruction of South Africa heavily emphasizes reconciliation, and it draws on

African cultural values to incarnate the Christian faith in their diverse socio-cultural realities.

Although some theologians do not accept inculturation theology, seeing it as "paganization" of Christianity, the greatest challenge facing inculturation theology is not theoretical but practical. Apart from changes in some liturgical vestments (often for special occasions), hymns in African languages, melodies from common folk songs, and the introduction of a few liturgical rites like the official **Zairean Rite** and other (unofficial) Eucharistic prayers in use in experimental centers in East Africa, very little has been done to inculturate other areas of Christian faith in Africa.

Zairean Rite: The Zairean Rite received official approval from the Catholic Church on April 30, 1988. It includes prayers that have links to the ancestral tradition, and its richly communal nature has an equally healing role in the community. It is also liturgically integral, allowing a celebration of the Word with free expression in song, body movements, and dance.

While theological reflection on inculturation has garnered sufficient attention, and some regrettably few changes in liturgy and church structure (which is to a large extent still Eurocentric) have occurred, inculturation has yet to be accomplished regarding marriage and family. This slow process of inculturation is truer of Africa west of the Sahara than of East and Central Africa. The practice of setting up Christian villages whereby converts to Christianity are separated from their so-called pagan kith and kin still continues, if only psychologically. Many African Christians separate themselves from their cultural values to embrace the Western lifestyle they consider definitively Christian. The various agents of social transformation and the manner of missionary enterprise in Africa have made many educated Africans and ordinary Christians ignorant of their cultures. This lacuna must be filled if the African inculturation of Christian faith is to become solid. Many cultural elements deemed evil are only believed to be so because missionaries with limited knowledge, or even total ignorance, of the cultures have branded them evil. People at the forefront of African inculturation theology include Vincent Mulago (known as "the first African theologian"), Tharcisse Tshibangu, John Mbiti, Charles Nyamiti, Kwame Bediako, François Kabasélé, Bénézet Bujo, Justin S. Ukpon, Elochukwu E. Uzukwu, Patrick A. Kalilombe, Jesse Mugambi, Kato Byang, Yusuf Turaki, and others.

A critical study of African cultures will make it easier to find elements of what can be considered the blind spot of African inculturation, and for which it has been severely criticized: the romanticizing of African cultures and the uncritical effort at recovering their purity while glossing over their weaknesses. This is important because while inculturation cannot take place without clear knowledge of African cultures, inculturation must not be approached in such a way that it appears ignorant of the effects of modernity on African cultures. Further knowledge of African culture should uncover unwholesome characteristics that exclude, marginalize, and oppress people while impeding progress and the common good. At the same time, better knowledge and appreciation of African cultures will lead some denominations, groups, and theologians who are suspicious of African cultures to realize that one cannot be Christian outside one's cultural ambience and values. A positive disposition toward inculturation and inculturation theology's appreciation of African cultures would mutually benefit those African cultures and the Christian faith. But when culture became the ideological tool of the apartheid regime in South Africa, the dialogue of faith and culture of Africa became inadequate in mainline churches in response to the struggle against segregationist rule.

African Theology of Liberation

The thrust of African theology of liberation is the human situation of Africans, particularly the question of human dignity and human worth of Africans. The African theology of liberation, which at times is modeled on Latin American liberation theology, is the recovery of African dignity and human worth degraded and demeaned by experiences of the slave trade, colonialism, neocolonial socioeconomic and political structures of the international communities, and corrupt African leadership. Its theological focus is the redemption of the common masses of Africa from the poverty and deprivation that dehumanize them and reduce their worth as human beings. This redemption implies recognition of the unjust economic structures comprising the activities of the transnational corporations (TNCs), international financial institutions such as the World Bank, the Paris Club, and the International Monetary Fund, and the unfair trade regimes (e.g., World Trade Organization) as well as the collusion of local commercial banks in Africa that militate against African economies. The nefarious activities of corrupt African leadership also trap Africans in a perpetual cycle of poverty and want in spite of Africa's abundant natural and human resources, resources that are often exploited to the benefit of international communities and selfish African elites and bureaucrats.

African theology of liberation is guided by the insight that the sociopolitical and economic plight of Africa is theological and urges African churches, through its hermeneutic of the poor drawn from the Exodus account, to be engaged in the struggle for the liberation of Africans from poverty. The foremost exponents of this theology are Jean-Marc Ela, F. Eboussi Boulaga, and Engelbert Mveng, as well as Barnabas Chukwudum Okolo and Laurenti Magesa. Apart from interest in inculturation theology, most African theologians' attention to the poor and oppressed, to social and economic justice, to the exploitation of the poor by the rich and other forms of marginalization draws on African liberation theology, as does their approach to Christology.

The challenge for African liberation theology is extricating African Christianity from colonial and neocolonial Christianity and Eurocentric attitudes to Christianity, theologically and in practice. For this reason, some African liberation theologians, such as Ebousi Boulaga and Jean Mac Ela, insist on the freedom of African Christianity from Eurocentric ideas and ideals; that is, they demand changes in ecclesial structures to reflect the concrete situations of Africans, structures Africans can maintain without dependence on financial assistance from overseas. The future of African liberation theology lies in its ability to theologize from the concreteness of diverse African conditions. This implies making sense of the structures of sin that continue to marginalize and impoverish Africans materially and mentally, locally and internationally. These structures are entrenched nationally by bad governance and internationally from the unjust structures that African governments must comply with in order to remain politically sovereign and yet not isolated in the international scene.

Beginning theology from the concrete situations of the everyday lives of people remains imperative for the future of African liberation theology because of the seductiveness of theoretical theology that seeks a kind of universalism. However, African liberation must be able to balance theory with practice within the praxis of African conditions; neglecting reflection while emphasizing action limits such theology to mere activism. Since theology and the Christian faith can be meaningful to people and prepare them for liberation only in the light of their concrete historical conditions, African liberation theology stands to lose when it fails to theologize and reflect on the Christian faith from the perspective of African conditions. The idol to be overcome in Africa is the idol of colonial Christianity through the incarnation of the Christian faith into African cultures and the neocolonial structures that impoverish Africans.

Black Theology of South Africa

The black theology of South Africa emerged from the experience of Africans living in white-dominated societies where blackness was used as an excuse to subject black people to oppression and exploitation. This attitude was based on the theological notion that white people's superiority to Africans is ordained by God. The African theological response to the decades of dehumanization arising from the deceitful and paternalistic white "goodwill"—by which whites believed themselves to be divinely ordained to civilize Africans—gave rise to black theology, as Africans read the Bible and realized that God takes the side of the poor and the oppressed. The black theology of South Africa can be traced first to the various forms of dissent African Christians expressed to the rigidly Eurocentric form of worship imposed by the various Christian missionary churches. There followed the rejection of the segregated worship enforced by the Dutch Reformed Church, the agent of the Afrikaner supremacist policy of domination and white privilege as early as 1857, when apartheid's segregationist policies gained ground.

The formation of the Black Theology Project of the University Christian Movement evolved from black discontent with white racial oppression and dehumanization. Its leaders were influenced heavily by the black theology of the United States, especially by James Cone's early writings. Of particular importance were his books *Black Theology and Black Power* and *A Black Theology of Liberation*. The relationship of black theology of South Africa to black theology in the United States can be attributed to the similarity of their situations. When black theology in South Africa was battling apartheid and racist exclusionary policies, black theology in the United States was also struggling against racist policies against blacks in America. The gains of the civil rights movement in the United States were an inspiration to the blacks in South Africa. For this reason, they drew upon American achievements.

The formation in 1968 of the all-black South African Students Organization (SASO) by Steve Biko was a boost to the black consciousness movement, which not only questioned the education of the Bantu by the apartheid regime but also championed the cause of correcting the miseducation of black people. This miseducation aimed at making black people despise their traditional cultural values as barbaric. The philosophy behind the black consciousness movement was to awaken blacks to a consciousness of being black, to their value as human beings, and to their dignity as children of God. Black consciousness became a way of life among black people who sought to embrace their blackness as God's gift and as not demeaning in any way. The formation of the African National Congress in 1912 strengthened black theology.

The praxis of black theology of South Africa was the liberation of South Africans oppressed by the apartheid regime. The major source of this theology is the Bible, read in the light of the Exodus motif of liberation. The majority black experience of deprivation, marginalization, and oppression under the minority white apartheid rule was compared to the slavery of the people of Israel in Egypt. Liberation was compared to awaiting entry to the Promised Land. Among other proponents of black theology were Manas Buthelezi,

Gabriel Setloane, Desmond Tutu, Simon Maimela, Frank Chikane, Dwight Hopkins, and Allan Boesak.

The major challenge to black theology of South Africa is determining what its task is to be now that the apartheid regime has ended. This has been problematic because black theology concentrated all its energies on freedom from apartheid and did not articulate broader theological approaches to liberation as a whole. Its future may lie in a paradigm shift that interprets liberation broadly to address such growing pains in post-apartheid South Africa as poverty, the spread of HIV/AIDS, disease, income inequality, class and gender discrimination, the brutality directed against immigrants from other African countries, and increasing crime and violence.

Theology of Reconciliation and Construction

Post-apartheid theology deals with issues left unaddressed so that black theology could concentrate on liberation from apartheid. Contemporary South Africa is faced with the two key issues of reconciliation and social change. The Truth and Reconciliation Commission seeks ways of restoring the justice that is essential to reconciliation. Post-apartheid theology asks, "In the face of bitterness and anger against perpetrators of heinous crimes against blacks, what Christian resources can be tapped not only to foster forgiveness but also to establish mutual relationship in a multiracial South Africa that ensures respect for the human rights of everybody?"

Theologies of reconciliation address questions of individual and corporate guilt, the healing of memories scarred by the crimes of apartheid, reconciliation and justice, and the Christian imperative of love and forgiveness. Important here is the relation between the gospel and improving living standards, healing in the context of the HIV/AIDS pandemic, the progress and development of South Africa through empowerment of citizens to overcome poverty, and fostering the contribution of all to the common good. In this regard, the African sense of community expressed in *ubuntu* is brought into play in addressing the South African way of being church in the wake of the segregationist policies of apartheid. The ecclesiology of inclusion emerges to integrate the differences that are no longer causes for segregation but proof of the belonging of many in the one people of God. Broadly, the emerging ecclesiology includes issues of gender equality and gay and lesbian rights. In countries that have experienced hatred, violence, war, and even genocide, as in Rwanda, the theology of reconciliation seeks to foster renewed relationships in the spirit of the gospel.

Although some theologians argue that theologies of reconciliation are a distinct form of liberative theology, ultimately they seek to reconstruct African countries emerging from political dependence or devastated by war. In this sense at least, the theology of reconciliation paves the way for theologies of reconstruction. In South Africa, for instance, many Christian movements whose identity was defined by the anti-apartheid struggle now face a crisis of identity. This crisis is further intensified by religious pluralism. Theologies of reconstruction redefine the potential role of such Christian movements in reconstructing a new South Africa where equality, justice, prosperity, and peace will be enjoyed by everybody. These movements champion the cause of justice by serving as voices for the voiceless, mediating for the marginalized, stamping out all traces of racism, and guaranteeing a just society in South Africa.

Appropriating the biblical symbol of the reconstructionist postexilic prophet Nehemiah instead of the Exodus motif of liberation theology, the major proponents of reconstruction theology are Archbishop Desmond Tutu, Charles Villa-Vicencio, and Brigalia Hlophe Bam (South Africa), Jesse Mugambi (Kenya), Kä Mana (Democratic Republic of Congo), Ukachukwu Chris Manus (Nigeria), and Jose Chipenda (Angola). They charge the church to resist the temptation of blaming Africa's woes on external factors such as Western countries and missionary activities in Africa. They urge Africans to instead recapture Africa's self-esteem, dignity, and integrity by thinking critically and contributing toward the reconstruction of their nations by enshrining the virtues of democracy that bring justice to all in the context of the new globalized world. Most proponents of reconciliation theology, Emmanuel Katongole, Desmond Tutu, John Rucyahana, Villa-Vicencio, Valentin Dedji, and Julius Gathogo among them, equally spearhead, in related but diverse ways, movements for the reconstruction of Africa. This reconstruction is to be achieved by replacing Africa's self-image as a continent of hatred, violence, and war with a self-image as a continent that fosters reconciliation, justice, and peace.

The major weakness of reconciliation and reconstruction theologies is their demand for a paradigm shift from liberation theology. This claim presupposes the existence of one African liberation theology that metamorphoses into various forms depending on the sociopolitical, economic, and cultural challenges of Africa. This demand remains a weakness even though reconstruction theologians understand "paradigm" in the sense of sublation, that is, of the new motif of reconstruction going beyond previous theological motifs without destroying them. The demand for a paradigm shift away from liberation weakens reconstruction and reconciliation theologies because theologies in Africa are by definition liberative. One does not evolve from one to the other, and none is exclusive of the others as well.

Furthermore, the reconstruction theological motif is based on a supposition that racism, oppression, and the Cold War ended with the attainment of the political independence of South Africa in 1994. But does this independence really mean the end of oppression in Africa? This claim of the reconstruction theological motif lacks concrete supportive facts; oppression remains prevalent in Africa not only from tyrants and corrupt politicians but also from the subtle international trade regimes that would keep African economies from growing optimally even if African leaders tackled the endemic issue of corruption. The future of reconciliation and reconstruction theologies depends on their abandonment of the claim of exclusivity, the demand for a paradigm shift, and the desire to collapse other liberative theologies into the theology of reconstruction.

African Women's Theology

African women's theology is different from the womanist theology of African American women. Although both theologies concern women of black skin color, their historical contexts are different. For example, African American womanist theologies struggle with racism, sexism, and classism in America. African women's theology addresses traditional societies, colonialism, and slavery and the after-effects of these contexts in contemporary African societies. These include a rise in poverty engendered by the impact of globalization and neocolonial economic structures in Africa.

African women's theology: African women's theology engages in an open critique of the patriarchy that keeps women faceless in society instead of coping by ploys and self-abasement in order to gain the attention and approval of men. African women seek autonomy, self-affirmation, to name themselves, and integrity in both religion and culture.

Liberative Theology in Action: Confronting Extreme Poverty

In spite of recent growth in Africa's economy, an estimated 414 million in the continent still live in extreme poverty, lacking food, good drinking water, electricity, and other infrastructure basics. According to the UN Food and Agriculture Organization 2010 estimate, 239 million Africans are undernourished. The United Nations Millennium Project estimated that more than 50 percent of Africans suffer from water-related diseases such as cholera and infant diarrhea. According to the World Bank, approximately 550 million people in Africa live without electricity.

Putting African liberative theologies into action has the potential to contribute to the elimination of poverty. For example, not only does inculturation correct the miseducation of Africans because of which they prefer other cultures and consume mostly imported goods, but it heals the anthropological crisis at the heart of African indigence of being that pushes Africans to the precipice of fatalism. African theology of liberation sensitizes not only Africans but the global community to the unjust terms of trade that exclude Africans from equal partnership in international trade and exposes the various ways and means that African corrupt leaders collude with some international financial institutions to loot their nation's treasury, thus perpetuating poverty. The agitation of South African black theology against the evil of racism helped bring about the dismantling of the apartheid regime in 1994. Today, black theology focuses on eliminating poverty and inequality by advocating for just wages, an end to all forms of discrimination, including against gays and lesbians, and an end to violence.

Poverty in Africa often affects women and children the most. The activities of the circle of African women's theologians in conjunction with women's development centers in different parts of Africa are engaged in bridging the gap between men and women in Africa's predominantly patriarchal societies. This struggle against the marginalization of women and the change in the status of women from being mothers restricted exclusively to childbearing are reducing poverty among women. Not only do more women have opportunities for education, but African women's rights are improving through African women's theology. Since poverty can never be made a thing of the past in Africa without a strong civil society capable of holding African governments accountable for their stewardship, African liberative theologies need also to work toward a civil society that integrates the Christian faith and human promotion. African liberative theologies can strive to help eliminate poverty by educating the people to stand up and hold their various governments accountable and can champion varieties of free trade that do not promote Africa's economic development in unjust ways.

For instance, Mercy Amba Oduyoye observes that the seeds of objectification and marginalization of women can be found sprouting within the African religio-cultural heritage. Colonial policies fostered them, and they flourish to the extent that they benefit men in Africa's highly patriarchal societies. African women's theology believes religion should liberate the human spirit for communication with God rather than alienate people from one another or manipulate them for the good of others. African women's theology therefore critically reexamines African cultures and resists men's manipulation of religion to oppress women.

African women's theology emerges from the inability of African theology and black theology to address issues of concern to women in Africa. Oduyoye calls for a focus on "women-beingness," which is opposed to female identity based merely on childbearing, marriage, procreation, biological continuity, purity, family, culture, and religion. African women's theology gained greater prominence in 1989 in Accra Ghana at the inaugural meeting of the Circle of Concerned African Women Theologians; it was attended by over seventy women theologians. The Circle comes together to reflect on what it means to be women of faith within their experiences of religion, culture, politics, and the social-economic structures of Africa.

The Circle was inaugurated to facilitate research, writing, and publication by a pan-African multireligious and multiracial network of women concerned with the impact of religion and culture on African women. In her keynote address during the inauguration, Oduyoye advocated a "two-winged" approach through which men and women could worship God. African women's theology advocates for a nongender-biased, nonpatriarchal, and nonsexist theology. Its scope includes issues of colonialism, female circumcision, racism, cultural and spiritual imperialism, ethnocentrism, violence, exploitation, women's poverty and its varied implications, the scourge of HIV and AIDS, etc. In response to these issues, especially the scourge of poverty and its attendant consequences, African women's theology constructs an integral liberating theology with an element of hope that serves the entire lives of women, men, and children. It arises from the concern to live rightly and put things right. African women theologians equally emphasize the dignity of women as human beings created as equals in a complementary relationship with men and their children within a harmonious creative community where dialogue is the best means of resolving issues and conflicts. Ecclesiologically, African women's theology adopts *koinonia* with an emphasis on justice and participation.

Methodologically, African women's theology uses the narrative theological approach of storytelling drawn from the rich African oral history and the Bible. It makes use of African literature in articulating theology because most African women live the scenes represented in this literature most days of their lives. According to Isabel Phir, one of the Circle's past presidents, the challenges facing the Circle include (1) the redefinition of the identity of African women theologians; (2) the promotion of more women to study theology and be on permanent staff; (3) the inclusion of African women's theology in the theological curriculum; and (4) collaboration with male theologians.

Some of the major proponents of African women's theology are Mercy Amba Oduyoye (who founded the Circle), Isabel Apawo Phir, Theresa Okure, Musimbi Kanyoro, Rosemary Edet, Rachel Tetteh, Bernadette Mbuy Beya,

Nyambura Njoroge, Denise Ackerman, Musa W. Dube, Mary Getui, Teresia Hinga, Hannah Kinoti, Anne Nasimiyu-Wasike, Elizabeth Amoah, Rose Zoe, Louise Tappa, Grace Eneme, Justine Kahungu, and Brigalia Bam. The Circle has more than six hundred members from different African countries, including Angola, the Republic of Benin, Botswana, Burundi, the Democratic Republic of Congo (Zaire), Cameroon, Egypt, Ethiopia, Ghana, Kenya, Lesotho, Malagasy Republic, Namibia, Nigeria, Rwanda, the Republic of South Africa, Swaziland, Tanzania, and Zimbabwe.

Conclusion

Responding as they do to the various forms of Eurocentric and North American Christianity spread at various times in different parts of Africa through the missionary activities of various Christian denominations, African Christian theologies are liberative theologies. This is true even of the initial conversations in African theologies around contextualization, including the application of general principles of theology to such concrete issues as polygamy, ancestral cult, festivals, initiation rites, etc., with the aim of solving particular cases. It is equally true of the efforts to adapt African elements into Christian theology by adopting the positive elements that have parallels in Christianity while confronting the negative elements in the light of the gospel. Moreover, African theologies are obviously liberative when the entirety of the African situation and Christian theology is taken into consideration; they are the African response to the Christian faith in the light of African sociocultural, political, economic, and religious conditions. Thus, the following characterize African liberative theologies: first, the inculturation of Christian faith, which appropriates the faith in the light of African traditional cultures and religions; second, the black theology of liberation in South Africa, which decries the racialism of the milieu and engages in liberation from slavery, dehumanization, and exclusion from governance of the country; third, African women's theology, which agitates against the patriarchal nature of the church that marginalizes women within the church; fourth, liberation theology, which emphasizes liberation from the structures of sin (economically, politically and socially, nationally and internationally) that inhibit the complete liberation of Africans from poverty, oppression, injustice, and bad governance. The same is true of the budding theology of reconciliation and reconstruction, especially in response to the hatred and injustice of violence and war and to the reconstruction of Africa after such wars and with political independence. As African liberative theologies, these all arise from reflecting in the light of the gospel upon the diverse concrete situations of various African countries.

The future of African liberative theologies depends on the ability of African Christianity to be truly contextualized and independent, the critical and prophetic response to the reality of historicity to which contemporary theology becomes relevant in a theologically pluralistic Christianity. This involves the ability of African Christianity to build a true sense of community different from the elitist, clergy-dominated church inherited from the missionaries by incorporating the laity as full and equal members of the church as the people of God. African liberative theologies will persevere and be fruitful through the consistent appropriation of Christian faith made possible by the inculturation that draws out meanings in African cultural values in the light of the changes and transformations these cultural values have undergone in response to various agents of social transformation on account of modernity and multifaceted globalizing trends. The future of the African church and its liberative theologies depends on a much more authentic and profound contextualization based on theological presuppositions of African theologians in such a way that they incorporate all aspects of African life and situations in their reflection on biblical faith and Christian belief.

Study Questions

1. How are African liberative theologies different from Latin American liberation theology? In light of Africa's colonial past, why are African liberative theologies necessary?
2. African theology emerged within the context of African nationalist movements' demand for political independence from colonialism. Why do you think African theologies are liberative? Do you consider a variety of contexts important for the emergence of theologies? Is it right to think of African theology in evolutionary terms, as constantly changing according to the socioeconomic and political exigencies of Africa?
3. How can the challenges of inculturation theology be overcome? What is the relationship between African theology of inculturation and African liberation theology?
4. With the dismantling of apartheid and the institution of multiracial democracy in South Africa, do you think black theology is still relevant? If so, what should be its goals? If not, can it be replaced by reconstruction theology?
5. Why is womanist theology different from African women's theology? In patriarchal societies like Africa, what chance does African women's theology have of achieving its aims? Do you think it will receive support from African Christianity?

Suggested Reading

Appiah-Kubi, Kofi, and Sergio Torres, eds. *African Theology en Route*. Maryknoll, NY: Orbis Books, 1979.

Baur, John. *2000 Years of Christianity in Africa: An African History 62–1992*. Nairobi, Kenya: Pauline Publications Africa, 1994.

Boulaga, Eboussi F. *Christianity without Fetishes*. Translated by Richard R. Barr. Maryknoll, NY: Orbis Books, 1984.

Carney, J. J. "Roads to Reconciliation: An Emerging Paradigm of African Theology." *Modern Theology* 26.4 (October 2010): 549-69.

Dedji, Valentin. *Reconstruction and Renewal in African Christian Theology*. Nairobi, Kenya: Acton Publishers, 2003.

Dickson, Kwesi, and Paul Ellingworth, eds. *Biblical Revelation and African Beliefs*. Maryknoll, NY: Orbis Books, 1969.

Ela, Jean-Marc. *My Faith as an African*. Translated by John Pairman Brown and Susan Perry. Eugene, OR: Wipf & Stock Publishers, 2009.

Gathogo, Julius Mutugi. "Black Theology of South Africa: Is This the Hour of Paradigm Shift?" *Black Theology* 5.3 (2007): 327-54.

———. "Reconciliation Paradigm in the Post-Colonial Africa: A Critical Analysis." *Religion & Theology* 19 (2012): 74–91.

———. "A Survey on an African Theology of Reconstruction (ATOR)." *Svensk missionstidskrift* 95.2 (2007): 123-48.

Getui, M. N., and E. A. Obeng, eds. *Theology of Reconstruction*. Nairobi, Kenya: Acton Publishers, 1999.

Gibellini, Rosino, ed. *Paths of African Theology*. Maryknoll, NY: Orbis Books, 1994.

Gichaara, Jonathan. "Issues in African Liberation Theology." *Black Theology* 3.1 (2005): 75-85.

Gunda, Masiiwa Ragies. "African Theology of Reconstruction: The Painful Realities and Practical Options!" *Exchange* 38 (2009): 84-102.

Martey, Emmanuel. *African Theology: Inculturation and Liberation*. Maryknoll, NY: Orbis Books, 1993.

Mot Uiabi, Mokgethi. "Phases of Black Theology in South Africa: A Historical Review." *Religion & Theology* 16 (2009): 162-80.

Mugambi, J. N. K. *Christian Theology and Social Reconstruction*. Nairobi, Kenya: Acton Publishers, 2003.

Oduyoye, Mercy Amba. *Introducing African Women's Theology*. Cleveland, OH: Pilgrim Press, 2001.

Torres, Sergio, and Virginia Fabella. *The Emergent Gospel: Theology from the Developing World*. Maryknoll, NY: Orbis Books, 1978.

3

Asian Liberative Theologies

Jonathan Y. Tan

Contemporary Asia, with around two-thirds of the world's population, is a continent of extremes, marked by such diversity and plurality as to defy attempts at easy classification. Although the term "Asian" is often used as a convenient label for a diverse range of peoples from different regions across Asia, in reality this label hides the significant diversity and plurality that differentiate them in terms of languages, ethnicities, cultures, social practices, and spiritual traditions across the six geographical regions that make up the continent of Asia.

North Asia consists of the sparsely populated Siberian region of the Russian Federation that is aligned politically, socially, and culturally more closely with the European region of the Russian Federation, especially after the resettlement of ethnic Russians in this region in the twentieth century. West Asia, the cradle of Abrahamic monotheism that birthed Judaism, Christianity, and Islam, is predominantly Muslim with significant pockets of Jewish and Christian presence. This region is torn by violence along ethnic, religious, and sectarian lines. Central Asia, which used to have thriving Buddhist, Assyrian Christian, and Zoroastrian communities, is now home to large communities of Muslims living in the various republics that broke away from the former Soviet Union. South Asia is predominantly Hindu in India, Buddhist in Sri Lanka, and Muslim in Pakistan and Bangladesh, with significant Christian, Sikh, and Jain minorities. Southeast Asia is a world of contrast, with the predominantly Muslim Malay and Indonesian Archipelago on the one hand, and the predominantly Buddhist Myanmar, Thailand, and Indochina on the other. This region contains significant diversity along ethnic, cultural, and religious lines. East Asia, encompassing China, Japan, and Korea, is influenced heavily by Confucian, Buddhist, and Daoist traditions, with a significant Muslim minority presence in the western region of China that overlaps into Central Asia.

Asia gave birth to several of the world's ancient civilizations, including the Mohenjo-daro, Harappa, and Dholavira civilizations in the Indus Valley (ca. 3000 BCE), the Yangshao civilization in the Yellow River basin (ca. 5000 BCE) and the Liangzhu civilization in the Yangtze River valley (ca. 3300 BCE). Asia is also the native soil from which the ancient great religions of the world sprang up. This includes the religious traditions of Hinduism, Buddhism, and Jainism in South Asia, Confucianism and Daoism in East Asia, Zoroastrianism in Central Asia, and the three monotheistic religious traditions of Judaism, Christianity, and Islam in West Asia.

In the aftermath of the Second World War, independence and postcolonial consciousness have led to a discovery of national pride, and with it, a massive revival and growth of traditional Asian religions throughout Asia. India is experiencing a Hindu renaissance and Islam is on the upsurge, making it one of the fastest-growing religions in the world. In East and Southeast Asia, Buddhism has a gained a new vitality as new Buddhist movements that first emerged in the early twentieth century blossomed in the decades after the Second World War. These religious traditions are very much alive and influential throughout Asia, nourishing the present spiritual needs of billions of Asians, very much intertwined within the sociopolitical and cultural fabric of diverse communities across Asia.

Unlike other continents, where Christianity has a dominant or significant presence, Asia remains the continent with the smallest Christian population, notwithstanding that Jesus was born in West Asia. Indeed, the Christian movement originally emerged in Asia and also moved eastward, propagated by Assyrian Christian missionaries who ventured across the vast expenses of Central Asia along the Silk Road to India and China in the first Christian millennium. According to the Pew Forum on Religion and Public Life's 2011 report, *Global Christianity: A Report on the Size and Distribution of the World's Christian Population*, Christians account for 7 percent of the total population of the Asia-Pacific region, which translates to 13.1 percent of the total world Christian population. *Global Christianity* further identifies the top three Asian countries with a significant Christian percentage of their total population as the Philippines (93.1%), Timor-Leste (99.6%), and South Korea (29.3%), and notes that Christians continue to comprise a small proportion of the residents of China (5%) and India (2.6%), who collectively comprise about one-third of the world's population.

More important, contemporary Asia is a continent of socioeconomic extremes. Asia has the world's oldest extant civilizations of China and India on the one hand, and newer nations such as Timor-Leste, which became an independent nation-state in 2002. The top three most populous nations in the world, namely China, India, and Indonesia, are not only in Asia, but they are so diverse such that they are, in reality, miniature continents with hundreds of languages and dialects, ethnic cultures, and sociocultural traditions. Asia also has extremes of economic disparities, with the richest nations in West Asia that are beneficiaries of an oil boom and cheap migrant labor, and countries at the bottom of the economic ladder such as Timor-Leste, Bangladesh, Myanmar, and Cambodia, where peoples are struggling to eke out a daily living.

Liberative Theologies from Latin America and Asia: A Comparison

Latin America	Asia
1. Overwhelmingly Christian	1. Christians comprise a small proportion of Asia's total population
2. The marginalized masses are Christians	2. The majority of the marginalized masses are adherents of the great religions of Asia
3. Liberation and social justice rooted in Christian theological thinking	3. Liberation and social justice must include the great religions of Asia
4. Liberative theologies take for granted a Christian framework in articulating principles of social justice and liberation	4. Liberative theologies cannot presume a Christian framework, but rather need to work from within the various religious frameworks of the masses from across Asia

Varieties of Liberative Theologies

What is unique about Asia, especially in contrast with Europe and the Americas, is its diverse and pluralistic religio-cultural context. Many of the poor and marginalized in Asia are followers of the great religions of Asia and practitioners of a variety of popular religious traditions that are related to Asia's great religious traditions that have shaped the dominant Asian cultures. It should not come as a surprise to us that liberative theologies have emerged in different religious communities across Asia.

In this chapter, we shall examine how liberative theologians from across the major religious traditions of Asia have sought answers from within their own religious traditions to the endemic persistence of mass poverty, exploitative socioeconomic structures, and oppressive political systems that often deny basic human and democratic rights to the masses of Asian poor and marginalized. We shall focus, in particular, on the liberative outreach of Mahatma Gandhi in Indian Hinduism, B. R. Ambedkar in Indian Buddhism, and Buddhadasa Bhikkhu in Thai Buddhism. From the Christian perspective, shaped by the sociocultural, economic, political, and religious challenges of the diverse Asian contexts, a variety of Asian Christian liberative theologies have emerged. In this context, we shall explore the insights of Aloysius Pieris (Sri Lanka), Dalit and indigenous tribal theologies from India, and minjung theology from Korea.

Mahatma Gandhi

An early advocate of liberative theologies from an Asian religious context is Mohandas Karamchand (Mahatma) Gandhi (1869–1948). Mahatma Gandhi is remembered best for his indefatigable campaign to liberate India through nonviolent means from British colonial rule and for social equality and justice for all Indians in the context of his Hindu faith. Indeed, Gandhi's vision of nonviolence was greatly influential in Martin Luther King, Jr.'s approach of nonviolence in his civil rights campaign against segregation in the Deep South. The seeds for Gandhi's nonviolent liberative approach were sown in his participation in the nascent South African civil rights movement. There, as a young lawyer defending Indian citizens from racist South African segregation laws against what were called colored peoples, he discovered the liberative power of nonviolent resistance against the segregationist legislation of colonial South Africa. His firsthand experience of social injustice from the grievous mistreatment for his colored status would shape his activism for liberative action.

Upon returning to India, Gandhi sought to use his new insight on nonviolent resistance to fight for the liberation of India from British rule. Drawing on the insights that he gleaned from reading the ***Bhagavad Gita*** and the Sermon on the Mount, Gandhi fleshed out the underlying philosophy for his nonviolent liberative approach that he called ***satyagraha***, which literally means "clinging to the truth," and is usually translated as "soul force" or "truth force." For Gandhi, nonviolence is more than practical strategy and pragmatic action. In reality, Gandhi understood it to be a core human attribute that empowers a person with courage, perseverance, and discipline to work for liberation of the oppressed and exploited. More important, Gandhi perceived *satyagraha* as the pursuit of one's ***dharma*** to work for solidarity, progress, and the empowerment of all without distinction, differentiation, or discrimination. In his writings, Gandhi insisted that the key element of *satyagraha* is the overarching power of ***ahimsa,*** not as a selective political strategy but rather as a consistent way of life to render unjust laws powerless through civil disobedience. Within the context of *satyagraha*, the path of *ahimsa* becomes a *nonviolence of the righteous* that is practiced even if one is justified to retaliate for unjust actions, because it is a way of life that accepts suffering as a means of purification and character building that is done out of free will. The efficacy of Gandhi's vision was demonstrated in the nonviolence mass civil disobedience movement of the 1930 Salt March, which overwhelmed the British colonial administration, gained crucial international recognition and support for Gandhi's campaign, and set in motion the negotiations for India's independence.

***Bhagavad Gita*:** the eighteenth book of the great Indian epic, the *Mahabharata*, in which Lord Krishna engages in conversation with Arjuna on the various paths to a deeper spiritual quest.

***Satyagraha*:** literally, "clinging to the truth"; it refers to the "soul force" or "truth force" that undergirds Gandhi's movement of nonviolent resistance for liberation from oppression and exploitation.

***Dharma*:** a Sanskrit term that is commonly translated as moral conduct, practical duty, path to righteousness, deeper spiritual insights, or religious practice.

***Ahimsa*:** a Sanskrit term that means nonviolence.

B. R. Ambedkar

Popularly acclaimed as the "Father of the Indian Constitution" for his active involvement in drafting the Indian constitution, Bhimrao Ramji Ambedkar's (1891–1956) lifelong fight for liberating the **Dalits** from **caste** oppression came from his own personal experiences of growing up as Dalit. This meant that he was marginalized as an untouchable in a society that was strictly delineated according to caste norms. At school, he often faced taunting and bullying for his outcaste status. His high-caste teachers refused to touch his work, and he was isolated from the other students, lest his untouchable stigma pollute the teachers and students from the higher castes.

Dalit: the preferred term for the group of Indians outside of the formal caste structure who are the outcastes and "untouchables" by virtue of their ritual impurity, which arises from handling corpses, dead animals, human waste, or garbage.

Caste: hereditary social segregation in a society on the basis of occupation and norms of purity and pollution.

The Indian caste system: More than 3,000 years old, the caste system of India is the oldest surviving hierarchical segregation of society based on status, purity, and pollution in the world. Historically, it originated as a division of labor among different groups of Indian society, which eventually became entrenched along hereditary lines by virtue of endogamy; that is, one could only marry within one's caste. As a result, caste identity became hereditary, passed down from parents to children.

The caste structure of India is shaped by the fourfold division of traditional Indian society along occupational lines. First, there are the *Brahmins*, who are priests and ritual specialists who possess the knowledge and skills to perform the complex ritual services of sacrificial offerings to the gods known as the *yajna*. Second, the *Kshatriyas* were the rulers and warriors in feudal Indian society who are responsible for proper administration and ordering of society, as well as defending the populace from attacks by rival kingdoms and brigands. Third, the *Vaishyas* are the merchants, traders, and landowners who comprise the economic backbone of society. Finally, the *Shudras*, who occupy the bottom rung of this fourfold caste structure, serve the other three castes as servants and manual laborers.

Excluded by this fourfold caste framework are the Dalits, relegated to the fringes of Indian society as *untouchables* and *outcasts* by virtue of being ritually unclean. Their ritually polluted status comes about because they perform the most menial and unclean of tasks, including handling dead animals, human waste, corpses, and garbage. While discrimination based on caste is expressly prohibited in the constitution of

Ambedkar struggled against all odds, excelling in school, winning scholarships to pursue doctoral studies at Columbia University and the London School of Economics. Notwithstanding his two doctoral degrees in economics and his status as a lawyer admitted to the Bar in London's Gray's Inn, Ambedkar continued to experience caste discrimination and harassment as a Dalit. His situation worsened when high-caste Indians took exception to his advocacy for caste reform and rights for Dalits.

Eventually, Ambedkar became disillusioned with Hinduism, convinced that caste reform within Hinduism was futile. He turned to Buddhism as an alternate path for liberating the Dalits from oppression and marginalization. In his seminal work *The Buddha and His Dhamma*, published posthumously, Ambedkar emphasized the relevance of Buddhist teachings to usher in much-needed social and political changes to reform the systematic injustices and inequities in the caste system, thereby liberating the Dalits from the vicious cycle of poverty, oppression, exploitation, and violence perpetrated by the high castes. Ambedkar and his wife converted to Buddhism in a public ceremony on October 14, 1956. Notwithstanding his death six weeks later, Ambedkar's embrace of Buddhism paved the way for Dalits to choose the liberative path of Buddhism to escape caste strictures.

Buddhadasa Bhikkhu

Buddhadasa Bhikkhu (1906–1993) was a well-known social reformer and critic of capitalism and its social ills. Growing up in the countryside in southern Thailand, he entered the Buddhist monastic life at the age of ten and came to the capital city of Bangkok for his monastic training. There, he became disillusioned by his many encounters with city-dwelling monks who were pursuing power and prestige instead of critically reflecting on the contemporary relevance of the Buddhist dharma to address the social ills of his day. He returned to his home province and established a hermitage for meditation and contemplation. His ability to explain deep insights in simple terms drew many to his hermitage. His strident critique of capitalism and the modern social and economic structures that were radically transforming Thai society in the twentieth century are deeply rooted in his insight that personal and social transformation must go hand in hand. In particular, Buddhadasa insisted that personal egoism and selfishness that cause individuals to be trapped in dissatisfaction and frustrations (***dukkha***) are linked inextricably to self-centeredness and selfishness, and give rise to social, economic, and political inequities and marginalization that entrap society in dissatisfaction and frustrations.

India that was drafted under the leadership of the Dalit activist B. R. Ambedkar, in reality discrimination and prejudice against Dalits continue to persist across contemporary Indian society.

***Dukkha*:** In Buddhist thought, the existential condition of living that is characterized by much dissatisfaction, frustrations, and unhappiness.

More importantly, Buddhadasa argued that capitalism is, as an economic system, based on a fundamentally flawed notion of destructive competition that reinforces individualism and egoism in search of selfish gains. It pits people against one another in a zero-sum game, thereby undermining the network of mutual interdependence in communities and societies, trapping individuals and communities in a vicious cycle of personal and social *dukkha*. By contrast, the Buddhist dharma provides the path for mutual benefit and support, promoting mindfulness and loving kindness to overcome egoism and selfishness, nurturing selfless endeavors to work for the betterment of society, alleviating the sufferings of the poor and marginalized, and empowering the fight for justice, equality, and peace in contemporary Thai society. Buddhadasa also went a step further than his Buddhist confreres in his willingness to engage in interreligious collaboration to bring about social and economic transformation in society, especially for the poor and marginalized.

Asian Christian Liberative Theologies

Moving on to explore the various Asian Christian perspectives, we begin with the insight of the Taiwanese theologian C. S. Song, who sums it up succinctly when he describes Asian Christian theologians as seeking to reclaim their Asianness within their diverse Asian heritages in order to carry out their theological reflections together with their fellow Asian peoples. Historically, Asian Christian liberative theologies were inspired by the Latin American liberative theologies that emerged in the 1970s that focused on Jesus Christ as liberator of the oppressed and on the goal of liberative theologies to bring justice to the poor and oppressed through sociopolitical transformation of sinful structures. In this section, we shall explore how Asian Christian liberative theologians seek to do theology with Asian realities as resources, discerning the divine presence and action in them and correlating them to resources in the Bible and the Christian theological tradition.

For many Asian theologians, the cultures of the peoples, the history of their struggles, their cultural and religious traditions, popular devotions, oral traditions, socioeconomic and political events, and experiences of exploitation and oppression, as well as the peoples' quest for justice, freedom, dignity, empathy, and solidarity in their lives, become resources for theological reflection. For Asian theologians, God is redemptively present in human history through the incarnation, and the Christian gospel is liberative only insofar as it is rooted in, and responding to, the totality of human life.

Liberative Theology in Action: Liberative Theologies and Asian Sexual Minorities

Sexual minorities across Asia often encounter prejudice and discrimination within their communities in the name of conformity and perpetuation of family lines. Many contemporary Asian LGBTs experience a double marginalization within their own ethnic communities and the global LGBT community. In the case of the former, Asian LGBTs are often compelled to marry and produce offspring to perpetuate their families. In the case of the latter, they must deal with the racism and orientalism of "rice queens," older white men who objectify Asian gay men as the exotic "other," fetishize them as "boy toys," and venture to Asia to engage in predatory consumption of younger Asian gay men.

Historically, Asian societies have been ambivalent toward same-sex relations. For example, Chinese emperors had male lovers; concubines in imperial Chinese households practiced "paired-eating"; transsexuals performed in Chinese operas; Chinese literary masterpieces such as *The Dream of the Red Chamber* and *Precious Mirror for Gazing at Flowers* celebrated same-sex romances; and Khajuraho temple art and Japanese woodcuts portrayed same-sex acts. Nonetheless, minority same-sex relations were accepted and tolerated only insofar as the male-female complementarity (e.g., the Chinese yin-yang and Indian tantric and yogic frameworks) and heterosexual family framework for perpetuating family lineages were upheld as normative. The arrival of Christian missionaries and European colonizers in Asia led to the imposition of Christian moral norms on marriage and sex and the outlawing of the diversity of poly-, same-, bi-, and transsexual relations historically tolerated within many Asian communities.

From the 1980s onward, a number of Asian Christian theologians have begun articulating Asian theologies that seek to liberate sexual minorities from shameful naming, coercive silencing of their voices, and oppressive suppression of their identities. First, they encourage these sexual outsiders to embrace both the multiplicity of their Asian ethnic and LGBT identities and be at home within their hybridized minority and sexual identities. Second, they seek to empower Asian sexual minorities in the face of stereotypes of same-sex relations as degenerate Western practices and ongoing pressure by their families and communities to conform to a heterosexual ideal of marriage and family life. Finally, they also challenge their faith communities to transcend narrow definitions of marriage and family and recognize the gifts and contributions that Asian LGBTs bring to their families, communities, and churches.

Working from a postcolonial theological framework in Hong Kong, Rose Wu and Lai-Shan Yip have constructed liberative Chinese theologies for the *tongzhi*, the preferred term for contemporary Chinese LGBTs. In their writings, both Wu and Yip are also committed to articulating liberative theologies for *nu-tongzhi* (Chinese women who love other women) that are rooted in both Christian social justice and traditional Chinese perspectives on same-sex relations and differently oriented persons. In addition, Malaysian-born Chinese queer theologian Joseph Goh, who has written on the intersection of interreligious spirituality and gender identity among same-sex and transgender Malaysians, has carried out groundbreaking theological reflections on the multiplicity and hybridity of the diverse identities of the *mak nyah* (male-to-female transgender Malaysians).

Contextual Theologies: Kosuke Koyama

The Japanese theologian Kosuke Koyama speaks of Asian theologies as having the following ten characteristics. First, Asian theologies are *contextual*, that is, they emerge from the experiences of the local community. Second, as contextual theologies, all Asian theologies take the Asian peoples' daily experiences and life struggles as a starting point. Third, Asian theologies seek to correlate these daily experiences and life struggles with the Christian gospel. Fourth, Koyama speaks of the need to use the tools of social analysis to interpret the experiences of Asian peoples. Fifth, social-scientific methods on their own are insufficient, and, therefore, indigenous thinking and logic are required to complement social analysis. Sixth, Asian theologies utilize Asian philosophical methods and conceptual tools to articulate insights and conclusions that are Asian in worldview and ethos. Seventh, Asian theologies also utilize the resources and realities of the Asian cultures that shape the worldviews and life experiences of the Asian peoples. Eighth, Asian theologies have to be formulated in the languages of the Asian peoples. Ninth, Asian theologies are not abstract or theoretical, but rather facilitate liberative action and commitment to social transformation. Finally, Asian theologies share the common goal of seeking the fullness of life for all Asians.

Asian Postcolonial Theologies

One of the earliest Asian pioneers in Christian liberative theologies was the Indian Jesuit theologian Samuel Rayan, who also served as an unofficial spokesperson for Asian theologies in general and Indian theologies in particular. Rayan was professor and dean of the Jesuit-run Vidyajyoti College of Theology in Delhi, India, in 1972, a member of the World Council of Churches' Faith and Order Commission from 1968 to 1982, and principal of the Indian School of Ecumenical Theology in Bangalore from 1988 to 1990. The underlying theme of much of his theological writings in English and his native Malayalam is a postcolonial thrust that seeks to *decolonize* and *liberate* Asian theologies in general, and Indian theologies in particular, from the clutches of "colonial" theologies.

By colonial theologies, Rayan refers to those theologies that originated in Europe and were brought to Asia by colonial-era missionaries and that the colonial administrations found convenient for keeping the locals subservient to colonial rule. He argues that these colonial theologies stressed hierarchy, power, submission, resignation, and otherworldly salvation rather than community, friendship, obedience to truth, pursuit of justice, and ushering in the reign of God in contemporary human societies. Rayan contends that indigenous postcolonial Asian theologies that focus on the concerns, needs, and hopes of the masses of the Asian poor and oppressed have to emerge, to liberate them from the unjust social, economic, and political structures that remain in spite of decolonization.

Complementing Samuel Rayan in East Asia is the Hong Kong Chinese theologian Kwok Pui Lan, who has done significant work in postcolonial liberative theology. In particular, Kwok makes the case for emergent postcolonial liberative theologies in Asia that seek to build on the political independence from colonial rule to construct autonomous indigenous theologies that are relevant to, address the challenges faced by, and respond to the hopes of the Asian peoples who confront significant economic and political challenges in their daily lives. By insisting on the need for theology to be postcolonial, Kwok is asserting that Asian liberative theologies have to confront how the experiences of colonialism and decolonization could help Asian Christians rethink how they read the Bible and construct indigenous Asian theology. Following in her footsteps, Angela Wong Wai-Ching, who teaches at the Chinese University of Hong Kong and is the former president of the Christian Conference of Asia, speaks of Asian theologies as having to take on an anti-imperialist task to challenge the hegemony of a Western Christian theological heritage. In turn, Wong explains that postcolonial Asian theologies have to be constructed in reference to the social location and identities of Asian peoples, to decolonize the economic and power structures left behind by the colonial elite that favored a small minority at the expense of the majority. For Wong, being liberative is synonymous with being anti-imperialistic and postcolonial in orientation.

Asian Interreligious Theologies

Among the many Asian theologians who have contributed significantly to the development of Asian Christian liberative theologies is the Sri Lankan Jesuit theologian Aloysius Pieris, who was the first Catholic to earn a doctorate in Buddhism at the University of Sri Lanka. Pieris seeks to make the case that Asian liberative theologies cannot be mere copies of Latin American liberation theologies. In his seminal work, *An Asian Theology of Liberation* (1988), Pieris argues that all discussions in Asian theology have to take seriously both the *Thirdworldiness* of the Asian context and its distinctive *Asian* character. He argues that an authentic Asian liberative theology has to be grounded in two important dimensions of the lived realities of Asia: the immense poverty and the multifaceted religiousness that characterize much of Asia. For him, both these realities are inseparable and must engage deeply with each other for any theology to be both Asian and liberative.

First, Pieris highlights the reality that, in Asia, poverty is not always simply forced but also can be voluntary, as in the poverty voluntarily assumed by the holy women and men. Hence, Pieris makes a contrast between the "imposed" or "forced" poverty that arises from injustice, marginalization, and exploitation on the one hand, and, on the other hand, the "voluntary" poverty freely assumed by many Asians within the context of traditional Asian religious practices as a way of life in solidarity with the masses of the poor and marginalized in Asia. He observes that the "imposed" or "forced" poverty in Asia arises from structural imbalances brought about historically by colonialism and perpetuated by neocolonial practices and economic exploitation by transnational corporations, the concentration of wealth in the hands of a few, the abuse and trafficking of women and children, the implications of dictatorship, and ongoing violence arising from civil strife. For Pieris, the involuntary or forced poverty is enslaving and oppressive, while the voluntary poverty is liberating and life giving.

Second, Pieris argues that unless theology enters into dialogue with Asian religions and integrates the introspective dimensions of Asian religiosity into its heart, it will remain foreign and nonliberative for the Asian peoples. For Pieris, the struggle with poverty and interreligious engagement are two sides of the same coin. In *An Asian Theology of Liberation*, he introduces the notion of the double baptism of Asian liberative theology. As he explains, for an Asian theology to be liberative for the masses of Asians experiencing crushing poverty and dehumanizing conditions in their daily lives, it must be baptized in the "Jordan of Asian religion" and the "Calvary of Asian poverty." In this regard, Pieris is adamant that interreligious engagements with other Asian religions are necessary for Asian Christian theology to be truly liberative for the masses of Asian peoples, the majority of whom are not Christian but devout practitioners of various Asian religions. The innate religiousness of the Asian masses and their experiences of material poverty must undergird any Asian liberative theology. To put it another way, the struggle for justice is doomed to failure if Asian Christians ignore the great religions of Asia.

Feminist Theologies

The Filipino feminist theologian Hope Antone, who also serves on the Christian Conference of Asia, has articulated an Asian feminist theology that draws upon the Filipino experiences of women and children. Her Asian feminist theological spiral is comprised of the following five elements: (1) naming the oppression; (2) identifying the agents and causes that reinforce the oppression; (3) identifying the dominant theology that justifies and perpetuates the oppression; (4) carrying out a feminist critique of the oppression, agents, and underlying theology; and (5) commitment to action to work toward change.

Building on the experiences of the huge contingent of Filipino migrants working abroad to support their families back home, the Filipino theologian Gemma Tulud Cruz has constructed a liberative theology for migrants that focuses attention on the powerlessness of the migrants in the face of economic exploitation and various forms of physical, emotional, and psychological abuse. She highlights the breakdown in family ties when one or more parents are forced to go abroad as breadwinners for their families. Drawing attention to the "irruption of the poor," she argues that the resistance of the poor and oppressed challenges not just the power of the powerful but also the way theology typically is done by, and for the benefit of, the powerful.

Minjung Theology

Emerging in the 1970s in the context of the Korean peoples' protest movement against the military dictatorship of General Park Chung Hee, *minjung* theology is a Korean liberative theology that challenged the Korean military dictatorship in the 1970s and 1980s and sought redress for the oppression and marginalization of ordinary Koreans. The term ***minjung***, which literally means "the common peoples" or "masses of peoples," captures the struggles and hopes of the powerless masses of Korea who suffer marginalization and exploitation by the economic and political elites. According to the Korean feminist theologian Chung Hyun Kyung, the term *minjung* may be translated as the popular masses from the underside of history who are oppressed, exploited, dominated, alienated, and discriminated against, especially the poor, women, ethnic minorities, and workers and farmers, as well as intellectuals who are persecuted and harassed for rousing the conscience of the nation. Chung Hyun Kyung argues that Korean women are doubly marginalized by society as sources of cheap labor in factories and by men in patriarchal familial structures. She explains the roots of this double marginalization in the twin contexts of the pervasive endurance of patriarchy and political oppression and economic marginalization, first by Chinese and Japanese colonialism, followed by military dictatorship and subsequent transnational neoliberalism that has emerged as the result of globalization.

***Minjung*:** literally "the common peoples" or "masses of peoples," this term is often used to refer to the exploited, oppressed, and marginalized masses of Korea.

More importantly, *minjung* theologians identify Jesus as being in solidarity and empathy with the Korean *minjung* by virtue of his solidarity and empathy for the poor and oppressed of the New Testament. In this context, one has to appreciate the unique history of the introduction of Christianity to Korea. Unlike many parts of Asia, Korea did not experience colonization by the European imperial powers, but rather by China and then Japan. Hence, Confucianism and Buddhism are perceived not as liberative but rather as enabling oppression and marginalization, as these two religious traditions were coopted by the Korean ruling class and therefore became tightly woven into the political landscape in Korean history.

By contrast, when Christianity arrived in Korea, it was not the faith of a colonizing power but rather a powerful liberative message for the Korean masses from Chinese and Japanese domination. More significantly, the proliferation of Korean Bibles in the vernacular *Hangul* script rather than the classical *Hancha* script of the Korean Confucian literati meant that the Korean *minjung* could appropriate the liberative power of the good news of Jesus concerning the coming of God's reign. Indeed, the good news of the in-breaking of God's reign served to empower the Korean Christians to rise up and break free from the chains of domination and oppression in their quest for peoplehood and dignity.

Minjung theologians argue that the *minjung* peoples are burdened by *han,* which arises from their oppression, alienation, and subjugation at the hands of the strong and powerful. Literally "resentment" or "frustration," the Korean term ***han*** refers to the unresolved frustrations and accumulated anger that emerge from the Korean peoples' sense of helplessness in the face of oppression and marginalization by the political and military elite. Properly harnessed and channeled in a responsible manner, the *han* that emerges from the grievances and anger of the *minjung* can be a powerful source of energy to spark a peaceful revolution for change against the powerful elite.

Han: a Korean word that refers to the accumulated and unresolved frustrations that emerge from the Korean peoples' sense of helplessness in the face of oppression and marginalization by the political and military elite.

In his essay "Minjung Theology: A Critical Introduction," the late Korean theologian Jung Young Lee describes the process of resolving the *han* as *dan*, literally "cutting off." Lee explained that *dan* occurs at the individual and collective levels. For individuals, *dan* entails the renunciation of material wealth and comforts that dull their sensitivity to human suffering and marginalization around them. For the community, *dan* involves a collective endeavor toward the transformation of community and society. As a Christian theologian, Lee asserted that *dan* comprises the following four steps: (1) realizing the presence of God in the world; (2) allowing the divine consciousness to permeate through life; (3) putting into action the good news of Jesus; and, by doing so, (4) overcoming injustices through radical action to transform society.

More importantly, *minjung* theologians speak of the Korean *minjung* perceiving Jesus as the compassionate one who is able to empathize with the deep pathos of their suffering. For the Korean *minjung*, Jesus is the messiah who liberates the oppressed and marginalized, who weeps with the suffering, and bears their burdens on his cross. Jesus is the liberator who has come to bring new life and freedom from oppression and exploitation to the *minjung*. In this regard, the good news of Jesus empowers them to release the *han* from their lives. The *minjung* are not merely the hearers of Jesus's good news. Rather, they become a part of the kingdom that Jesus sought to establish with his outreach to the poor and outcast of his day.

Hence, *minjung* theologians seek to address the oppression and exploitation of the masses, emphasizing the triumph of God's justice in Jesus that liberates the *minjung* from oppression and marginalization. *Minjung* theologians emphasize that God is in solidarity with the *minjung* in their sufferings and struggles. After the collapse of military dictatorship and return to democracy in South Korea in the 1990s, *minjung* theologians broadened their horizons to explore the emerging social issues of environmental justice, eco-feminism, and rampant consumerism, as well as the struggles faced by migrant workers and foreign brides in Korea.

Dalit Theology

Dalit theology in India highlights the social injustice and oppression that the Dalits, who are marginalized as outcastes and untouchables, have experienced at the hands of the higher castes of India. In general, Jesus is perceived as liberating the Dalits from oppression and enabling them to gain equal status with the other castes.

The Dalit theologian Arvind Nirmal defines Dalit theology as undergirded not just by the pathos of the Dalits' daily life experiences but also by their protest against the social oppression and economic injustices that they encounter and their liberative dream to break free and seize control of their own destiny. Nirmal further identifies three important dimensions of Dalit theology. First, Dalit theology is *experiential* in orientation, rooted in the Dalits' experience of pathos in their lives. Second, Dalit theology *anticipates* the coming liberation of the Dalits from such pathos and oppression. Third, Dalit theology seeks to *dismantle* the caste framework that has enslaved them for generations.

Another Dalit theologian, Sebastian Kappen, emphasizes the implications of Jesus's good news of God's reign for the Dalits' struggle for new life and their quest to be treated as full human beings. Specifically, Kappen has articulated a Dalit Christology in which Jesus's liberative actions among the marginalized of Galilee continue with the quest for the Dalits' liberation in India. For Kappen, Jesus is a prophet who models the "praxis of subversion" that liberates the Dalits from oppression by the upper castes, as well as exploitation by global capitalism.

In a similar vein, the Indian Jesuit and Dalit theologian Maria Arul Raja speaks of Dalit theology as a liberative theology arising from the context of the Dalit experiences of exploitation and oppression. Moreover, Dalit theology seeks to address the challenges that the Dalits encounter in their daily life experiences, criticizing the status quo and proposing alternatives. Postcolonial in orientation, Dalit theology also rejects attempts by outsiders, especially the higher castes, to impose top-down solutions. Dalit theology is also eclectic in approach, integrating the divergent interdisciplinary critical methods and engages in critical dialogue with other Asian contextual liberative theologies.

Tribal/Indigenous Theologies

The indigenous (or "tribal") theologian Wati Longchar hails from the tribal peoples of northeast India. His theology seeks to express the tribal peoples' struggle for identity, justice, and participation, linking their precarious situation with the greedy exploitation of the land's resources. In northern India, the tribals are confronting the reality that land and natural resources that have sustained life for centuries are forcibly being taken away in the name of economic development. For Longchar, the liberation of the tribals from their oppression cannot be detached from the liberation of nature from human exploitation, and indigenous or tribal theology cannot occur apart from ecological liberation. Both humans and their environments are in a symbiotic relationship, and for theology to be liberative, both must be considered a single whole.

Liberative Theologies and Migration in Asia

Contemporary Asia is dealing with significant migratory movements of people that are transforming the sociocultural, religious, and economic-political landscape across Asia, leading to the breaking up of traditional social order as well as the loss of stable familial and communal structures. The phenomenon of migration in Asia is not new. Beginning with the nomadic tribes that wandered the vast expanse of the Asian continent in search of water and grazing lands, the trade caravans that traveled on the Silk Road across vast stretches of Asia, and the invading armies that displaced peoples and communities from their ancestral lands, migration has defined the Asian continent in every age.

While nomadic tribes and trade caravans have come and gone, large-scale migration continues unabated in Asia. Indeed, to say that we are currently living in an age of migration in Asia is an understatement. Today's migration patterns in Asia include internal migration from rural to urban centers, external migration from economically depressed countries to economically booming countries, and refugees fleeing violence and persecution. Migration can be voluntary, as in the case of economic migrants, or forced, as in the case of refugees, asylum seekers, and internally displaced persons who are fleeing civil strife.

More problematic is the reality that contemporary large-scale globalized migration patterns are caused in large part by immense poverty, extreme social-economic imbalances, and violent ethnic and religious strife, as well as the insatiable demand for cheap labor and cheap products. The magnitude of this problem is especially marked in Asia. The many Filipinos, Indians, Chinese, and others who seek better opportunities outside their homelands as construction workers, domestic helpers, and factory workers are examples of voluntary migrations. Involuntary migrants include not just refugees who are fleeing wars, social strife, economic upheavals, political instability, religious tensions, and persecution, but also the many economic migrants, especially vulnerable women and children, who are exploited and trafficked by underworld gangs, smuggling networks, and secret societies for cheap labor and sex trafficking. The sheer violence and abject dehumanization that many of these women and children experience reveal the dark underbelly of migration and call for a concerted response on the part of all of society to redress these problems.

The late Indian Jesuit theologian S. Arokiasamy spoke of migration as revealing the reality of uprootedness, vulnerability, and exploitation in the treatment of Asian migrants as outsiders and foreigners by xenophobic communities that welcomed them for their cheap labor yet refused to integrate them as residents with full rights and opportunities. The Vietnamese theologian Peter C. Phan, a refugee and asylum seeker himself, has written of his own feelings of violent uprootedness, anxiety, and loss of national identity and personal dignity as he and his family fled Vietnam in the aftermath of the fall of Saigon in 1975.

Federation of Asian Bishops' Conferences (FABC): A transnational body established in 1970 and comprising fifteen Asian Catholic bishops' conferences as full members, namely Bangladesh, India, Indonesia, Japan, Kazakhstan, Korea, Laos-Cambodia, Malaysia-Singapore-Brunei, Myanmar, Pakistan, the Philippines, Sri Lanka, Taiwan, Thailand, and Vietnam; as well as ten associate members, Hong Kong, Kyrgyzstan, Macau, Mongolia, Nepal, Siberia, Tajikistan, Turkmenistan, Uzbekistan, and Timor-Leste.

The **Federation of Asian Bishops' Conferences (FABC)** has taken the lead to articulate a liberative theology of migration in the contemporary Asian context. At their Fifth Plenary Assembly in Bandung (1990), with the theme "Journeying Together toward the Third Millennium," the FABC stated:

> We are deeply conscious, therefore, that within our context of change there is the unchanging reality of injustice. There remains in Asia massive poverty. . . . Poverty likewise drives both men and women to become migrant workers, often destroying family life in the process. Political conflict and economic desperation have driven millions to become refugees, to living for years in camps that are sometimes in effect crowded prisons. (FABC V, art. 2.2.1)

In response, FABC V asserts that Asian Christians "must live in *companionship*, as true *partners* with all Asians as they pray, work, struggle and suffer for a better human life, and as they search for the meaning of human life and progress" (FABC V, art. 6.2). The Asian bishops insist that Asian Christians must walk in solidarity with the "exploited women and workers, unwelcome refugees, victims of violations of human rights." They should seek to "denounce, in deeds, if it is not possible to do so in words, the injustices, oppressions, exploitations, and inequalities resulting in so much of the suffering that is evident in the Asian situation" (FABC V, art. 6.4).

A groundbreaking document on migration from the FABC is the final statement of the Fifth Faith Encounters in Social Action (FEISA), organized by the FABC Office of Human Development in Kota Kinabalu, Malaysia, in 2002. FEISA V sought to make explicit the connection between migration, mission, and engagement with the pluri-religious Asian milieu. Its final statement, which is entitled "Pastoral Care of Migrants and Refugees: A New Way of Being Church," is a thorough discussion of the challenges faced by undocumented migrants and refugees and what the Asian church could do to respond to these challenges. Specifically, FEISA V insists that the human-rights migrants in general, and undocumented migrants in particular, must be respected. It insists that Asian Christians should begin by listening to migrants and asylum seekers to ascertain their needs and provide the needed assistance and support in a spirit of Christian solidarity and empathy. As it explains,

> Christian solidarity simply sees the need to take care of human beings, especially young people, minors and children who are incapable of defending themselves because they lack protection under the law and often do not know the language of the country in which they have been obliged to seek refuge due to natural catastrophes, wars, violence, persecution, even genocide in their own country or due to existing economic conditions such as to endanger their physical integrity or life itself. (FEISA V)

On the issue of poverty and migration, the document acknowledges the reality of poverty as the force behind much of the mass migrations in Asia, whether internal or external, voluntary or involuntary, and recommends that the Asian church should stand in solidarity with the poor and marginalized. More importantly, FEISA V goes a step further to insist that in addressing the needs of migrants, the Asian church must work together with people of other faiths. FEISA V states that the Asian church should take the initiative of reaching out to migrants from other religious faiths to care for their pastoral needs. It explains that the Asian church should not only see and understand the dignity of peoples from other faiths but also receive and assist them in their moment of greatest need.

Conclusion

Contemporary Asia is a continent of contradictions and contrasts, with both wealthy and poor nations, ancient lands and newly emerged states, and huge movements of peoples in search of economic livelihoods for the survival of their families, as well as immense religious diversity. The great religions of the world that emerged in Asia continue to nourish billions of Asians who find their spiritual needs fulfilled by these vibrant religious traditions. Compared to other regions of the world, liberative theologies in Asia emerged from the deep spiritual and religious roots of the Asian peoples. In one sense, the preferential option of liberative theologies in Asia is more than just a preferential option for the poor and marginalized. It is also a preferential option to search for liberation in the multifaceted religiousness that defines Asia and, in doing so, privileging indigenous Asian spiritual and religious traditions.

In other words, Asian liberative theologies are committed to serving Asian peoples and responding to their needs and hopes amidst great diversity and pluralism of multireligious, multi-ethnic, multilingual, and pluricultural Asian worlds. Asian liberative theologies are inspired by the intense religiosity of the Asian peoples and their struggles to achieve a better quality of life beyond crushing poverty, oppression, marginalization, and exploitation. Unless liberative action emerges out of and is nourished by Asian spiritual and religious traditions, it cannot be a truly liberative path to transform the daily lives of Asian peoples.

Study Questions

1. How do the various Asian religions understand the Asian peoples' quest for liberation from various forms of oppression and exploitation in their daily lives?
2. What are the various forms of liberative theologies that have emerged in Asia?
3. How do Asian liberative theologies compare with liberative theologies

from other parts of the world, for example, Latin American or African liberative theologies?

4. This chapter discusses several types of Asian liberative theologies, Christian as well as from other Asian religious traditions. Which of these appeals the most to you? What elements or insights from that theology do you find meaningful or important?
5. Which of these liberative theologies from Asia is relevant to your own social location?

Suggested Reading

Amaladoss, Michael. *Life in Freedom: Liberation Theologies from Asia*. Maryknoll, NY: Orbis Books, 1997.

Ambedkar, B. R. *The Buddha and His Dhamma*. Third Edition. Bombay: Siddharth Publications, 1984.

Kappen, Sebastian. *Jesus and Freedom*. Maryknoll, NY: Orbis Books, 1977.

Koyama, Kosuke. *Waterbuffalo Theology*. Maryknoll, NY: Orbis Books, 1974.

Lee, Jung Young, ed. *An Emerging Theology in World Perspective: Commentary on Korean Minjung Theology*. Mystic, CT: Twenty-Third Publications, 1988.

Massey, James, ed. *Indigenous Peoples: Dalits, Dalit Issues in Today's Theological Debate*. Delhi: ISPCK, 1998.

Nirmal, Arvind P., ed. *A Reader in Dalit Theology*. Madras: GLTCRI, 1991.

Pieris, Aloysius. *An Asian Theology of Liberation*. Maryknoll, NY: Orbis Books, 1988.

Queen, Christopher S., and Sallie B. King, eds., *Engaged Buddhism: Buddhist Liberation Movements in Asia*. Albany: SUNY Press, 1996.

Song, C. S. *Jesus, the Crucified People*. New York: Crossroad, 2000.

4

Jewish and Islamic Liberative Theologies

Sophia Rose Arjana

Judaism and Islam are distinct traditions that share commonalities based on linguistic, historical, and theological contingencies. For example, at one time Muslims prayed toward Jerusalem, and even today many dietary laws and other customs are based upon Talmudic law. Both of these religious communities are "Abrahamic," tracing their beginnings to the patriarch who rejected polytheism. Both Jews and Muslims abstain from pork, bury their dead before sundown, and have an inherited religious legal system (the Jewish *halakah* and Islamic *shariah*). Perhaps more interesting, however, their respective theologies encourage individual and social liberation—the subject of this chapter.

Judaism, with its spirit of individual and community liberation situated in the Exodus narrative of oppression, exile, and renewal, offers a vision of social change that has been influential both within and beyond the Jewish tradition. We see this in the writings of Jewish thinkers such as Martin Buber, the efforts to formulate a modern, equitable Judaism as articulated in the Reform and Renewal movements, and the various Jewish political actions that are inclusive of feminist, queer, and other voices formerly muted by the tradition's patriarchy and authoritarianism. The Jewish vision of liberation is found in the writings and speeches of Dr. Martin Luther King, Jr., Catholic liberation theology, and other diverse movements inspired by verses like "Let my people go, so that they may serve me" (Exod. 8:20). We also find it in the liberationist

Abrahamic traditions: The Abrahamic traditions include Judaism, Christianity, and Islam, which all identify Abraham as a patriarch of their tradition. Although serious differences exist among these three religions, many things are shared. One can find the same individuals in the Torah, New Testament, and Qur'an, though they may be known by slightly different names. For example, Moses is known as Musa in Islam and Mary is called by her Arabic social critiques of prophets like Hosea and Jeremiah, and the verses about remembering their lessons, "Tie them [God's words] to your hand and wear them on your forehead as reminders" (Deut. 11:18).

Islam is foremost an articulation of remembrance and renewal, as evidenced in the Qur'an's numerous references to earlier prophetic messages and the ethical imperatives for needed re-engagement in the world. From the beginning, Islam has insisted on a better way, one that is situated in reflection and action. Prophet Muhammad's message was clearly anti-establishment and was met with accusations that he was a rambling poet or simply insane. As his detractors said, "Shall we abandon our gods to follow a mad poet?" (47:36). The madness that Prophet Muhammad was accused of was, in fact, a radical love that overturned the existing tribal order and replaced it with a better community. For Muslims, liberation from poverty, oppression, and pain is achieved through social action that is rooted in the mercy and compassion of God and the example of the last Abrahamic prophet. It is to this message that Muslims often turn in times of struggle, oppression, or grief. This is why the Qur'an says, "He is the Merciful, the Mercy-Giving" (59:22), because Allah helps those who help relieve the suffering of others. As the Prophet said, "The best jihad is to speak a word of truth to a tyrannical ruler."

Today, these two faith traditions exist in diverse communities that at times represent radically different readings of their foundational prophetic traditions. More traditionalist readings insist on maintaining a patriarchal and authoritarian stance, excluding the voices of women, queers, and others who would speak out in their communities and shape the future of their faith. At the same time, many other Jews and Muslims insist on a liberationist view that puts the voices

name, Maryam. Scholars have pointed out other commonalities, such as the fact that all three of the Abrahamic faiths are monotheistic, prophetic, and messianic (to one degree or another).

***Jihad* and liberation**: *Jihad* is a concept that today is commonly associated with violence. In actuality, *jihad* is classified into two types, "lesser" and "greater"; the former is the type used in warfare. The greater jihad, *jihad al-nafs*, literally, "the struggle with the self," represents a lifelong fight against the ego that when won leads to personal liberation. According to Islam, when the lower self can be annihilated the true self can be restored, bringing one closer to Allah and creating justice in the world.

of many in place of the voices of a few. We find these voices in the synagogue and the mosque, in academia, and in the streets protesting capitalism, poverty, war, and other forms of physical, emotional, and moral violence.

This chapter will provide a brief overview of the teachings and beliefs in Judaism and Islam that allow for personal and social emancipation. By asking what religious values address the need for liberation in these communities, identifying the important figures in Jewish and Islamic liberative theology and offering resources for the teaching of these theologies for future generations of students, activists, and community leaders, we can see that liberation is a natural consequence of these traditions.

History and Development of Jewish Liberative Theology

The prototype of Jewish liberation is situated within the Torah, and in particular, the exodus and the various stories of Hebrew prophets. The story of the exodus is the primary narrative for Jewish redemption, an important testament to the struggles of an oppressed people. Today, the story of the exodus is recounted in daily prayers, as part of Pesach (Passover), and in other rituals and traditions, such as the wearing of *tefillin* (phylacteries). The centrality of this story to Jewish identity lies in its resolution—Jewish enslavement is ended through the intervention of Yahweh (Adonai), creating the covenant between Israel (the people) and God and establishing the Jews as the chosen people. The story, which is told in the Jewish books Exodus, Leviticus, Numbers, and Deuteronomy, begins with the death of Joseph, then tells of the enslavement of the Jewish people in Egypt, the exodus of the Jews under Moses, the Sinai revelations, and finally, the wandering of the community in the wilderness.

B'tzelem Elohim: "in the image of God." This idea gives value to each and every human being regardless of race, ethnicity, gender, sexual orientation, or religion and guides our moral actions with others.

The exodus story of the victory of the Jewish people over adversity has influenced numerous social, religious, and political movements focused on justice, but colonizing readings also exist. As one example, white colonists in the Americas used it to legitimize their conquest of Native American lands, insisting that God ordained the invasion. The naming of American Indian land as "Promised Land" is a hideous perversion of the exodus's language of freedom into the language of white supremacy and genocide. The Exodus narrative also influenced U.S. government policies of expansion and subjugation of nonwhites, serving as the inspiration for Theodore Roosevelt's vision of white Americans as the chosen people and the expansionist policies into the Philippines and other distant lands. The results of these policies are seen in institutional violence against humans today, in the imprisonment of immigrants, African Americans, and others.

Better known are the ways in which the language from Exodus functions in numerous social struggles of the twentieth and twenty-first centuries such as the American civil rights movement, Catholic liberation theology, and other social justice struggles. Several African American spiritual songs, including adaptations of "Go Tell It on the Mountain" and "Go Down Moses," contain the line, "Let my people go," referencing the 1960s civil rights struggle. The long march to freedom was likened to the exodus, a journey that would result in the emancipation of all God's children. Dr. King was likened to Moses and white supremacists to the pharaohs. The night before his assassination, Dr. King described himself as an individual who had seen the Promised Land, but, like Moses, might not be there with his people when they reached it. These words resonate with the exodus tale of liberation.

Outside of Exodus, the Torah narrates the challenges posed to Jewish prophets, which, when overcome, formulate a theology of hope. Foundationally, Judaism is a faith tradition focused on a cycle of oppression, struggle, and redemption. The traditions associated with the Hebrew prophets provide a moral instruction for liberation. The prophet Amos, for instance, was a vocal proponent of social justice, known for preaching against poverty and his criticism of the disparity between the haves and have-nots. From the southern kingdom of Judea, Amos focused his message on those living in the North and in particular, the cities of Samaria and Bethel. His focus on the poor, the oppressed, and the abused helps explain why civil rights leaders such as Dr. King often cited the prophet Amos. At the Civil Rights Memorial in Montgomery, which stands just a few blocks from Dr. King's former church, we find Amos's words as Martin applied them to the struggle for freedom: "We will not be satisfied *until justice rolls down like waters and righteousness like a mighty stream.*"

V'ahavtah l'reicha kamocha: "Love your neighbor as yourself." This value was cited by Rabbi Hillel as a fundamental teaching of the Torah and provides a rule for our interactions with those with whom we are in relationship.

The Torah provides ample material that has been adopted by liberation theology movements outside of Judaism. But how have the Jewish people formulated liberation within their tradition, especially given the events of the past century? The Holocaust has had a profound effect on the ways in which Jewish liberation is envisioned. The loss of most of the world's Jews introduced a crisis of faith for survivors such as Elie Wiesel and Primo Levi that has found its way into contemporary Jewish thought, whether religious, philosophical, or political. The American diaspora, while safe from the horrors of the Shoah, was faced with the challenge of formulating a Jewish theology that could deal with the unimaginable heartbreak and loss associated with the Holocaust. Jews have had to ask how God could allow this to happen to his chosen people—a question that has directly impacted the ways Jewish identity and theology are formulated today.

Since its foundation in 1948 Israel has served as the dominant symbol of Jewish survival in the post-Holocaust world. Almost seventy years later, the foundation of the state of Israel continues to be a major influence on American Judaism, including as a source of schisms among different communities whose support, critique, or rejection of Zionist policies has become more vocal in recent decades. Some Jews have taken the reference in Isaiah 42:6 to the priesthood as the source of moral guidance, as the "light of all nations," and applied this to the state of Israel. Israeli politicians such as David Ben-Gurion and Benjamin Netanyahu used this phrase often, describing Israel as a morally righteous country that serves as the example for other modern states. Jews more critical of Israeli policies have also cited Isaiah 42:6, saying Israel is not living up to the standards set for it in the Torah. Martin Buber, for example, challenged the way in which this verse was understood, arguing that the Jewish people needed to act in accordance with their role as "the elect." Buber's view has since been adopted by Israeli intellectuals such as Ella Shohat to argue for a responsible, ethical Zionism.

Over the past century, American Jews have wrestled with questions of identity, pluralism, and survival. The civil rights movement, the sexual revolution, and the antiwar movement have had profound effects on American Judaism. One of the results of these interactions has been the development of new articulations of Jewish traditions by those who see themselves as religious as well as those who identify as secular, cultural, or even postreligious.

Modern Jewish denominational movements have often promoted a liberationist agenda. In all these iterations of Judaism, from Orthodox to Renewal, the liberation of Jews from oppression is an experience that carries with it a certain responsibility. More traditional iterations of Judaism, including Orthodox and Conservative, have voiced concerns over issues ranging from military action to gender discrimination. As one example, the late Rivka Haut, an Orthodox Jew, campaigned for women's rights in family law as well as equal participation in prayer. The Reform movement's concern with gender equity is seen in their liturgy, which replaces patriarchal terminology

Jewish activism: Jewish involvement in numerous social change struggles over the past century has been well noted by scholars who identify the labor movement, antifascism, and feminism as causes with a major presence of Jews. In the twentieth and twenty-first centuries, this array of movements is often described as the "Jewish left" and includes Jews in Europe, North America, South Africa, and Israel. Today, the Zionist left, sometimes referred to as "socialist Zionists," contribute to the political culture of Israel as well as the United States. Much of the American leftist intelligentsia is Jewish, including the philosopher and scholar Judith Butler, the late historian Howard Zinn, and linguist Noam Chomsky, all of whom are champions of the underclass, women, and others who suffer under systems of domination and oppression.

with a gender-fluid language that is inclusive of females. The Renewal movement's dedication to social justice is seen in their allegiance to feminism, inclusiveness of LGBTQ Jews, a commitment to human-rights concerns in Israel/Palestine, as well as social action work to eliminate modern-day slavery.

Progressive Jews are another group that while not organized along congregational lines constitutes an important community of activists made up of entertainers, scholars, and political figures who advocate social justice causes, including some, like the journalist Amy Goodman, who are critical of Israeli policies and the treatment of Palestinians under occupation. Some progressive Jews, like Rabbi David Wolpe, are deeply religious, while others are "cultural Jews" whose political activism is situated in ethical values located in a religion they may not actively practice or even publicly identify with. Some Jews are what is called trans- or postdenominational, identifying with Jewish moral teachings but seeking a better articulation of Judaism than they find represented in the current offerings of congregations. trans- or postdenominational

Liberative Theology in Action: The Issue of Occupation in Israel-Palestine

In the summer of 2014, tensions between Israel and Palestine erupted into violence with deadly results, including the death of more than 1,800 Palestinians in Gaza, many of them children. The events leading up to this particular conflict in Israel-Palestine included the kidnapping and murder of three young Yeshiva students and the abduction and murder of a Palestinian youth, who was burned alive. Despite the pleas of the parents of two of these victims, the murders escalated an already tenuous situation in Gaza. As a result of the ensuing violence, which included the destruction of most of Gaza's infrastructure, the bombing of hospitals, and the apparent targeting of children, American Jews came out in unprecedented numbers in vocal opposition to Israel's occupation of Palestinian land, arrest, detainment, and abuse of Palestinian children, and the war in Gaza. Among the most important voices is the Jewish Voice for Peace (JVP), which launched protests across the United States and Israel in July and August 2014. As this organization has stated, "Jewish Voice for Peace members are inspired by Jewish tradition to work together for peace, social justice, equality, human rights, respect for international law, and a U.S. foreign policy based on these ideals. JVP opposes anti-Jewish, anti-Muslim, and anti-Arab bigotry and oppression." Protests included the media campaign #GazaNames in which prominent Jews, Muslims, and other public figures such as Gloria Steinem, Chuck D, Jonathon Demme, Brian Eno, and Nobel Laureate Bishop Desmond Tutu held signs with the names and ages of Gazans who had died in the war.

An important development emerging out of the work of JVP is the bridging of American Jews and Muslims. American Muslims, who have often felt isolated in their critique of Israeli policies, have welcomed these Jewish calls for divestment from Israel, policy changes, and full rights for Palestinians—a recognition that has resulted in numerous protests and campaigns with both Jewish and Muslim individuals standing side by side. The joining of Jewish and Muslim voices for peace and justice in a small but growing group signals hope that a transreligious anticolonial movement has the possibility of transforming the quagmire in Israel and Palestine. As the Jewish philosopher Judith Butler has stated, "But for me, given the history from which I emerge, it is most important as a Jew to speak out against injustice and to struggle against all forms of racism. This does not make me into a self-hating Jew. It makes me into someone who wishes to affirm a Judaism that is not identified with state violence, and that is identified with a broad-based struggle for social justice." Such a rearticulation of Jewish ethics provides hope for the future for not only Israelis and Palestinians but for all those living under occupation, war, and oppression.

New articulations of Judaism have resulted in many successful media projects. Rabbi Michael Lerner has articulated a vision of Judaism as a network of believers dedicated to interfaith dialogue and a more just society. From his perspective, Lerner's religious beliefs necessitate commitment to social causes. As Lerner sees it, being a Jew entails taking the social justice mission of the Hebrew prophets very seriously, engaging with and putting the prophetic example into practice. Lerner's vision is situated in the Jewish concept ***tikkun olam***, "repairing the world," which inspired the name of his interfaith magazine, *Tikkun*. For Lerner and others, the performance of ***mitzvot*** or "good deeds," is seen as a fundamental part of Jewish practice that can influence the larger society, creating a more balanced and just world.

***Tikkun olam*:** "repairing the world." This expression is a central focus of contemporary Jewish life and is viewed as a religious duty.

***Mitzvot*:** "commandments." These deeds are also understood as moral deeds or acts of kindness, which contribute to a better world for all.

The Jewish Tradition and the Need for Liberation

Although the Jewish tradition provides an excellent theological argument for liberation, the problems of traditionalism, patriarchy, heteronormativity, and political injustice plague Jews much as they do other religious communities. While the emergence of several new Jewish movements in the twentieth century has ameliorated some problems, they still exist in many communities in the United States and elsewhere.

Judaism, like Islam, is a religion intertwined with patriarchy. At the same time, Jewish texts such as the Torah, the Talmud (rabbinic commentaries), and the Zohar (the most important text in the Kabbalistic tradition) offer spaces in which liberation can take place. As the discussion of the exodus shows us, the stories in the Torah with which we are so familiar can be read in both oppressive and liberative ways. One of these readings is presented by Rachel Adler, who argues that *halakah* (the law) must be reimagined and that Judaism has to be reconstructed and enacted in people's lives as it is *lived*. This reimagining of the law takes the form of a bridge, which requires listening (*nishmah*) by both men and women. In the case of marriage, the traditional view of ownership (of the wife by the husband) is replaced with the lover's covenant (*b'rit ahuvim*), a relationship that encourages equality and endearment.

Jewish attitudes toward nonheterosexual identities and lifestyle vary greatly by community. Orthodox Judaism is perhaps the most stringent with regard to questions of sexuality. However, since 2013, Orthodox rabbinic authorities have relaxed their critique of LGBTQ individuals. This includes the rejection of reparative therapy by the Rabbinic Council of America, which represents a shift in Orthodox attitudes toward gay Jews. The Renewal movement has been perhaps the most affirming regarding LGBTQ individuals. This is actually quite remarkable when one considers the lack of affirmation gays, lesbians, and the transgendered receive in other traditions. Contemporary Judaism exhibits an impressive degree of tolerance toward nonheterosexual Jews, one that other religious communities might draw inspiration from.

The state of Israel is a difficult subject for Jews who subscribe to a liberationist theology. Speaking out against injustice is, according to some, a value inherent to the Jewish tradition. Judith Butler has described her activism as situated in a Jewish ethical imperative that has its roots in the twentieth-century experience. Specifically, what Butler points to is the moral crime of silence in the face of state violence. Jews are morally required to speak out against injustices, especially when they are committed by modern states. This is why Butler advocates a two-state solution for Israel—for her, true emancipation is seen as impossible within a state that restricts citizenship.

A sizeable number of Jewish intellectuals have voiced concern over Israeli policies; some of these voices have focused on Jewish theology. Marc Ellis's work addresses the problem of Israel-Palestine as a theological problem, situated in the Jewish experience of suffering and the empowerment and violence that have been born out of historical contingencies. He urges a shift away from the overidentification with the Holocaust, which has generated a worship of the past that denies the suffering in the present, and asks whether a prophetic voice can survive the current Jewish problem of privilege (what he calls "empowerment"). Ultimately, Ellis sees that the suffering of all people must be the focus of contemporary Jews, something that requires a rejection of "pre-Holocaust and Holocaust categories on the contemporary world," which results in the closure of our "eyes and ears to the pain and possibility of the present."

Political injustice is a complex topic made more so by the controversies surrounding Israeli policies toward Palestinians that exist both within and outside Jewish communities in Israel and elsewhere. Within Israel, many human-rights and social-justice organizations exist, including many that deal solely with Palestinian and Arab rights. Several challenging theological problems that emerge from the Israeli/Palestinian dilemma merit consideration. One is the issue of expulsion, an important Jewish experience that is now shared by Palestinians. The right of return, of both Palestinians to Israel and Jews to the numerous spaces from which they have been expelled, is an issue that plagues peace talks as well as Israeli relations with neighboring Arab states. Related to this problem is that of guardianship, based on the idea that Israel is, or should be, a paradigm of justice, a state to which the world can look for moral guidance. Israeli policies often make this concept problematic, providing yet another challenge to Jews, who struggle with reconciling their love of Israel with social-justice concerns.

Leading Scholars and Figures in Jewish Liberative Thought

The large number of Jewish theologians, philosophers, and activists cannot be covered fully in this chapter. A few of these individuals have pushed for a liberative reading of their traditions, engaging the texts in new and interesting ways and allowing for more inclusiveness in Jewish communities. This list is designed to orient the reader to a few of the important thinkers in twentieth- and twenty-first-century American Jewish thought. It is important to note that these individuals have a range of different ethical concerns, from political justice to feminism. They represent a diverse group of men and women, philosophers, religious leaders, and scholars.

Anyone interested in Jewish liberative thought should begin with Martin Buber, arguably one of the most important intellectuals of the twentieth century. As a conscientious Zionist who believed in a just alliance with Arabs, Buber argued for a kind of Jewish humanism that was moderated by social-justice concerns. His most famous work, *I and Thou*, focuses on the importance of human relationships, which help bring individuals closer to God. In other writings, he focused on Hebrew humanism, linking the situation of Jews to that of humanity at large. Much of Buber's influence on later Jewish thought is situated in his understanding of religion as experiential and mystical, rather than focused on religious authority and dogma, an articulation later seen in the modern Jewish reformation and, in particular, the Renewal movement.

Reb Zalman (Rabbi Zalman Schachter-Shalomi) is the individual most immediately associated with the Jewish Renewal movement. Educated in both leftist Zionism and the Hasidic tradition, he formulated an engaged, humanistic, and mystical reading of the Jewish tradition. His personal theology includes public commitments to feminism and LGBTQ individuals as well as to interfaith dialogue. Reb Zalman is also known for his high-profile relationship with Muslim Sufis like Muzaffer Ozak and his appointment as a sheikh (Sufi master) in the Sufi lineage of Hazrat Inayat Khan. In 2004, he founded a Jewish-Muslim Sufi group, the Inayat-Maimuni order, evidence of his commitment to interfaith engagement as well as to mystical practice.

Zalman's articulation of Judaism is one that is fully liberative in body, mind, and spirit and has been adopted by such Jewish women as Rabbi Tirzah Firestone, the founding rabbi of Nevei Kodesh in Boulder, Colorado, cited by Reb Zalman as the flagship temple of the Renewal movement. Firestone argues for a return to the Jewish calling *kedoshim tihiyu*, "to be holy," an action that requires, among other things, care of the stranger—including the Palestinian.

The movement away from doctrinal and dogmatic understandings of Judaism that Zalman and others have encouraged includes the emergence of new readings of Judaism. Rachel Adler is among the most important scholars in Jewish feminism. In 1971, she published the article "The Jew Who Wasn't There," widely considered to be a groundbreaking work that launched Jewish feminist theology. Since then, Adler has published numerous works on Jewish theology, liturgy, and law. Today, Jewish feminism is a broad movement that includes scholars such as Rachel Adler, Naomi Janowitz, Margaret Wenig, and Judith Plaskow.

Possible Future Trends in Jewish Liberative Movements

Jews in Reform and Renewal circles have already modified the patriarchal language in some Jewish texts, a move that has had an impact on liturgy and ritual. Where this goes in future decades remains to be seen. The reading of the Haggadah at Passover is recognized as a liberative practice that now includes versions of the reading that are geared toward LGBTQ individuals and many other communities. At this annual retelling of the exodus, Jews have the opportunity to reflect on social problems such as modern-day slavery, exile, and the right of return. The reading culminates with the hopeful statement "next year in Jerusalem," referencing the return of the Jews to their ancestral homeland after captivity, exile, and homelessness. In future iterations of Jewish liberation, Jerusalem may be refashioned as a symbol for all people, an imaginary homeland for all people who suffer injustice and find their way to a safe abode.

History and Development of Islamic Liberative Theology

Islam began as a localized social-reform movement that, due to historical circumstances, including crumbling empires and unchecked tribalism, and to its message of human liberation through unity, was transformed into a global religion. When the Prophet Muhammad first called for the abandonment of the tribal system,

The Haggadah: The Haggadah ("telling") is a text read on the evening of the Passover Seder. Although its reading fulfills the duty to tell the story of the Jewish liberation to children, in recent decades it has been altered to be inclusive of oppressed peoples outside the Jewish community. Today, an almost endless number of modern, liberative versions of the Haggadah exist addressing modern slavery, civil rights, LGBTQ Jews, the environment, and other current social issues. In 2011, *Tikkun* published a Passover Haggadah supplement that included a section titled "Solidarity with Contemporary Egyptians Seeking Democracy" and "Liberation Today in Israel/Palestine." It ends with a wish that messianic redemption begin with each and every Jew who will build a more just world together with others.

he was immediately met with resistance. Eventually, this led to the persecution of the early Muslim community (*ummah*), assassination attempts on the Prophet, and the exile of the *ummah* to the city of Yathrib, later named Madinat-al-Nabi, or "City of the Prophet," now known as Madina or Medina.

Muhammad's struggle was much like that of other prophets in the Abrahamic tradition, for his message was not unlike that of Musa (Moses), Isa (Jesus), and earlier prophets whose prophecies were met with closed minds and hearts. Prophet Muhammad's experience as an orphan is reflected in both the Qur'an and *hadith* (traditions surrounding his life). Islamic jurisprudence, which begins to be formulated in the ninth century, incorporates these traditions into laws concerning slaves, the poor, widows, and orphans. However, we find a troubling disconnect between Qur'anic revelation and the Prophet's example and the continuation of certain tribal practices. Slavery, of war captives in particular, continued to be practiced for centuries, and many scholars have argued that this, like the quick erosion of improvements surrounding the treatment of girls and women, came with the death of the Prophet in 632. At this point, we see an almost immediate breakdown of the liberative attitudes and policies that were a part of the Medinan community, including equal access to the *masjid* (mosque) and economic justice. In their place, women were placed behind a curtain or barrier; the leadership of the *ummah* was characterized by greed, corruption, and decadence; and slavery became a large part of the quest for empire.

***Azaadi*:** "liberation." This concept is central to the work of 'Ali Shari'ati, who argued that an activist Islam that regained the spirit of the early *ummah* (community) could lead to personal and social liberation.

Less than fifty years after the Prophet's death, in the year 680, his grandson Husayn was killed on the plains of Karbala in an epic David and Goliath–style battle between a small band of men, women, and children and the Umayyad dynasty. This became the formative event for Husayn's followers, the *Shi'at 'Ali*, or "Party of Ali," a movement that later became the Shi'a. This group, which remains relatively small even today, is responsible for much of the liberative theology in Islam historically and in contemporary times. This chapter examines both Sunni and Shi'a liberative theology but is largely concerned with the latter, which influences much of Islamic thought.

Islamic liberation thought is difficult to identify as separate from the basic theology Muslims subscribe to, which places a number of demands on Muslims that are designed to alleviate the misery in the world. The Qur'an contains numerous instructions about the fair treatment of widows, orphans, and the poor, and the institution of *zakat* (one of the five pillars of Islam) is a legal remedy for the inequities of wealth that exist in the world. The Hadith of the Prophet often reads like a manual of liberation theology; for example, "feed the hungry, visit the sick, free the captive." However, these religious prescriptions are not always seen in Muslim ethics, at least not to the extent they should be. One look at the human-rights record in Islamic religious states such as the Kingdom of Saudi Arabia (KSA), or the treatment of workers in the United Arab Emirates (UAE) provides evidence that there is a widespread lack of Islamic consciousness. It is this lack of consciousness or awareness about the world (***aghfala***), this forgetfulness, that contemporary Islamic theologians are largely concerned with.

***Ijtihad*:** "diligence." This practice, often explained as the exercise of independent judgment, is necessary for the opening of Islamic legal thought to new and liberative readings.

***Aghfala*:** "unmindfulness." Islamic reformers often cite this lack of awareness to explain the state of Islamic decline or stagnation and the condition of *taqlid* (blind imitation).

Much as in Judaism, Islam includes many rituals that are liberative for both the individual performing them and the larger community. Ramadan, the month of fasting, is in many ways an exercise in liberation—from food, water, swearing, gossiping, gluttony, and greed. When one abstains from all of these things, the individual is liberating the body and the mind but also, through the process, identifying with the poor. Muslims often remark that the thirst caused by sunup-to-sundown fasts makes them think of those who have no water. In this way, Ramadan is an exercise that makes one think about liberation.

Islamic liberation theology that specifically addresses political struggle begins with the Islamic modernists who critique European colonialism. For the generation of Muslim intellectuals active in the eighteenth and nineteenth centuries, two central concerns—oppression and stagnation—were the focus. These were seen as the result of colonialism, European systems of dominance, and Muslim apathy. Shah Waliullah, Jamal al-din al-Afghani, Muhammad Rashid Rida, Muhammad Iqbal, and others encouraged an awareness that is still important today among Muslims living under colonial and neocolonial rule. Since this period, a number of political movements concerned with emancipation from foreign rule have emerged, some of them violent (Hezbollah) and others peaceful (Nahdlatul Ulama).

Arab Spring: The Arab Spring is the name given by Western journalists to the series of revolutions in the Arab world beginning on December 17, 2010, when a Tunisian street vendor named Muhammed Bouazizi set himself on fire to protest government abuse. In the Arab world, the revolution in Tunisia was called *Thawrat-al-Hurriya-wa-l-karima*, "The Revolt for Freedom and Dignity," and as the revolutions spread to other Arab states they became collectively known as the Dignity Revolutions. The regimes of Tunisia, Egypt, and Yemen were toppled, but in other cases—Syria and Bahrain—prolonged civil wars resulted. Still, the revolutions and protests that spread across the Arab world have represented a widespread movement for freedom, justice, and dignity.

Need for Liberation and the Muslim Tradition

Since its beginning, Islam has been concerned with political tyranny. Beginning with the early battles between the nascent Muslim community and those resistant to Islam's message of God's unicity (*tawhid*), economic justice, social reform, and political change have been core Islamic themes. In early theological and philosophical writings, we see a focus on just rulership, perhaps most notably in the words and letters of 'Ali. In modernity, the battle for moral government has been a key concern of Islamic reformers. More recently, the Dignity Revolutions, known in the West as the "Arab Spring," exemplify these concerns. It is worth noting that these revolutions began with a self-immolation, an act that signals the desperation of many Muslims who seek a way out of their moral despondency. At present, it remains to be seen how these struggles for justice will be won, given the capitalist and neoliberal structures in place.

Related to the problem of corrupt and unjust government is economic inequity. Relieving poverty and its effects are key themes in the Qur'an and *sunnah* (the tradition of the Prophet), seen in numerous instructions to house, feed, and care for the poor, especially orphans. In Islam, charity is legislated through the institution of *zakat* (charitable giving), and a second type of charity known as *sadaqa* (spontaneous giving) is also encouraged. These practices are designed to redistribute wealth, which according to the Qur'an should be shared equally and justly (2:261).

Gender inequities are a central concern for Muslims today, seen in the separation of men and women at the mosque, the violence perpetrated against girls and women, and the relegation of females to subservient roles. Muslims are beginning to reassess the tradition and its history in order to reformulate traditions that are liberative for women. For example, when arguing against gender segregation today, scholars point out that the barrier between men and women in the mosque was not instituted until after the Prophet's death. Related to issues surrounding gender are those concerned with sexual orientation and identity, topics that are largely taboo in Muslim communities. As scholars such as Khaled el-Rouayheb have observed, before modernity homosexuality was envisioned as one of many options on a wide spectrum. It may be that a greater understanding of this history is necessary to reclaim it.

Islamic feminism: Islamic feminism is a broad movement that addresses women's rights in numerous spaces, including the home, mosque, university, and government. Female Muslim scholars who have dealt with these issues include Kecia Ali, Amina Wadud, and Laury Silvers, all of whom base their arguments within the Islamic tradition, at times using the same texts to argue against patriarchal interpretations of the Qur'an and other traditions. Activists are found in every Muslim community imaginable, from Afghanistan to Turkey, Iraq to Indonesia, and in between. Among the most famous of these is Nawal el Saadawi, whose work on a variety of issues is known not only in Egypt and the region but worldwide.

Issues and Questions for Islamic Liberative Theology

Islamic liberation is often explained as a process in which Muslims or Islam itself must change, progress, or even reform. The most obvious problem with these descriptions is that they reflect more of a Protestant reality than a Muslim one. Muslims whose work in liberation requires a critical eye often insist that Islam does not need a reformation but a renewal. This stance is based in the Islamic practice of *dhikr* (remembrance), which is reflected in the Qur'an ("Remember me, I shall remember you"—2:152) and found in much of the reformist literature of the past two centuries. Despite the efforts of Muslim intellectuals to remain true to the values of the Qur'an, many are still anxious about the new ways in which it is being interpreted.

A fundamental question that Muslims must contend with involves the veracity of religious texts. In particular, the status of extra-Qur'anic texts collectively known as the *sunnah* (tradition) of Prophet Muhammad is in question. Amina Wadud is one of several liberationists who takes a clear position on which texts formulate her theology. In her view, the Qur'an is the foundational text for Muslims, and *hadith*, while culturally important for some, are not to be trusted. The reasoning behind this is quite simple. The Qur'an is considered the word of Allah, and while it can be interpreted differently, it is completely infallible. *Hadith*, the stories and traditions that tell us of Prophet Muhammad's life and his example for us, are fallible.

Ali Shari'ati: Ali Shari'ati (1933–1977) was an Iranian sociologist of religion who wrote on Islamic theology, politics, and liberation. Influenced by Marxism, Shari'ati viewed Islam as the solution to the capitalist dilemma. From his perspective, the recovery of a liberationist Islam was necessary for the establishment of a just and moral society that would result in the *ummat* and *nezam-i tawhid*—the activist community and unitary society that disappeared after Prophet Muhammad's death. Shortly after moving to England to escape persecution by the regime, Shari'ati mysteriously died at the young age of forty-four. His most famous quote, "Every day is Ashura; every place is Karbala," is one of the most popular expressions of the Shi'a revolutionary spirit even today.

Leading Scholars/Figures in Islamic Liberative Thought

Prophet Muhammad is undoubtedly the most important figure in Islamic liberative theology. All later teachings come through him, either through his revelations as recorded in the Qur'an or in the corpus of sayings and actions attributed to him that are collectively known as the *sunnah*. One Qur'anic verse that encapsulates the example of Muhammad as a warrior for justice is, "And we have not sent you except as a mercy to mankind" (21:107). In addition, the numerous attempts on his life speak to the threat he posed to those in power, who failed to exhibit the mercy and compassion practiced by the Prophet and exemplified by his interactions with others.

Much of Islamic thought is dedicated to liberation of the poor and oppressed, and this is in particular a focus of Shi'a theology. Shi'ism is identified as a theology of liberation concerned with the condition of the oppressed, an orientation that emerges out of hundreds of years of subjugation by Sunni Muslims and others. These concerns are seen in the words of the imams (the twelve teachers who are descendants of the Prophet's cousin 'Ali and his daughter Fatima), the writings of 'Ali Shari'ati, Ayatollah Khomeini, Ayatollah Montazeri, Ayatollah Mutahhari, and others. Among twentieth-century thinkers, Shari'ati is among the most important; he is counted as an influence on Khomeini and many others and cited by both the current Iranian regime and its detractors.

Among contemporary Sunni thinkers, Tariq Ramadan is influential with European Muslims and among the intelligentsia in the American academy. A prolific writer, he is most concerned with the position of Muslims in Europe, which in many cases is characterized by alienation from the larger society in which they live. Unlike some of his contemporaries who argue that Muslims should assimilate into Western culture and alter their religious values, Ramadan argues that Muslims, through a positive engagement with their fellow citizens, can improve the European landscape socially, culturally, and morally.

It is impossible to talk of Islamic liberation theology without including several important African American thinkers. Malcolm X is perhaps the single most important of these individuals, influential today with Muslims and non-Muslims, appealing across racial and economic lines and serving as an example of prophetic leadership. More recently, a number of other African American Muslims have been influential. Dr. Amina Wadud is arguably the most important female Muslim scholar of the late twentieth century. In her work, she argues that the Qur'an has been subjected to patriarchal readings that betray the original intent of the text. In particular, Wadud argues that a faithful reading of the Qur'an makes it clear that men and women are equal, invested with moral worth and sacredness that must be reclaimed through a more faithful reading of the revelations.

Possible Future Trends for Islamic Liberative Thought

Islam has a gender problem. Despite the examples set by the Prophet's wives and his daughter Fatima and the historical record of numerous female queens, sultans, scholars, and other powerful individuals, Muslim women today face challenges in several areas, including mosque space, government, family law, and education. Related to the issue of gender is sexuality, a subject that many Muslims are uncomfortable even discussing. In the past few years, mosques led by females and queer Muslims have begun to emerge, a sign that a shift may be under way.

Contemporary Islamic liberation theologians include a number of figures, including Ali Shari'ati, Ayatollah Khomeini, and Amina Wadud. Ali Shari'ati viewed Islam, and in particular Shi'a Islam, as the solution to society's problems, but only in its activist form. The revitalization of humanity was possible, but required a direct apprehension of the Qur'an, which, for Shari'ati, was the foundational key to liberation. Some of these ideas were adopted by Khomeini, whose use of Shari'ati's language in the revolution is well documented by scholars. For Khomeini, the religion of Islam was the key to social liberation. The universality of Islamic liberation is seen in the attempted export of Khomeini's message to oppressed peoples in the United States, Africa, and Asia.

Outside of these Shi'a examples, many other liberationist theologians have been active in the twentieth century. Amina Wadud is known for her liberative reading of the Qur'an, which definitely states the moral equality of men and women, defining them as complementary partners. In addition to her exegesis of Qur'anic verses, in particular those addressing the worth and treatment of females, Wadud has been influential on an entire generation of

Islamic scholars, male and female, whose work argues that the Qur'an—the literal word of God for Muslims—unequivocally states the equality of all peoples.

In recent years, much of Islamic theology has dealt with issues around Israel-Palestine. Palestinian liberation theology is often linked to the religious leadership of Hezbollah and Hamas, who have often advocated violent strategies to combat Israeli colonization, subjugation, and violence against the Palestinian population. However, not all Palestinian liberationists see violence as the only solution. *Sabeel* is a Palestinian Christian liberation theology movement that sees prayer and nonviolent actions as the path to lasting peace and liberation. With the example of Jesus, who himself lived under occupation and injustice, Palestinians—Christians and Muslims—can identify, for Prophet Isa (Jesus) is called "al-Masih" (literally, the liberator) by Muslims. This suggests that at least one possible place of transformation is found in the example of Jesus/Isa, who in Islam appears at the End of Days with the *Mahdi* (an Islamic messiah) to redeem humankind and slay the false messiah (*Dajjal*), an evil figure who is associated with greed, oppression, and suffering.

Study Questions

1. How does the exodus narrative provide inspiration for both colonialist and liberationist/revolutionary ideologies? What types of challenges do Jewish texts present to liberation theology and to liberative views of social justice?
2. What are the different types of Zionism? Can this ideology be liberative, not just for Jews but also for Palestinians?
3. Name two figures in the Jewish left and comment on why they are important. What Jewish value(s) do their examples reflect? Name an important liberationist figure in contemporary Islam. How does this person's work reflect Islamic values?
4. How did Prophet Muhammad challenge the oppressive structures of Meccan society? What changes regarding gendered space and sexuality took place between the Prophet's lifetime and the period immediately following his death? Why is this important today?
5. What historical experience is Shi'a liberative theology situated in? Why is the *jihad al-nafs* important for liberation?

Suggested Reading

Adler, Rachel. *Engendering Judaism: An Inclusive Theology and Ethics*. Philadelphia: Jewish Publication Society, 1988.

Blumenthal, David. *Facing the Abusing God: A Theology of Protest*. Louisville, KY: Westminster/John Knox Press, 1993.

Boyarin, Daniel, Daniel Itzkovitz, and Ann Pellegrini. *Queer Theory and the Jewish Question (Between Men—Between Women: Lesbian and Gay Studies)*. New York: Columbia University Press, 2003.

Buber, Martin. *A Land of Two Peoples: Martin Buber on Jews and Arabs*. Chicago: University of Chicago Press, 2005.

Dabashi, Hamid. *Islamic Liberation Theology: Resisting the Empire*. New York: Routledge, 2008.

De La Torre, Miguel A. *The Hope of Liberation in World Religions*. Waco, TX: Baylor University Press, 2008.

Ellis, Marc H. *Toward a Jewish Theology of Liberation*. Maryknoll, NY: Orbis Books, 1987.

Heschel, Susannah, ed. *On Being a Jewish Feminist: A Reader*. New York: Schocken Books, 1983.

Malcolm X. *The Autobiography of Malcolm X: As Told to Alex Haley*. New York: Penguin, 2010.

Plaskow, Judith. *Standing Again at Sinai: Judaism from a Feminist Perspective*. New York: HarperOne, 2001.

Rahnema, Ali. *An Islamic Utopian: A Political Biography of Ali Shari'ati*. New York: I. B. Tauris, 1998.

Ramadan, Tariq. *Radical Reform: Islamic Ethics and Liberation*. New York: Oxford University Press, 2004.

Safi, Omid, ed. *Progressive Muslims: On Justice, Gender and Pluralism*. Oxford: Oneworld, 2003.

Schachter-Shalomi, Zalman. *First Steps to a New Jewish Spirit: Reb Zalman's Guide to Recapturing the Intimacy and Ecstasy in Your Relationship with God*. Woodstock, VT: Jewish Lights Publishing, 2003.

Shari'ati, Ali. *On the Sociology of Islam: Lectures by Ali Shari'ati*. Translated by Hamid Algar. Berkeley, CA: Mizan Press, 2000.

Taleqāni, Ayatullāh Mahmūd, Ayatullāh Murtadā Mutahhari, and Dr. Ali Shari'ati. *Jihād and Shahādat: Struggle and Martyrdom in Islam*. Edited by Mehdi Abedi and Gary Legenhausen. North Haledon, NJ: Islamic Publications International, 1986.

Wadud, Amina. *Qur'an and Woman: Rereading the Sacred Text from a Woman's Perspective*. New York: Oxford University Press, 1999.

Part II

The U.S. Racial, Ethnic and Class Context

5

Hispanic Liberative Theologies

R. J. Hernández-Díaz

The conquest of America . . . heralds and establishes our present identity.

—Tzvetan Todorov, *The Conquest of America*

Las palmas son novias que esperan: Y, hemos de poner la justicia tan alta como las palmas!

—José Martí, "Discurso en el Liceo Cubano"

But God knows that we are not beasts of burden, agricultural implements or rented slaves; we are men locked in a death struggle against man's inhumanity to man. . . . And this struggle itself gives meaning to our life and ennobles our dying.

—César Chávez, "Letter from Delano"

The United States was created on the basis of colonial conquest, genocide, and displacement of indigenous peoples, as well as on the enslavement and exploitation of African peoples. Early settlers—already a mix of British, German, Dutch, Swedish, and Irish populations—interacted with American Indians, Africans, and other waves of large immigrant groups from all over the globe. Racial/ethnic and cultural tensions have resulted from this diversity. The dominant Anglo-Protestant American group claims racial/ethnic and cultural superiority, while various racialized communities seek racial/ethnic parity and political power. Hispanics constitute one community in this diverse population.

The term "Hispanic" was adopted in the 1970s as the official U.S. government term to refer both to the descendants of early Spanish settlers in North America and immigrants from Central America, the Caribbean, and South America, as well as their progeny. Hispanics, by 2015, were the largest minority group living in the United States—about 50.5 million people, or

16.3 percent of the population according to the 2010 census. Hispanics represent an enormously varied people along the lines of national origin, history, language, social class, and legal status. Altogether, the category "Hispanic" includes groups of over twenty different nationalities, including Mexicans (about two-thirds of the U.S. Hispanic population), Puerto Ricans, Cubans, members of other Caribbean nations, and Central and South Americans. Yet the dominant Anglo-American culture in the United States largely perceives Hispanics as a monolithic group, partly as a strategy to understand and thereby achieve some measure of control over them. Some Hispanics also perpetuate the fiction of unity as a way of gaining political and social power through the use of terms such as ***Latinidad*** or ***Hispanidad***.

***Latinidad*:** the state of "Latina/o-ness." A broad term used to capture a general sense of the character of Hispanics. Often equated to *Hispanidad*, *Latinidad* is laden with numerous conflicting connotations, sometimes divorced of historical or linguistic uses. While some theologians celebrate the term, others counter that the Eurocentric concept of *Latinidad* has no place in a critical, liberative theology.

The term "Hispanic" is derived from the Latin *hispanicus*, from *Hispania*, the Roman name for the Iberian peninsula. Etymologically speaking, then, Hispanic refers to peoples who have their origins in Iberia. By this definition, most of Latin America, over one-third of North America, and some of Europe is Hispanic. This chapter focuses mostly on the transnational communities of Hispanics living in the United States, though some of what is said is applicable to Hispanics living elsewhere.

The Hispanic community in the United States has its origin in the Spanish conquest of the American Indians in the late-fifteenth and early-sixteenth centuries. The mixing of different ethnic groups that resulted in *mestizo/a* and *mulato/a* people paralleled a religious hybridization. The religious-cultural mix of Aztec, Mayan, and Taino practices deeply altered the Spanish brand of Catholicism that was forced on these populations. Home altars, religious tattoos, processions, animal sacrifices, and candlelight vigils constitute various expressions of the Hispanic religious culture. *Corridos* (stories), *leyendas* (legends), art, poetry, drama, and dances also transmitted history and religious meaning. Religious-cultural practices provided a space to resist the oppression of colonial masters, first the Spanish and then the Anglo. A number of theologies of self-affirmation and resistance have emerged from the religiously hybrid experiences and traditions of this oppressed people. These theologies inquire into the meaning, purpose, and intent of sacred symbols and rituals—from baptism to funerals—that form part of the daily struggle to survive.

The term "Hispanic liberative theology" (HLT) encompasses a family of critical reflections on the hybridized traditions and religious-cultural practices of Hispanic communities as they relate to the conditions of oppression under which many Hispanics live. Hispanic liberative theologies have been described using a multiplicity of terms, including Latino, Latina feminist, Latin American, *mujerista*, Chicano, *mestizaje*, Mexican American, and Afro-Cuban theology. These descriptors refer to racial/ethnic, gender, regional, and/or ideological distinctions. As part of its development, HLT has addressed a series of difficult questions arising from the issue of authorship and representation. Is HLT "Hispanic" because of its author, because of its subject, or because of its intended audience? Can a Hispanic theologian speak for the community at large? Which Hispanics, by whom, and for whom?

In attempting to answer these questions, Hispanic theologians have been informed by the theories of representation and domination of Indian postcolonial theorist Gayatri Chakravorty Spivak (see her article "Can the Subaltern Speak?"). Some have considered how their own writing constitutes a form of colonial discourse along the lines of what Homi Bhabha, another important postcolonial theorist from India, describes in *The Location of Culture*, representing their communities as "other" even as they attempt to speak on behalf of/for the Hispanic community. Addressing the question of authorship and representation in their own theological construction offers a way for Hispanics to counter the use of colonial logic in their writings. Hispanic theology can be liberative only if it exposes how marginalization and domination work in its own intellectual projects.

A second set of questions arise as part of HLT's

***Peregrinaje* (pilgrimage):** *Peregrinaje* or *peregrinación* (pilgrimage) is a journey undertaken for religious purposes or to fulfill a *manda* (vow) to a sacred space, shrine, or sanctuary. Traditional pilgrimage sites in the U.S. Southwest include Chimayó in New Mexico and *La Virgen de San Juan* in Texas. Sites that are in Latin America but attract U.S. Hispanic pilgrims include *La Virgen de la Caridad del Cobre* shrine in Cuba, *La Basilica de la Virgen de Guadalupe* in Mexico City, and *El Santo Cristo de Esquipulas* in Guatemala. However, destinations for pilgrimages have expanded to sites that are significant for Hispanics, such as the tombs of Gloria Anzaldúa and César Chávez, or the shrines to *curanderos* (healers) and folk saints such as El Niño Fidencio in Espinazo, Nuevo León, Mexico, and Don Pedrito Jaramillo of Falfurrias, Texas. Traditionally, the *peregrina/o* (pilgrim) travels to a holy site to ask for a blessing, healing, or special favor. Pilgrimages formed a popular aspect of medieval Catholic practices in Europe, but sacred sites in the Americas predate conquest. Thus, the

Roman Catholic Church encouraged the tradition that was already in place of journeying to venerated sites.

development: What should count as HLT and what criteria should be used to make that determination? No one would dispute that figures such as Virgilio P. Elizondo, Justo L. González, and Ada María Isasi-Díaz are Hispanic liberative theologians. They are uniformly accepted as being part of the canon of Hispanic theology. There are some theologians who clearly are not Hispanic, such as Alfred North Whitehead and Hans Urs von Balthasar, even though their work has had a direct influence on the work of HLT. The categories are less clear when we consider figures and works such as the *Popol Vuh* (the sacred text of the Quiché Maya), Bartolomé de Las Casas, Sor Juana Inés de la Cruz, José Martí, and Frantz Fanon.

The *Popol Vuh*, a collection of the founding narratives of the Quiché Maya, is perhaps the most important religious text of the period before the Spanish conquest. It would be difficult to understand the indigenous American religious cosmology without the *Popol Vuh*. Should it be considered a work of Hispanic theology? Bartolomé de La Casas represents a different problem. He was Spanish but wrote about the exclusion and oppression of pre-Columbian people. How should we balance his place of origin against his concern with issues arising from the Hispanic context and advocacy for the oppressed? Sor Juana Inés de la Cruz was Mexican, but she was not, strictly speaking, allowed to write theology because she was a woman. Yet, her poems and other writings have ethical and moral relevance for the work of Hispanic theology. José Martí, the Cuban national poet and revolutionary, did not write theology either. Still, Martí's focus on the liberation of all suffering bodies has had an undeniable influence on Hispanic political and religious imagination. Frantz Fanon's concerns with the plight of colonized people, violence, and historical change directly apply to the Hispanic context, and his work is another important influence on HLT. Born in Martinique, he wrote in French and spent most of his adult life in France and North Africa. On what basis do we exclude Fanon from HLT, especially given the centrality of his work to many liberative thinkers? What should count as HLT and what criteria should be used are not clear-cut issues. An examination of the history of HLT, to which we turn next, helps to further define the field.

History

Hispanic liberative theology has its origins in the work of sixteenth-century humanist theologians, in particular Bartolomé de Las Casas (1484–1566), whose advocacy for the humane treatment of Indians against Spanish oppression is an important foundation of later liberative theological movements.

He spoke unequivocally for justice for the oppressed and argued that the well-being and future of Spanish society depended on the humane treatment of American Indians. For example, Las Casas, in his book *Historia de las Indias*, criticized the Royal Council for its ignorance of the American situation, in effect condemning American Indians "to perpetual servitude, and to the death necessarily ensuing therefrom." Of course, Las Casas was Spanish, not a hybrid product of Spanish, American Indian, and African peoples that is often identified with HLT. He played an ambiguous role in the American Indian cultural genocide and advocated for (although later regretted) African slavery. Despite his mixed legacy, his protests against exploitation and oppression played a pivotal role in constructing a theology that limited Spain's power over the American Indians.

The wave of colonization continued in the nineteenth century, with the U.S. invasion of Texas and California and the conquest of the North American Southwest and Puerto Rico marking a second context for the development of Hispanic liberative thought. Euro-Americans believed that it was their God-given destiny to spread westward and disseminate their republican and Christian values to the inferior races, such as the American Indians and Hispanics. The doctrine of Manifest Destiny provided the political and religious rationale for U.S. territorial expansion and domination of the "less civilized" people.

The belief that their conquest of the West was God's will led to forcible confrontation between Anglo-American Protestantism, its churches and institutions, and Spanish-Mexican Catholicism. Protestant missionaries followed on the heels of the Euro-American prospectors, squatters, and soldiers into California and the Southwest. The imposition of Protestantism became a form of cultural imperialism in these areas, just as Catholicism had been in earlier centuries. These incursions resulted in few converts. Those who did convert were persecuted by Catholic neighbors, according to Juan Francisco Martinez, Jr., in his book *Los Protestantes*. The violence, racism, and marginalization of the past, coupled with the denial of atrocities of the past, continue to shape the political and religious imagination of Hispanics, as evidenced by the HLT emerging from Hispanic communities.

The contemporary articulation of HLT begins with Latin American liberation theology. Peruvian theologian Gustavo Gutiérrez's *Teologia de la Liberacion* (*A Theology of Liberation*) articulated a theology committed to reading the "signs of the times" (a central concern of Vatican II) by expressing solidarity with the poor, centering the activities of *comunidades de base* (base communities), and attending to the lessons of Marxist-inspired Latin American revolutionary movements. Gutiérrez defined theology as a "critical reflection on historical praxis" and emphasized the "preferential option for the poor" as the chief hermeneutical tool for theology. He articulated a new form of theology, one that does not stop at critical reflection on the world but "tries to be part of the process through which the world is transformed" into a new, just society. U.S. Hispanic theologians adopted this approach to doing theology in their own work.

Some important differences exist between these two schools of theology. Latin American liberation theology is more concerned with sociopolitical injustice caused by economic exploitation and oppression, while U.S. Hispanic liberation theologies address sociopolitical injustice caused by white supremacy and anti-Hispanic racism. Despite the differences, both of these theological movements confront distinct yet interrelated forms of oppression through critical reflection on social and historical events.

Virgilio Elizondo's book *Galilean Journey: The Mexican-American Promise* (1983) is commonly identified as the beginning of HLT as a formal academic discourse distinct from Euro-American and Latin American theology. Elizondo introduced ***mestizaje*** as a theological concept describing the hybrid experience of Mexican Americans and their struggle to survive on the border between Spanish and Anglo America. The Catholic-Spanish conquest of the American Indians produced a first *mestizaje,* and the Protestant-Anglo conquest produced a second. The result is an autonomous, distinct *mestizo/a* people, with elements of the parent races and cultures, "but with an originality of its own." Elizondo reads the gospels through the hermeneutical concept of *mestizaje*, arguing that Jesus was *mestizo* and suffered on the cross, thus connecting him to the identity and suffering of the Hispanic community.

***Mestizaje*:** a racial/ethnic, cultural, and social hybridity resulting from the mixing of European and Native American peoples. The term has been criticized for homogenizing racial differences through the trope of inclusiveness. *Mestiza/o* is the form used to refer to people.

***Mulatez*:** a racial/ethnic, cultural, and social hybridity resulting from the mixing of European and African peoples. It is sometimes used in conjunction with *mestizaje* for a more inclusive sense of the mixing of peoples, as in *mestizaje-mulatez*. It is related to the terms "creolization" and "Africanization." *Mulata/o* is the form used to refer to people.

The identification of Jesus the Galilean with the Hispanic *mestizo* constitutes a radical expression of solidarity with the oppressed Hispanic community. Through the Galilean's life in the **borderlands**, at the crossroads of empire, Jesus reveals a God who works in history through weakness and love.

Jesus as *mestizo* becomes the point of departure for understanding the socio-economic oppression of the Hispanic community as well as a way to interpret the eschatological event of the resurrection. Having set the precedent, many other Hispanic theologians began to use Hispanic experiences, concerns, symbols, and rituals to construct new theologies. Not everyone accepts *mestizaje* as a legitimate theological paradigm. *Mestizaje*'s fusing of races and cultures has been used in the past as justification for Euro-American racial domination and the erasure of indigenous and African identities. Some find the eugenics connotations of *mestizaje* insurmountable. Despite its problematic history, *mestizaje* continues to be investigated for its liberative potential.

Borderland: a physical, metaphorical, and symbolic site of contact between communities of asymmetrical relationships. The borderland emphasizes the fluidity and permeability of Hispanic communities that shape religious practices on both sides of the border.

Elizondo's reflections were born out of his rumination on Latin American liberation theology and his life experience on the Texas borderland. He attempted to make European and Latin American theologies relevant to the context of his community. Since Elizondo's *Galilean Journey* (1983) there have been dozens of anthologies, monographs, and hundreds of articles devoted to constructing theology, sociology of religion, critical and comparative religious studies, and the like relevant to the Hispanic community. There are at least four books devoted to "introducing" the subject: Justo L. González's *Mañana: Christian Theology from a Hispanic Perspective* (1990), Eduardo C. Fernández's *La Cosecha: Harvesting Contemporary United States Hispanic Theology (1972–1998)* (2000), Miguel A. De La Torre and Edwin David Aponte's *Introducing Latino/a Theology* (2001), and Luis G. Pedraja's *Teologia: An Introduction to Hispanic Theology* (2003). Many articles and chapters in books rehearse what has been said in the discourse of HLT theology (see my entry, "Latina/o Theology," in *Encyclopedia of Hispanic American Religious Cultures*). In part because of this wealth of introductory writing that captures the main themes and topics of HLT, this chapter focuses on the most recent developments.

Need for Liberation

The main goal of HLT is liberation from unjust sociopolitical structures and institutions. This goal leads to two questions: What constitutes an "unjust" structure? and What constitutes "liberation"? According to political theorist

Hannah Arendt, social structures emerge from the accumulation or institutionalization of human activity. These structures transmit common communal values, instructing the new generation of a community how to act in the world. When these structures no longer serve the common good, when they become compromised and endanger the conditions of the good life, they become unjust. For example, although the Treaty of Guadalupe Hidalgo (1848) guaranteed full rights of citizenship to Mexicans living on the U.S. side of the border, these Mexican Americans continued to face violence, intimidation, and a refusal by Euro-American settlers and their officials to recognize the rights of the new citizens. This mistreatment continued long after the "settling of the West" because of the moral framework embedded in the institutions and structures of society. The assumption that Mexicans were at best second-class members of society permeated Euro-American thinking. There was very little an individual could do to overcome the institutionalization of this value.

Unjust structures represent realities that constrain Hispanics and prevent human flourishing in Hispanic communities. They generate impossible choices, binding people in social situations that are difficult to escape. For example, a migrant laborer may be paid less than was promised or not paid at all. He or she may have little recourse but to resort to theft or other wrongdoing to feed his or her hungry family. This choice is not a result of the moral failing of the individual but because of unjust structures. Among the unjust structures Hispanics face are colonial racial logics, political domination and economic exclusion, and cultural imperialism.

Colonial Racial Logics

Hispanics continue to face the legacy of racism produced by colonial conquest and invasion. The categorization of human beings into various racial types, half-breeds, *mestiza/os*, *mulata/os* and the like, was an explicit colonial project that remains in force. These racial hierarchies support the myth of Euro-American superiority and render other populations, including Hispanics, as expendable or amenable to colonial improvement. As Anne McClintock explains in *Imperial Leather: Race, Gender, and Sexuality in the Colonial Contest*, Europeans represented national and racial/ethnic formation as an evolutionary progress of family types, from the "primitive," child-like races to the "enlightened" Europeans. The family metaphor for racial hierarchies led to catastrophe: "projecting the family image onto national and imperial progress enabled what was often murderously violent change to be legitimized as a progressive unfolding of natural decree." Although the understandings of racial differences have shifted in response to historical circumstances, the underlying racial logic is never far below the surface. The arrival of new immigrant populations from Latin America (about 30 percent of the U.S. Hispanic population is foreign born) continues to stoke the fires of "threat" to the Euro-American way of life. The threat, of course, is an illusion: Hispanics are not homogenous but diverse, as noted earlier. Hispanics are united by little more than historical circumstances and the continued oppression by Euro-Americans.

Some might object that according to official U.S. government categorization the identity of Hispanic is not a race but an ethnicity, and therefore cannot be subject to "colonial racial logics." Race, the argument goes, refers to genealogy or phenotype. Ethnicity refers to culture, tradition, and sometimes language. Race is unchosen; it is simply an accident of birth, while ethnicity is learned. However, this sort of natural/social distinction reveals a shallow understanding of race and ethnicity. Social scientists have long since abandoned the natural definitions of race for social ones. Moreover, the features associated with Hispanic ethnicity, such as unassimilatability, being less rational than Europeans, etc., are not considered mutable features. Sociologists Michael Omi and Howard Winant argue in *Racial Formation in the United States from the 1960s to the 1980s* that the construction of minorities as an ethnicity ignores the distinct historical experiences and imposes a monolithic immigrant story that blames the victim. The recognition of race as a result of social processes and the construction of ethnic characteristics as fixed make the commonalities between race and ethnicity much stronger. In terms of understanding the unjust structures that Hispanics face, the strong dividing line often drawn between race and ethnicity is largely misplaced. Whether understood as racism or ethnic prejudice, Hispanics have suffered, and continue to suffer, discrimination, violence, and abuse.

Political Domination and Economic Exclusion

Another unjust structure Hispanics face is political domination and economic exclusion. Despite the overblown claims that Hispanics were a deciding voting bloc in the 2012 presidential election, Hispanics have not had a significant effect on political outcomes in the United States. Moreover, Hispanics have historically been excluded from full political participation. In the nineteenth century, Hispanics faced seizure of their lands, the imposition of laws enacted against them, including taxes for citizens of Mexican ancestry, the refusal of courts to uphold Hispanic legal claims, and the withholding of the right to vote. Many Texas and California *rancheros* lost their land to squatters, in part due to the domination of the courts by Anglo legal officials. A new tax system also helped in the disposition of Mexican landowners. When Anglos took over lands owned by Mexicans, they paid the back taxes at a reduced rate. In the twentieth century, the tactics of domination changed from direct legal barriers to indirect manipulation. The political machinery of the U.S. Southwest encouraged Hispanic electoral participation and even helped ensure Hispanic officeholders as long as they promised to serve the interests of non-Hispanic whites. Anglos continue to control all southwestern state legislatures, even though Hispanics are more politically active.

Dispossessed from the land, Mexicans became laborers, sometimes on the very land that had been taken from them. Systematically excluded from the main source of the accumulation of wealth, Hispanics were locked into the lowest economic stratum of society. They found themselves in a racially stratified labor system with Anglo owners at the top and Mexican pickers and cowhands at the bottom. In the New Mexico mines, Mexicans did the most dangerous work. In California, they were hired as ditch diggers and unskilled laborers. As documented by Ronald Takaki in his book *A Different Mirror*, when they did work side by side with Anglos, Mexicans were paid less than their counterparts.

El Plan Espiritual de Aztlán (The Spiritual Plan of Aztlán) is an important document that marks a turning point in Chicana/o consciousness and religious imagination. Drafted for the 1969 National Chicano Youth Liberation Conference held in Denver, Colorado, *El Plan* declares the Chicano desire to liberate Aztlán—the ancestral home of the Aztecs identified as the U.S. Southwest—from its colonialist oppressors. As well as a geographic space, Aztlán also represents a counter-discursive site of resistance and functions as a symbol through which many Mexican American activists articulate a transnational identity. *El Plan* became the foundational philosophy of *Movimiento Estudiantil Chicano de Aztlán* (MECHA), an organized student movement of the early 1970s.

The situation for Hispanics at the lower end of the economic ladder has deteriorated over time. Their material conditions are limited by the structures of the U.S. political economy, its labor markets, and their exclusion from access to wealth-building assets like homes. The poverty that results from perennial unemployment and underemployment has led to their being deprived of the experience of social recognition that comes from meaningful and well-remunerated work. Yet, Hispanics have proven they continue to hold a sense of self-respect and dignity through social movements, including repeated *huelgas* (strikes) in the early twentieth century, the Chicano Student Movement of the 1960s, including the development of *El Plan Espiritual de Aztlán*, the organized agricultural labor movement of César Chávez and the United Farm Workers of America (UFWA), and Latina/o participation in the civil rights and women's movements. Liberation from political domination and economic exclusion are linked.

Demographic shifts among the U.S. population raise a number of questions in terms of liberation from political domination and economic exclusion for Hispanics. The steady stream of Hispanics arriving on U.S. shores and the higher-than-average birthrate have led many to predict that Hispanics will become the plurality if not the absolute majority in the United States. Given these demographic shifts, some have suggested that a new Hispanic consensus will emerge with enough political power to turn the tables on Anglos. The threat of a unified and politically motivated community of Hispanics has resulted in calls to establish English-only policies, demands for stricter laws to further limit immigration, and outright attempts to disenfranchise Hispanics from the political process. The fears driving these reforms are based largely on fear and ignorance. The portrait of Hispanics as subversives plotting to take over the U.S. political process gives Hispanics too much credit: Hispanics are neither that organized nor that devious. Many Hispanics do not identify pan-ethnically, nor do they share a common set of preferences that distinguishes them from other political constituencies. Diversity, not homogeneity, characterizes the Hispanic community in politics, as in most other areas. Hispanic liberation from political domination means liberation from fear-driven, xenophobic, and irrational policies. At issue for the dominant Anglo-Protestant American culture is concern over the loss of long-held privileges.

Liberative Theology in Action: The Issue of Immigration

Contemporary debates on Hispanic immigration are often framed from a nativist perspective. The debate becomes about legality, border security, and what to do with the poor, "huddled masses" arriving on our shores or crossing our borders (deportation has become the standard answer). The issue of immigration is broader and more complex than this framing presupposes. A combination of cultural, historical, and economic forces either "push" or "pull" immigrants to leave Mexico and other Latin American countries. Among these forces are the potent combination of U.S. foreign policies and the ascendancy of neoliberal economics. In Mexico, for example, neoliberalism's effects through NAFTA and the actions of U.S.-based corporations create intolerable living conditions that "push" Mexicans to take the dangerous journey northward, even as the U.S. demand for cheap, low-skill workers "pulls" them across the border.

The diverse migration experiences of Hispanics as exiles, refugees, migrant laborers, and dreamers suggest a need for a complex theology of immigration. Hispanic thinkers have drawn on a wealth of sources in constructing a theological response to the oppression and discrimination associated with immigration. The image of God, the Hebrew Bible's portrayals of migrants, the theme of hospitality (as well as restitution), borderlands/border crossing, and Jesus's special attention to aliens and strangers all provide rich themes from which to reflect on the situation of Hispanic immigration. The idea that the divine image is found in the *mestiza/o-mulata/o* Hispanic person, for example, has profound implications for how immigrants should be treated. HLT suggests that not only should individuals, communities, and governments take care of the immediate needs of immigrants and their families, but they should also challenge the global political-economic system that drives immigrants into alien territory. HLT on the issue of immigration calls for an embrace of the stranger that develops into a deep respect, as well as a mutuality that works toward the dismantling of oppression. HLT insists that one encounters the divine image in the experience of sojourners, outsiders, and foreigners—in short, Hispanic immigrants. Immigration policy decisions must stem from solidarity through the lens of the immigrant experience.

Cultural Imperialism and Suppression

Hispanics also suffer from institutionalized cultural imperialism and suppression. Cultural imperialism refers to the practice of appropriating another's culture for one's purposes or normalizing one culture as a universal. Everything from Hispanic music, food, dress, and style has been appropriated and commoditized, packaged and sold to the consuming public. The Anglo media sells Hispanic stereotypes, portraying them as illegal immigrants, criminals, gardeners, and maids or as hot-blooded, "sassy" beauties. Cultural suppression occurs through, for example, the under-emphasizing of Hispanic literary production as a part of public education or the dismissal and/or rejection of Spanish language in schools. The suppression of language is particularly troubling, since it is the chief transmitter of culture. Bilingual education is on the decline, despite the strong evidence of its cognitive and social benefits. One problem is the view of Spanish, spoken by 37 million U.S. residents, as a foreign language. The U.S., however, contains one of the largest Spanish-speaking populations in the world. In what sense, then, is Spanish "foreign"?

When injustice becomes institutionalized, individuals who perpetuate injustices do not recognize themselves as participating in wrongdoing. Unjust structures cannot be undone by the exercise of an individual's will—or by universalizing their will, as Kantians would insist. Dismantling unjust structures is only possible through social transformation that includes both the perpetrators who maintain unjust structures and the victims who suffer from them. Confronting socialized and institutionalized forms of injustice such as colonial racial logics, political domination, economic exclusion, and cultural imperialism is a long and difficult process and possible only through organized action in solidarity with the victims of the "underside of history."

Questions of Identity

Hispanic theologians continue to wrestle with questions of identity. What should Hispanics call themselves and on what basis? Whose purpose is served by doing so? What does it mean to be Hispanic in a neocolonial world? No consensus exists as to what term should be used to refer to the community of Latin American origin. Hispanic and Latina/o are the two most prominent choices, but simple ways of distinguishing them—"Hispanic" tends to be used by conservatives, "Latina/o" better captures the mix of Latin people—are gross oversimplifications. Despite the fact that some have criticized these debates as more identity politics, an inflexible political positioning based on self-interested perspectives, labeling matters since there is power in the act of naming oneself, as *mujerista* theologian Ada María Isasi-Díaz notes in her book *En la Lucha*. The process of naming is rooted in a need for validation of one's self and one's group. It is tied to dignity and reveals a way that Hispanics can assert themselves within a larger social context and reclaim autonomy that challenges imposed characterizations of Hispanics as a static social group. There is little reason to doubt the good faith behind whatever label is used to refer to this diverse community, whether it is Hispanic, Latin@, or some other term. Given the centrality of establishing identity and the process of naming, the question about identity is one that must perennially be addressed.

More recent debates have centered on the very nature of theology and its place among other disciplines. Much of HLT, like other forms of liberative thought, emphasizes "critical reflection on historical praxis" and the "preferential option for the poor." How do we access the reality of Hispanic poverty, racism, sexism, and other oppressive conditions? There has emerged a growing impatience with the repeated treatment of theological themes without references to ethnographic, sociological, and other sources of hard data. The fields of religious studies, sociology, anthropology, and history have engaged in focused study on the same marginalized communities that concern HLT. Hispanic theologians, who have been by and large too fixated on disciplinary boundaries, have emphasized cultural and social context to such an extent that it reduces the applicability of their work to broader discussions. The new generation of Hispanic theologians insists that HLT can and should benefit from the (historical, ethnographic, and more) studies of the communities they claim to represent. There is a need to bridge the gap between HLT and the many other disciplines that contextualize and theorize the rituals and practices of the Hispanic community beyond a narrow (and often conservative) theological meaning.

Questions about the nature of theology are often situated in questions of religious authority within Hispanic communities. Who should define the agenda for HLT? The church or the academy? The voices of the marginalized or the popular practices of Hispanic faith communities? If the Hispanic church, then which congregations—the charismatic, Pentecostal, Protestant, or the Catholic? What authority should be given to the official documents of the Roman Catholic Church? If hermeneutical preference is given to the oppressed, does this not constitute a radically new vision of theological authority? The implications for theology are far reaching. Communal and personal experience influence theology alongside scripture, tradition, and reason. The shared lived experience of oppression becomes a way to challenge ecclesial authority as well as theology that fails to take oppression seriously. Yet this raises additional questions. How do we negotiate the place of Hispanic lived experience in theological construction? And what is the role of the autobiographical voice? A danger lies in claiming that a set of one particular group's experiences represents the community as a whole. Appropriating one set of experiences can perpetuate a set of cultural-religious values that leads to the exclusion of others or, in the case of the autobiographical voice, one individual speaking for all. Care must be taken when giving epistemic privilege to one individual or group on the basis of their social location. Clearly, the concept of the lived experience/autobiographic voice has severe limitations. Yet, as Michelle A. González argues in *A Critical Introduction to Religion in the Americas*, HLT should resist the insider/outsider dualism, not by resolving it through hybrid language but by resisting it as a false construction. At their best, Hispanic liberative theologies represent a dynamic drawing on religious authority of both the institutional and the everyday faithful.

Popular Religion

The place of popular religious expressions in HLT is another question with which the group wrestles. To what extent should Hispanic popular religion be included as a source of theological reflection? By and large, the debate has taken place within the framework of institutional versus popular religious expressions, especially with reference to Catholicism. Popular religion refers to the large number of religious activities that take place outside the boundaries of official religious institutions. It is defined by what it is not: unofficial or not sanctioned by a formal religion. Autonomy over their devotional practices has allowed Hispanics to continue many practices since colonial times. Popular religious expressions from African-based religions, spiritualism, and indigenous traditions symbolically preserve Hispanic memory and ways of making sense of life. Theology, like history and other fields, has long favored the written documents, official statements, and primary works of religious insiders. The danger of this methodological preference is that it leaves much of what constitutes religious practice and belief among Hispanics "undocumented." Orlando Espín, one of the chief proponents of popular religion, argues in *The Faith of the People* that popular religiosity is a key source for constructing an adequate HLT. Given HLT's emphasis on identity as the bearer of important values, it is not surprising that it has devoted so much attention to popular religious experiences.

Fiesta worship: a celebratory and ecstatic experience of worship that often characterizes Hispanic liturgical practices. *Fiesta* literally means "party" or "celebration." The fiesta style of worship constitutes both an expression of communal faith and a form of cultural resistance. In the face of suffering and alienation Hispanics respond by celebrating the gift of life through fiesta worship.

Public Theology

A central concern for HLT is how to make theology "public." The question is sometimes framed in terms of finding ways of translating the personal and spiritual to what is political and material. If theology is poetic, imaginative, and irrational, then some work needs to be done to make it prosaic, plain, and rational. As Argentinian theologian Nancy Bedford argues, without this work of translating, HLT's denunciation of justice amounts to ideological rhetoric rather than a position open to critique. There are some problems with this formulation, notably that it defines theology as "irrational." Theology is both irrational and rational—it draws on quantifiable social realities even while exploring new imaginative possibilities for justice. Nevertheless, the impulse to make theology public is based on a desire to move HLT beyond the boundaries of group interest to more tangible social change. But this begs the question: Should we do the work of translation to make theology publicly accessible? What is lost by doing so?

Making something "public" requires subjecting it to the moral and discursive rules of common political life. The common rules of moral discourse have created the structures and institutions that oppress Hispanics. Should Hispanics instead endorse only the political values that cohere with liberative values—like equality of opportunity—while undermining and challenging the laws, institutions, and values that lead to racist, exclusionary, and destructive activities? There are also some concerns that this reclaiming of the traditional role of theology in U.S. society—as the moral authority for society—is simply an attempt to reestablish Christian privilege. One way of making HLT public is to bridge the gap between liberative theology and religious studies. HLT can reconceptualize the theological task for a broader audience through a collaborative interdisciplinary approach. This requires rethinking liberative theology along the pattern outlined above. Yet there is no reason to stop at dialoging only with religious scholars. Serious efforts at social change will require meeting with critical thinkers in the fields of economics, politics, and sociology. It is clear that if HLT is to be taken "public," it will require a complex and nuanced methodology with selective attention to what is supported and what is critiqued.

Leading Scholars and Figures

As mentioned above, there are a number of historically important Latin American intellectuals who set the stage for the possibility of HLT. The most immediate influences are the Latin American liberation theologians of the 1950s, '60s, and '70s, including those who founded the Latin American Episcopal Council (CELAM) in 1955. Among the progenitors of the movement were the Peruvian Gustavo Gutiérrez, the Brazilian Hugo Assmann, and, on the Protestant side, the Argentinian José Míguez Bonino. The leading scholars and figures can be divided into three distinct groups, organized chronologically and corresponding to methodological commitments. The first generation is marked by initial attempts to articulate what it means to construct theology from an unabashedly particularized perspective, to use the experiences of oppression, marginalization, displacement, immigration, and **exile** to spark the theological imagination and reflect on the symbolic purpose and power of Hispanic religious culture. The first generation of scholars awoke to the creative possibilities of focusing on Hispanic American identity and culture as a liberating methodology, reflecting a growing sense of self-worth and dignity in Hispanic faith communities as authors of their own future by drawing on their own values and religious-cultural metaphors. This generation of scholars did nothing less than develop a new form of theology, relevant for Hispanic churches, institutions, and communities. They argued from the beginning that this "contextual" theological reflection has broader implications for the wider church and society. It is difficult to overstate the significance of their contributions, since the initial steps in creating a new discursive field are always the hardest. These scholars boldly asked difficult questions about the sociopolitical status of Hispanics that challenged the nature of the theological task.

Exile: a state of forced separation from one's homeland, causing alienation and, often, sadness. As a religious metaphor, the state in which the impossibility of returning meets the eternal need to return, to *patria*, childhood/innocence, and happiness. The metaphor is particularly prevalent among the Cuban community but also among Chicana/os, as evidenced by Jose Antonio Villarreal's 1959 novel *Pocho*.

This first generation formulated a number of concepts in their construction of HLT. Theology, Hispanic theologians insist, takes place at the level of *lo cotidiano*, the approach to everyday experience, especially the cultural and socioeconomic struggle to survive. Everyday experience drives the tasks of observing, interpreting, and understanding social realities, as well as of constructing visions for a better life. For *mujerista* theologian Ada María Isasi-Díaz, *lo cotidiano* becomes a form of liberative praxis, a way of uncovering effective strategies for surviving oppression (*Mujerista Theology: A Theology for the Twenty-First Century*, 1996). HLT expresses the experiences and practices of *lo cotidiano*, which becomes a theoretical and epistemological starting point for theological reflection. Analysis of, for instance, *corridos*, popular adages, devotional practices, artistic expression, and *remedios*, yields important lessons about how Hispanics interpret and understand theology.

Oppression constitutes an embodied everyday experience of many Hispanics. *La lucha*, or the struggle, refers to survival in the face of multiple forms of oppression, along economic, political, social, gender, and sexual dimensions. *La lucha* as a category for Hispanic theology signifies not just the struggle against oppression but also the hope for liberation and fullness of life. The "already but not yet" eschatological tension is captured by *la lucha*. Hispanic scholar Miguel A. De La Torre later expands and extends the meaning of *la lucha*. De La Torre, in his book *La Lucha for Cuba*, argues that *la lucha* names the religious expression, a "holy war," of the Cuban exilic community against the displacement and pain caused by Fidel Castro and his regime. In De La Torre's interpretation, *la lucha* has the unintended effect of masking today's oppression, that is, the oppression of the current ruling elite, by focusing on the hope of tomorrow's liberation. *La lucha*, like other terms discussed earlier, has both repressive and liberative potentialities.

Acompañamiento (accompaniment) is another term formulated by Hispanic theologians of the first generation. Making a radical option for Hispanics necessarily includes the practice of solidarity and *acompañamiento*, the act of being present and affirming the personhood of the other. Hispanic theologians have noted that popular religious practices provide an opportunity for Hispanics to accompany one another and express their cultural bonds, shared sufferings, and collective hopes. Systematic theologian Roberto Goizueta, in his book *Caminemos con Jesús*, grounds Hispanic theology in the praxis of *acompañamiento*, arguing that its aesthetic and liberative dimensions are distinct yet mutually interrelated elements of Hispanic spirituality. In light of the continued marginalization and exploitation of the Hispanic community, *acompañamiento* becomes a religious and liberative act, not just for Hispanics but also for the community that obtains privileges as a result of their oppression.

The first generation of Hispanic liberative theologians used Hispanic identity rather than fixed categories as a conceptual framework for theological reflection. It was an enormous achievement that nevertheless left a number of important questions unaddressed. The following generation of Hispanic theologians advanced the discussion by framing the discourse differently, providing new directions and focus. Over the past twenty years, HLT has split into two methodological schools. Both schools have scoured and mined the foundational concepts of the first generation and have sought to build upon them. The first of these remained heavily grounded in the ecclesial context. The *Hispanidad* identity of their work depends on the cultural and racial/ethnic identity of the author. The second school centers on a greater complexity of social commitments. Their work focuses on approaches to the study of Hispanic religion from comparative, historical, philosophical, and anthropological perspectives.

The ecclesial school remains concerned with questions of theology in a ministerial and pastoral context. It seeks to construct a liberative theology *latinamente* through sustained engagement with Hispanic literature, music, art, and other cultural experiences and practices. The purpose of the theological task is to guide the church by taking stock of the place of the community and carefully considering how the church can cultivate the growth of ***convivencia***. Thus, liberation is understood as cultivating the conditions through which marginalized communities secure their own inclusion and full participation in society. At the same time there is an insistence that this confessional theology of the faith community advance a publicly relevant discourse. For Latin@ theologians, HLT is necessarily public, since its place of theorizing is the living faith of Hispanic churches and communities. This school takes its methodological guideposts from the first generation and generally takes a celebratory stance toward the earlier work. By and large the scholars of this school are Catholic theologians, though not exclusively.

***Convivencia*:** literally, "living together." The term consciously draws on the idyllic coexistence of Jews, Christians, and Muslins in Spain from the early eighth century to the late-fifteenth-century *Reconquista*. Some have argued that *convivencia* is merely a historical construct. As a theological term, *convivencia* amounts to a communal accompaniment, a shared living experience characterized by peace and justice between privileged and marginalized.

The second, comparative school of Hispanic scholars critically examines the assumptions of Hispanic liberative theologies. They ask whether liberation amounts to more than just participation in a liberal, democratic society. They question whether liberation, defined by the first generation of scholars as achievable through the sacrifice and resurrection of Jesus Christ and the reign of God, can be found in non-Christian religious traditions. These thinkers wonder if highlighting oppression in one's work qualifies as "liberative" engagement and if the concerns of the scholar represent the concerns and struggle of the community. Through a critique of the internal colonialism of U.S. society, its militarism and capitalist exploitation, they elevate the prophetic critique in the work of the first generation. In challenging the occultation of African and American Indian sources and the racial logics that are behind such decisions, a new theology emerges. This new theology engages with religious studies, critical theory, philosophy, and other disciplines. This group of scholars is also much less concerned with defending disciplinary boundaries and writes under categories as diverse as theological anthropology, decolonization, transcendence, historiography, and pragmatism.

Possible Future Trends

Postcolonialism and Transnationalism

Some Hispanic theologians, in their efforts to overcome the sway of the larger culture, have found an ally in postcolonial studies. Postcolonial analysis understands the phenomenon of empire, imperialism, and colonialism as the larger structural reality that determines political, economic, social, and cultural conditions. This structural reality functions in terms of a center/margins binary that includes a number of other subordinate binaries: civilized/barbarian, developed/undeveloped, Anglo/Hispanic, male/female. Postcolonial theory helps Hispanic theologians to challenge these binaries and the social structures based on them. It also provides a productive way of dismantling the presumption of transparent, disinterested, and dehistoricized agents and structures, and of revealing fundamental asymmetries of power and highly partisan points of view. Biblical scholar Fernando Segovia introduced postcolonial hermeneutics and theory to HLT at an early stage. A few scholars, among them Miguel A. De La Torre and Mayra Rivera Rivera, have incorporated postcolonial paradigms into their work. A possible future trend in HLT would involve a critique of the modes of colonial domination within HLT and an elaboration of a thoroughgoing postcolonial Hispanic theology.

Related to the move toward postcolonialism is the growing trend toward transnational analysis. Despite the categories of borderlands, *nepantla* (the Nahua term meaning "middle place"), and other related terms in HLT, the tendency by and large has been to focus on the nation-state as the primary context for analysis. This has severely limited interregional theological dialogue. Transnational analysis contextualizes the movement across national borders—not just communities and religious-cultural practices but active networks and organizations. Transnationalism can help to make sense of, for example, the remittances from Mexican Americans to their families back home, which represent a staggering transfer of wealth across boundaries. Transnational analysis has the ability to improve on the local and national conceptual frameworks already developed by Hispanic theologians. The creation of unjust social societies is a transnational and global phenomenon. The struggle against injustice should capture the transnational effects of broad global forces without devaluing contextual analysis at the local level.

Religious Diversity

Another emerging trend takes more seriously the complex religious landscape of the Americas. Until recently, HLT has largely ignored indigenous and African religious traditions, focusing instead on a politically progressive form of Christianity. Scholars such as Miguel A. De La Torre, Luis D. León, Michelle Maldonado González, and Edwin David Aponte are documenting the incredible religious diversity among Hispanics. Hispanics identify with *Curanderismo* (a tradition of faith healing), Seventh-Day Adventists, Jehovah's Witnesses, *la Regla de Ocha* (popularly known as *Santería*), Judaism, Islam, and Buddhism. The largest growing religious identities among Hispanics are the charismatic/pentecostal and evangelical movements. The image of the Afro-Cuban *santero* priest sacrificing chickens and goats are as Hispanic as the procession of penitents marching under the image of *La Virgen de Guadalupe* or sweeping graves on the Day of the Dead. Even if these are stereotypical images of Hispanic religious experience, they provide a sense of the range of religious vitality in the community. It is increasingly clear that Hispanics can no longer be viewed as a monolithically Catholic population. The future of HLT will move away from studies focused on varieties of Catholicism and mainline Protestantism and be replaced by more attention to the enormous variety of religious traditions within Hispanic communities.

Class and the Political Economy

Another possible future trend is a turn toward greater analysis of class and the political economy. Despite the insistence by a number of theologians that U.S. Hispanics suffer injustices based on economic exploitation, classism, and inequality, few efforts have been made to study these issues among Hispanics. Instead, the tendency has been to note class inequality and economic injustice and then move on to issues of cultural or religious identity. In "Reclaiming Marxist Analysis for U.S. Latina/o Theology," I argue that among the many reasons for the hesitancy to engage in class analysis are a desire to disassociate from the Marxist-inspired regimes from which some Hispanics fled and a loyalty to the United States, which sees itself largely as a classless society. Whatever the reasons for the scholarly omission, economic injustices remain a central form of oppression in Hispanic communities. Hispanics are disproportionately the victims of a capitalist political economy that creates poverty, unemployment, and underemployment at higher rates in their communities than the general U.S. population. Class analysis would provide a way of identifying unequal power relationships that produce oppressive structures. One of the reasons that HLT has not been able to respond effectively to oppression in the Hispanic community has been because critical class analysis and evaluation of policies and structures of the political economy have been lacking.

Sexuality and Heteronormativity

Chicana feminist Gloria Anzaldúa, theorizing about a new "mestiza consciousness" in *Borderlands/La Frontera,* created space for analysis of the interstices between sexuality, gender, race/ethnicity, and culture. Since then, the number

La Virgen (the Virgin): *La Virgen*, an archetype corresponding to the Virgin Mary, is an enduring, ubiquitous, and highly malleable religious symbol among Hispanics. Stories of appearances of *La Virgen* vary from one region to the next. Two popular manifestations are *La Virgen de Guadalupe* (or alternatively *Nuestra Señora de Guadalupe* or simply *La Morenita*), particularly prominent among Mexican Americans, and *La Virgen de la Caridad del Cobre* (or *La Caridad* or *Cachita*), primarily among Cubans. According to the legend, *La Guadalupana* appeared to an indigenous peasant by the name of Juan Diego in 1531 on a hill in Tepeyacac. A *mestiza* of both American Indian and Spanish ancestry, *La Guadalupana* provides a sense of meaning and religious-cultural belonging and speaks in terms of motherly love for the oppressed. *La Virgen de la Caridad del Cobre* has a number of origin stories. In one version, three Cuban fishermen—two Indian brothers, Juan and Rodrigo de Hoyos, along with a young slave named Juan Moreno—searching for salt at the Bay of Nipe around 1687 discovered an icon of Mary floating on the water with the words "*Yo soy La Virgen de la Caridad*" ("I am the Virgin of Charity"). *La Caridad del Cobre*, represented as a biracial figure, is strongly associated with Afro-Cuban devotion, in particular with the *orisha* (diety) Oshún. Nearly everywhere *La Virgen* is found, she functions as a beloved symbol of religious and national identity.

of works examining the intersection of LGBTQ studies and Hispanic communities has proliferated. While analysis of Hispanic sexuality takes place in fields such as sociology, political science, and queer and feminist studies, theological and religious reflection around sexuality/orientation/heteronormativity and *Hispanidad* is very much in its initial stages. A possible future trend consists of attending to the plethora of strategies used by scholars to study sexuality in the Hispanic communities as liberative performances and forms of resistance. This new line of scholarship should not confine itself to LGBTQ subjects, but also a broader examination of heteronormativity, representations of masculinity and femininity, and their interaction with the global capitalistic complex of consumption and desire. Research questions should not merely add homosexuality to their work, but integrate the methodologies of queer studies into their work of addressing oppressive gender and sexual representations among Hispanics.

Study Questions

1. How would you define Hispanic liberative theologies? Do they provide primarily a cultural, political, or racial/ethnic critique of unjust structures and institutions? In what ways does HLT provide a pragmatic, prophetic, and public critique to socialized and institutionalized injustice?
2. The large and increasing number of Hispanics in the United States makes the nation the fifth largest Hispanic country in the world. What are some of the ways that U.S. society and public policy should respond to an increasing Hispanic population? How should churches respond? How should it alter theological construction?
3. Some Hispanics did not immigrate to the United States; rather, the border moved on them. How does the perspective of the borderlands challenge a Euro-American-centric approach to history? What difference does it make to think of the United States with a south-to-north orientation rather than an east-to-west one?
4. Samuel P. Huntington has argued that the increasing numbers of Hispanics and the influence of Hispanic language, culture, and power constitute a threat to U.S. Anglo-Protestant identity (*Who Are We? The Challenges to America's National Identity*). How would you rebut this argument? What

does it look like to stand in solidarity with a rejected and marginalized people?

5. Unlike earlier European groups that quickly assimilated, many Hispanic communities have managed to retain their own language and cultural practices within small enclaves. Why do you think many Hispanics consider the process of assimilation undesirable? How would you feel if you were asked to abandon your mother tongue, religious-cultural practices, and traditions in order to "fit in"?

Suggested Reading

Aponte, Edwin David. *¡Santo! Varieties of Latino/a Spirituality*. Maryknoll, NY: Orbis Books, 2012.

De La Torre, Miguel A., ed. *Encyclopedia of Hispanic American Religious Culture*. Volumes 1 and 2. Santa Barbara, CA: ABC-CLIO Publishers, 2009.

De La Torre, Miguel A., and Gastón Espinoza, eds. *Rethinking Latino(a) Religion and Identity*. Cleveland, OH: Pilgrim Press, 2006.

González, Michelle A. *A Critical Introduction to Religion in the Americas: Bridging the Liberation Theology and Religious Studies Divide*. New York/London: New York University Press, 2014.

Isasi-Díaz, Ada María, and Eduardo Mendieta, eds. *Decolonizing Epistemologies: Latina/o Theology and Philosophy*. New York: Fordham University Press, 2012.

Martell-Otero, Loida I., Zaida Maldonado Perez, and Elizabeth Conde-Frazier. *Latina Evangélicas: Theological Survey from the Margins*. Eugene, OR: Cascade Books, 2013.

Martínez, Juan Francisco, Jr. *Los Protestantes: An Introduction to Latino Protestantism in the United States*. Santa Barbara, CA: ABC-CLIO, 2011.

Martínez-Vázquez, Hjamil A. *Latina/o y Musulmán: The Construction of Latina/o Identity among Latina/o Muslims in the United States*. Eugene, OR: Wipf & Stock Publishers, 2010.

Valentín, Benjamin, ed. *New Horizons in Hispanic/Latino(a) Theology*. Cleveland, OH: Pilgrim Press, 2003.

6

African American Liberative Theologies

Cheryl A. Kirk-Duggan and Travis T. Judkins

Long before Columbus "sailed the ocean blue" and Puritans landed at Plymouth Rock, African persons lived and practiced their faith in North America, from Christianity and Islam to African indigenous religions. Most Africans on this continent, kidnapped into enslavement, then packed in the bellies of slave ships and transported across the **Middle Passage**, were not *tabula rasa* upon arrival to the shores of the so-called New World or colonial America. They came with rich cultures and traditions, framed by philosophical and theological praxis: their embodiment existed years before analysis and reflection. This praxis framed their quest and desire for freedom.

Middle Passage: named for the middle leg of a voyage that started in Europe, in which the ship carried cargo: iron, cloth, brandy, firearms, and gunpowder. Once on Africa's "slave coast," they exchanged cargo for Africans, loaded them on ship, and sailed for the Americas, where they exchanged the enslaved for sugar, tobacco, or other products; then the ship returned to Europe.

The rich, complex tapestry of religious practices and lived reality of African peoples has been shaped by colonial inventions, discrimination, and economics within the black Atlantic world, connecting Africa and her peoples who arrive in the United States—Jewish, Christian (Protestant and Catholic), Muslim. Liberative theologies are critical to the construction of just systems for African peoples, because some religious systems are antithetical to justice and freedom. Much of this systemic oppression stems from postcolonialism, which can problematize the objectives of those liberative theologies that are necessary for African American communal unity and progression.

This chapter explores African American liberative theologies as theory and praxis, viewing them as critical to the lived realities of particular Africans in the United States who embraced Christianity, Islam, and Judaism. While there are numerous other religions and faith practices followed by African peoples in the United States, the limits of space only afford room to provide a brief overview of three theistic religions.

Seeing through a Lens Darkly: A Womanist Postcolonial Approach

Womanist theology names, exposes, and seeks to liberate and transform systemic and personal oppressive violence. Womanist theology is the interpretation or hermeneutical engagement about who God is and how womanists profoundly relate to this God, to others, creation, and themselves. This discipline- and justice-based way of life, informed by works of art, music, literature, poetry, and scripture, marries theory and praxis. Womanist theology articulates the meaning of being made in God's image, yet oppressed due to class, race, gender, physical/mental/emotional ability, sexual orientation, and age, as it presses toward what constitutes liberation despite one's sociocultural and economic location. Alice Walker coined the term "womanist," and many black women scholars have adopted her terminology and notion of "outrageous, audacious, courageous, or willful behavior. Responsible. In Charge," as an emancipatory rubric of hope, for change. Womanist theology names ways that systems and people oppress others, invites those victimized to not be victims, and emboldens victimizers to mindfulness and transformation—sentiments in postcolonial theology.

Postcolonial theology explores the ramifications of colonialism on the postmodern world. Colonialism is a system of beliefs in which one group of people acquires, exploits, and perpetuates their oppressive beliefs and identity over the territories and bodies of others; they take what is not theirs as their own. What was once overt racism, gender biases based on color and ethnicity, has become more veiled. Such tyrannical biases stem directly from the colonialized system of separatism and enslavement impressed on African descendants. Although centuries have passed, these heinous acts are alive, though veiled by skewed interpretations of the Christian canon, which informs politics, racism, sexism, and religious diversity. Postcolonial theology deconstructs oppression within the academy and disrupts oppressive perspectives within faith communities, and serves as a catalyst to destroy inequalities of class, race, gender, and deplorable acts within religious belief systems. Womanist and postcolonial theories create a powerful lens for viewing African American liberation theologies.

Womanist postcolonial theology bridges "town and gown," church and academy, to dialogue around systemic oppression and communal/personal identity, agency, integrity, and justice. To some, oppressive actions and beliefs by a few individuals holding the majority of societal power are in the past. The possibility for justice embraces a womanist postcolonial theology that listens to the "least of these," to poor black women's lived experience, and to all of God's impoverished, to extract an epistemology (way of knowing), and theological anthropology (way of relating) that honors all beings made in God's image. We meet this God amid authentic goodness and systemic and personal sin, within intricate relationships forged by complex human beings. We embrace the beauty of humanity, of their bodies, as we interpret and do God-talk. The postmodern world is full of continuous changes. Diverging ideals are normative even within faith communities. A theology that speaks to diverse voices and changes is critical, because it exposes oppressive actions by the world's hierarchical power brokers. As global violence intensifies, fueled by unchecked biases, a womanist postcolonial lens helps us speak truth to power about African American liberative theologies via black Judaism, Christianity, and Islam.

Building Blocks: Basic Tenets of African American Liberative Theologies

When thinking about the African American experience in the three Abrahamic religions, we can see that they share geographical ties to ancient Israel and Africa, and are monotheistic. These faiths have developed in the United States among complexities and tensions of "Du Boisian double consciousness": what does it mean to be African and American in the United States? To engage liberative theology requires exploring oppressive history and faith, the quest for freedom and justice, questioning how African American Jews, Christians, and Muslims deal with blackness, black suffering, and liberation.

African American Judaism

The term "Black Jews," also known as "Black Hebrews," refers to groups that combine **pan-Africanist** and **black nationalist** thought with Jewish symbols and principles. While they often relate to Beta Israel (Falasha), a group of Ethiopian Jews, they are separate and not connected to African Americans born Jewish or who convert to Judaism. Black Jews engage idiosyncratic interpretations of Judaic teachings and history, sometimes with a militant stance, categorizing themselves as God's chosen people. They seek identity with blacks in the Old Testament, have pride in a marvelous African past, predict a phenomenal future as the true Israel, uphold

Ethiopia: Officially the Federal Democratic Republic of Ethiopia, Ethiopia is a country located in the Horn of Africa. In the fourth century, after the rise of Christianity in Ethiopia, Jews who refused to convert were persecuted and withdrew to the Gondar region. In the tenth century, they sought to eliminate Christianity. Ethiopian Jews enjoyed great influence for some 350 years, often brokering power

Ethiopia/Africa as motherland, and desire true liberation. From the seventeenth century, sources used the Israelite trope to define Native American origins. From the nineteenth century, some used the Israelite trope to create a racialized, religious identity of various Europeans as descendants of the ten lost tribes, identifying Jews as imposters, assuring extinction of so-called lesser breeds, and endowing Anglo-Saxons with biblical promises. Through time, many religious groups vied for the coveted pedigree of the lost tribes.

Pan-African: philosophy and movement that encourages solidarity of Africans worldwide, based on the idea that unity is vital to socioeconomic and political progress and intends to unify and uplift people of African descent.

Black nationalism: Gaining major national influence through Nation of Islam and the 1960s black power movement, advocates of black nationalism promoted economic self-sufficiency, racial pride for African Americans, and black separatism.

The earliest black Jewish congregations established in the United States were the Church of the Living God, the Pillar Ground of Truth for All Nations, by prophet Frank S. Cherry, Chattanooga, Tennessee (1866), and the Church of God and Saints of Christ (1896) by William S. Crowdy (1847–1908), in Lawrence, Kansas, which moved to Philadelphia (1900). Some sources indicate Crowdy's group emerged in Washington, DC, and Belleville, Virginia. Nigerian Wentworth Arthur Matthew, rabbi for a time at Pentecostal Church of the Living God founded in Steele Springs, Tennessee (1903), also organized the Ethiopian Hebrew

between Muslims and Christian forces. From the thirteenth through the seventeenth centuries they faced persecution. The first modern contact with this community occurred in the eighteenth century, when an explorer found them in a quest for the Nile river. Israeli Jews began sending educational support to the Ethiopian Jews in 1954 as they prepared to migrate to Israel. Other groups followed with aid. During Haile Selassie's reign, Ethiopian Jews often became scapegoats for any difficulty that befell the land. The government closed Jewish synagogues and schools in Ethiopia, limited their travel, and imprisoned those speaking with tourists. Many fled to Sudan, and Israel's government vowed to save Ethiopian Jews.

Lost tribes (of Israel): The lost tribes are ten of the original twelve Hebrew tribes who took possession of Canaan, the Promised Land, under the leadership of Joshua, after Moses's death. The tribes were named Asher, Dan, Ephraim, Gad, Issachar,

Manasseh, Naphtali, Reuben, Simeon, and Zebulun, all sons or grandsons of Jacob. In 930 BCE the ten tribes formed the northern independent kingdom of Israel, and the two other tribes, Judah and Benjamin, set up the southern kingdom of Judah. Following the conquest of the northern kingdom by the Assyrians in 721 BCE, the ten tribes were gradually assimilated by other peoples and disappeared from history. A belief persists that one day the ten lost tribes will be found.

Commandment Keepers Congregation in New York City (1913). Arnold Josiah Ford, who believed blacks descended from blood Hebrews, organized the Beth B'Nai Abraham congregation in Harlem (1924), after **Marcus Garvey** expelled him from UNIA (Universal Negro Improvement Association).

Garveyism—describes the thought and organizational activities related to Marcus Mosiah Garvey of Jamaica, who organized the Universal Negro Improvement Association and African Communities League (UNIA/ACL), fostering aspects of black nationalism.

Many such groups believed that prophets and other biblical characters, including Jesus, were black. Black racialized theologies, antithetical to bigoted white theologies, explained how blacks descended from the lost tribes, including texts such as Olaudah Equiano's 1789 classic, *The Interesting Narrative of the Life of Olaudah Equiano, or Gustavus Vassa, the African. Written by Himself,* which posited Jewish descent for the Igbo. Black Hebrews included many migrants from the U.S. South and the West Indies during the Great Migration. This sociocultural milieu marked the change from Black Hebrewism rooted in the literal interpretation of the Hebrew Bible or Old Testament to a faith shaped by Talmudic tradition and oral law. Many southern migrants either flocked to Black Judaism, to Garveyism, or to figures like **Father Divine**. Symbiosis, empathy, and cultural exchanges of ideas and practices increased between Jews and blacks. Much interest surrounded the Lemba, Beta Israel of the Ethiopian mountains, and the Falashas. Beta Israel evolved from a Judaic-like faith out of Ethiopian Christianity. The quest for authenticity also resounded within African American Christian communities.

Father Divine: a twentieth-century social reformer who championed racial equality and advocated for economic self-sufficiency in the 1930s for African Americans. He founded the Peace Mission. Followers of Father Divine live communally and are celibate.

Liberative Theology in Action: The Issue of Battered Love

Renita Weems, in *Battered Love: Marriage, Sex, and Violence in the Hebrew Prophets,* demonstrated that many Old Testament scriptures utilize language that oppresses women, and perpetuates and justifies the abuse of women by their male counterparts. Simply put, words of scripture justify domestic violence. Various norms and attitudes regarding women, their bodies, and sexuality lent themselves to exploitation and manipulation by biblical prophets because they used gender-biased language to persuade their male audiences. Sacred texts have been used to abuse women, just as these texts were used to keep enslaved persons oppressed. The language of battered love legitimated sexual abuse and domestic violence against many women within biblical history and in the twenty-first century. Reading these biblical texts literally can make males feel they are divinely ordained to rule over women. Yet such a view does not consider that Jesus, the savior of the world in Christian doctrine, was born of a woman. Language can be twisted to uplift some and destroy others. A liberating theology is a theology that seeks to uplift the entirety of humanity, because God is the creator of all.

African American Christianity

Christianity has never been far removed from people of African descent. Within African traditional religions exists a critical understanding of humanity within a religious universe. Saint Augustine, in his *Confessions,* describes the reciprocity of divine sovereignty. All things originate from and return to God. African American Christianity recognizes God, reflected in all things, within the universe. John S. Mbiti suggests that God is manifest in every creature. One also cannot separate African American Christianity from African traditional religions, from the Middle Passage to enslavement in the United States.

Undoubtedly, through the corridors of slavery, integration of African traditional religions and Western Eurocentric thought emerged. African American Christianity, a distinctive religion born out of slavery, has a sovereign creator who desires that all humanity be free. A people shackled in bondage perpetuated this faith. Such bondage was antithetical to a liberative theology of a Jesus-based biblical theology. While many Christians have used biblical narratives to oppress not liberate, freedom within Old Testament narratives and in Christ's life anchor African American Christians' faith.

James H. Evans asserts that Jesus is so much a part of the African American religious experience that it should be referred to as "Jesusology." This expression concerns Jesus's struggle as a member of an oppressed minority, not his redemptive suffering. African Americans' struggle and pain correlate with Old Testament Yahwistic narratives of the oppressed. The theology of liberation is birthed out of a theology of pain. This theology of pain cultivates and nurtures liberative religious experiences. African American Christians identified with the ancient Hebrews, a persecuted, exiled, but ultimately delivered people. A parallel kinship occurs in Christ as God in flesh, who was socially marginalized, religiously/theologically criticized, publicly crucified, but ultimately resurrected.

African American Islam

Islam, as both a religion and a culture, first arrived in the Americas with Spanish explorers, Muslim soldiers or sailors who came from Africa, as enslaved or free, or as independent contractors. Other scholars posit that enslaved Africans brought by English planters were the first Black Muslims on American shores. Black Muslims' numbers were substantial by the late 1800s in South Carolina. While Muslim slaves were forbidden to practice their religion, clandestine services occurred, and their faith continued in stories and memories. Religious and other cultural values survived and re-emerged through Noble Drew Ali. Born Timothy Drew, Ali received the call, in a dream, to restore the "Lost-Found Nation" for Moors/Asiatic blacks kidnapped to the Americas. He created the Moorish Science Temple, an expression of Black Islam. After he founded the Temple in Newark, New Jersey (1913), the movement spread to many major midwestern, northern, and southern cities. After Ali died (1929), other leaders emerged, notably the Honorable Elijah Muhammad, born Elijah Poole.

In Detroit, Poole became a follower of Wali Farad, who was committed to rescuing the Lost-Found Nation by using the teachings of Islam. Farad and Ali differed on some of their doctrines but essentially agreed that African Americans, a people of noble heritage, could be raised up by knowing and practicing Islam, their true, natural religion. When Farad moved to other priorities, Elijah, now deemed the "Messenger of Allah," received the mantle of leadership, and he wore it until his death in 1975. Elijah built the Nation of Islam (NOI). Under Elijah's forty-year leadership, NOI grew exponentially. For thirteen years, Malcolm X served Muhammad as national spokesperson, recruiter, and minister, articulating his own ideas and establishing credibility for the Messenger's teachings. During these years, Muhammad shifted from ranting about white devils to being a respected black leader; he focused on the transformational possibilities that every black man could become disciplined, have dignity and respect, without integration. Muhammad gradually nudged NOI into new ways of understanding and functioning.

Tensions eventually emerged between Muhammad and Malcolm. Muhammad sanctioned Malcolm for his "chickens coming home to roost" statement after the Kennedy assassination, then made a complete severance after Malcolm's so-called discovery and condemnation of Muhammad's sexual liberties with some young women on his staff.

Malcolm and Muhammad are a study in contrasts, despite the respect the former had for the latter. A southerner, Muhammad knew the importance of patience and submission, and that life and death depended on adhering to written and unwritten rules. Malcolm, who grew up on northern streets of Detroit and New York, faced tensions from naysayers within the Nation and his aficionados who could not fathom Malcolm's support of the Messenger. After Malcolm's pilgrimage to Mecca (1964) wedded him to Islamic orthodoxy, he grew beyond NOI and his debt to Elijah Muhammad. Because of the furor around Malcolm's untimely remarks and Muhammad's desires to continue garnering emerging respect within the United States and his prospering network, reconciliation became more and more difficult. Malcolm told C. Eric Lincoln days before his assassination on February 21, 1965, that he would die soon; the police also knew of the assassination plot.

With the death of Elijah Muhammad on February 25, 1975, his son, Wallace Deen Muhammad (Warith Deen), became prime minister. Deen exacted many changes, decentralizing authority and downsizing NOI businesses. Deen was now an imam; temples became mosques and later Masjids. Individual "Nations" developed in Detroit, Baltimore, and Atlanta. Minister Louis Haleem Abdul Farrakhan, born Louis Eugene Walcott, succeeded Malcolm as minister of Mosque 7, in Harlem, New York. In 1977, Farrakhan broke with Warith's World Community of Islam in the West to rebuild the Lost-Found Nation of Islam. Farrakhan rebuilt and reconstructed NOI, reinstituting many of Muhammad's teachings. Farrakhan accomplished many firsts: from appointing Sister Ava Muhammad to be a minister in NOI and registering to vote in 1993, to providing Jesse Jackson with security when he was a presidential candidate and forming political coalitions with Native and Latino/a Americans. He was also central to the success of the Million Man March.

Since 1978, the original Nation of Islam has been divided into three groups: two calling themselves the Nation of Islam and the third identifying as the World Community of al-Islam in the West.

Along with indigenous Muslim African American movements such as the Moorish Science Temple, Ansar Allah, and the NOI, African American Sunni and Shi'a communities also exist in the United States. The African American Shi'a community focuses on preserving, not extending, its boundaries. Because the diverse ethnic Shi'a communities depend on foreign-based ayatollahs, Black Shi'ism has not yet forged a distinct identity nor fully engaged its distinct black consciousness, though Shi'ism's spirit of resistance and opposition to injustice is often viewed as greater than that of Sunni Islam.

Rituals of protest: The 1963 March on Washington for Jobs and Freedom indelibly marked the United States of America and the world. This was a time when people of all races, creeds, genders, denominations, ethnicities, and religious backgrounds came together to the nation's capital to speak out against the injustice of racial inequality. The dream of Martin Luther King, Jr., was stated clearly on this day: to unify the nation's people to destroy racism and injustice. This day perhaps concretized the vision of African American liberation theologians of the past, individuals who did not have formal education but believed that liberation could occur when faces of many shades would gather for a like purpose. Similarly, the country saw another great gathering at the nation's capital during the Million Man March in 1995. Men gathered together from across the country to restructure the public opinion of the black male, stating clearly with their voices and bodies that the black male was more than a person of low quality, but held character, integrity, and desired only to be

The fervor of the Iranian revolution and the quest for socioeconomic justice have inspired Black Shi'ism. Lack of financial resources made Black Shi'as dependent on immigrant Shi'as regarding law, ritual, and culture. While immigrant Shi'as view Islam through the lens of what they left "back home," Black Shi'as view Shi'ism as a way to overcome struggles of oppression, to engage unemployment, housing, education, social justice, affirmative action, economic empowerment, finding suitable marriage partners, and relationships with immigrant Shi'as. Immigrants tend to focus on theological and historical differences between them and Sunnis.

While these faiths are not monolithic and have a variety of expressions, African American Judaism, Christianity, and Islam have all made freedom and transformation of their people, individually and collectively, a major priority.

Need for Liberation

The three Abrahamic religions provided African Americans with essential avenues for faith development, worship, hospitality, education, pastoral care, congregational empowerment, communal activism regarding civil rights, and a quest for justice and liberation. Liberation has been at the vanguard of their theologies and missions because the larger society systemically oppressed persons of African descent. Questions of identity and agency were critical as these congregations struggled to define what it meant to be a black person of faith and to be free, within their particular religious faith and larger society, which used **Black codes** and **Jim and Jane Crow** practices to limit access by blacks and poor people, and recently processes like gentrification, redistricting, and steeper sentencing laws for illegal drugs.

Black Codes—In the United States, after the abolishment of slavery, southern states enacted a series of restrictive laws (1865, 1866) known as "black codes" to limit freed blacks' activity and ensure their availability as a mandatory conscripted labor force. Failure to comply meant they could be arrested as vagrants and fined or forced into unpaid labor.

Jim and Jane Crow—Jim Crow laws and Jane Crow laws are terms used to describe laws that reinforce discrimination and segregation. Jim Crow Laws were enacted (1876–1965) to support forced racial segregation of all public facilities, especially in the South; they established an allegedly separate but (not) equal status for blacks; Jane Crow laws supported sexism, or the oppression of women.

treated as equal. These two major protest events are forever engrained in the psyche of both the United States and the world: liberation theology in action. At no time can a theology be liberating if it is simply on the page. Only when it becomes alive is it truly a liberative theology.

Liberative Theology in Action: The Issue of Social Dislocation

Despite the Emancipation Proclamation and the various nineteenth- and twentieth-century civil rights movements and landmark laws of the Great Society programs, socioeconomic, historical, and political gains have often been sabotaged through social tools such as disenfranchisement. With the new legal oppression, "New Jim Crow" and related laws, the right to vote is being obstructed by mandatory IDs, redistricting, gerrymandering, and the denial of civil rights to persons formerly incarcerated, such as the lack of access to voting, loans for higher education, food stamps, or public housing. With gentrification, which comes with renewal and rebuilding of low income or deteriorating areas, poor residents are displaced because either their former homes are torn down or they can no longer afford the property taxes, as the influx of middle-class or affluent people move in. These contextual matters are impediments to the liberation of peoples in these communities, and their faith communities, the academy, and governmental entities need to address these matters.

African American Judaism

Using biblical themes of hope, revenge, and deliverance, black Israelites honed a new metaphorical identity, in which as Israelites under the scourge of U.S. pharaohs, they awaited their Moses to bring them to freedom. Some black Jews took biblical narratives, spirituals, and Bible plays in the West Indies and used them as liberative source materials, viewing their traumatic displacement redemptively. The exodus motif helped the enslaved recast their destiny as a divine drama. White Jews often did not take black Jews seriously. Black Judaic religions did not try to emulate their white counterparts; Judaism, like Christianity, is not monolithic. Authors such as James William Charles Pennington, in his *A Text Book of the Origin and History of the Colored People,* refuted notions of inherent black inferiority because of the Hamitic curse (for Noah cursed Canaan, not Ham). Some black Jews argued that only Africans were Jews; white Jews were imposters or of secondary significance.

African American Christianity

Framed by the crucible of oppression wherein the dominant culture works to inculcate blacks with a sense of inferiority, black Christian worship celebrates the beauty of faith and the gift of survival and overcoming. Black Christian faith engages the tradition of prophetic resistance against systemic, social evils, steeped in a firm theological foundation: apocalyptic, liturgical, and eschatological, one that responds to historical and present lived experiences of diasporan Africans, promotes black self-esteem and self-determination, and values religious culture and creative liturgical expression. Black Protestant and Catholic worship embraces a Soul theology, the psychological foundation innate to black culture. The Holy Spirit anoints the worship event to engage the theology of the folk. Despite uncertainty and ambiguity, God is in control and extends grace and mercy. Amid chattel apartheid, oppression, and discriminatory practices, black Christianity used black homiletics and communal activism, prophetic, kerygmatic pronouncement, to connect its African roots and Eastern sensibilities with the antebellum United States and ancient Israel. Contemporary black Christian ministry is Christocentric, challenges oppression, and embraces a moral imperative.

African American Islam

The quest for an Islamic identity and Islamic practice involves a culture that offers numerous responses to the United States environment and a unique synthesis of Islamic philosophies and legal theories. Law is foremost, and

Allah is critical to Islam. Technically, NOI is a "proto-Islamic sect," which often practices concepts antithetical to orthodox Islam. For example, while most Muslims believe in one God, Allah, an eternal, omnipotent, omniscient God who is interested in humanity, NOI believes that Allah, a corporeal being, is black. The NOI, reinvented by Farrakhan following Elijah Muhammad's tenets, supports black superiority and views the white race as demonic and promotes global work against white imperialism. The NOI shares an Islamic vocabulary and has a common interest, not a common faith.

Many U.S. Muslims are Sunnis, though some are Shi'as: both follow Qur'an and the Five Pillars. Many Shi'as settled in the United States from the Indian subcontinent, the so-called Middle East, and parts of East and North Africa during the twentieth century. Many African Americans who initially converted to Sunni Islam or NOI have converted to Shi'ism. Shi'as settled in Michigan, New York, Illinois, Iowa, Ohio, and North Dakota. Changes in immigration laws and political realities have increased the linguistic, national, ethnic, and racial U.S. Shi'ite population. As a minority within Islam and the United States, Shi'as began more outreach: creating institutes, sending out information to interested parties and correctional facilities, particularly after the Iranian revolution in 1979.

Main Themes

Traditionally, the sources used by theologians to ponder how we know and experience God include revelation, scripture, tradition, culture, experience, and doctrine. Within liberative theologies, methodologies and hermeneutics place heavy emphasis on experience, from the Middle Passage and lynching, to sociocultural activism, through infrastructural needs in community. With African American liberative theologies, questions arise around the nature of God, human agency, and, when that agency is compromised, the quest for justice. Black theologian James Cone posits that God is the God of the oppressed; thus God can only be a figure of power, justice, and peace if this God cares about persons who know pain and rejection because of their color. Good theology is an inclusive, liberating theology that welcomes all to the table.

African American Judaism

African American Judaism engages themes of slavery and freedom from bondage, and parallels the experience of African Americans with those of the Hebrew children in Exodus. Positing that African Americans were truly Hebrews before the travesty of enslavement, they embrace repatriation and often return to homelands in Israel and parts of Africa. Influenced by messianism, Black Hebrews usually follow a charismatic leader who claims

Homophobia: In childhood, most individuals in African American churches are taught that God hates homosexuality; if God hates it, the church must also hate. Congregants are told that if they live a homosexual lifestyle they will be condemned to burn in hell forever. Yet much of this reflects poor biblical interpretation. Most individuals never learn enough about biblical languages to analyze texts on their own, but accept another's interpretation or take biblical texts out of context. Christian theology teaches the providence of God; but if God's agenda has already been designed, this suggests that God has not made a mistake as to how individuals are born in terms of their sexuality. In the African American church context, many homosexuals have been forced to live in the shadows. It is the liberating purpose of the church to accept all.

Cheap Grace: Cheap grace is the grace we confer on ourselves. Cheap grace can mean preaching forgiveness without needing repentance. Cheap grace avoids discipleship, the cross,

divine inspiration and assures ultimate redemption from spiritual and material poverty. Black Hebrews believe themselves to be Hebraic, authentic descendants of Old Testament patriarchs and matriarchs, desiring authentic identity beyond what the majority culture seeks to impose.

For example, the Hebrew Israelites, a sect of black Americans, immigrated to Israel in 1969, because some Black Hebrews felt alienated from the larger so-called Christian society that excluded them and contradicted Christ's teachings. In 1995, Rabbi Capers Funnye gathered black Jews at the synagogue he led, Beth Shalom B'nai Zaken Ethiopian Hebrew Congregation of Chicago, to create a new national organization, the Black Alliance, that celebrated their wide-ranging blackness and Jewishness and to bridge gaps within their sociocultural, political, and religious diversity. Funnye posited that being Jewish reclaimed his heritage, for his African ancestors were Jews. His congregation also has direct ties to Wentworth Matthew's Commandment Keepers.

African American Christianity

African American Christianity retains a strong focus on liberating the physically, socioeconomically, and spiritually oppressed. Religious themes include the journey of the oppressed Hebrews who are eventually restored by God's providential will. Jesus, in the New Testament, brings salvation to Jew and Gentile, destroying all barriers. Jesus's resurrection from the dead suggests a resurrection of minorities from the death-dealing sociocultural oppression within the human societal condition. However, this faith was not so liberating much of the time. African slaves were immersed in distorted Western Eurocentric Christian theological, philosophical, ethical, and moral ideologies via the degrading, dehumanizing actions of slaveholders. The offensive and repulsive nature of such Christianity led many slaves to find their hope with a Christ envisaged through their own oral traditions. African ancestral traditions shaped this new religious faith. Slaves engaged a Christianity that called for their redemption, restoration, salvation, and liberation. They developed a new cosmology and eschatology, in which liberation is in the present, defining and affirming their human dignity.

From slave religious ideology and Christianity emerged churches independent of their white counterparts, such as the African Methodist Episcopal Church. A gospel was preached that shed new light on biblical interpretation, foregrounding social/civil justice, and motivating the liberation of the demoralized. Some black Protestants and Catholics remained within white church establishments. African American Christianity gave transformative power to the 1950s and '60s U.S. civil rights movement, on into the twenty-first century.

African American Islam

Black Muslims in the United States grew into a vibrant, living movement of African American self-reliance though self-actualization—helping themselves, one another, and their communities. Self-care, sisterhood and brotherhood, and prayer undergird equality for a people outside of the critical, racist, destructive aims of their Anglo-Saxon counterparts. Black Muslims work to develop, create, implement, and promote the growth of people of color. Much of this eventually would help persons not identified as Black Muslims.

Methodologies

Religious traditions usually include prophets, revelatory experiences, sacred texts, tradi-

or the living, incarnate Jesus Christ. German theologian Dietrich Bonhoeffer made this term a Christian theological staple, but Adam Clayton Powell, Sr., a pastor who developed the Abyssinian Baptist Church in Harlem, New York, as the largest Protestant congregation in the country, with ten thousand members, coined the term "cheap grace." Powell was a community activist, author, and the father of Congressman Adam Clayton Powell, Jr., Bonhoeffer attended Abyssinian Baptist while studying in New York at Union Theological Seminary before World War II. He was greatly influenced by Powell's preaching and teaching, social work, and the black spiritual music of the congregation.

Passing: a sociocultural phenomenon that has occurred with the beginning of intercultural, interracial contact, in which a person presents her- or himself as a member of social groups other than his or her own (e.g., different race, ethnicity, caste, social class, gender, sexuality, age citizenship, and/or disability status), generally with the purpose of gaining social acceptance or to cope with difference. Marcia Dawkins posits that everyone "passes" to some degree. Passing concerns perceptions and privileged status in which people struggle to identify themselves and relate to a larger world, amid tensions, ambiguities, projections, estrangements, and connections.

tions, ethical norms, personal and communal piety, and a God, sometimes multiple gods (in theistic religions), or a philosophy that shapes the believer/practitioner's lived reality. African American theologies include another characteristic: they are protest-oriented against any oppression. Frederick L. Ware posits that African American theologies use diverse analytical tools, with black experience being significant, for defining, investigating, evaluating, clarifying, reviewing, or rejecting beliefs. African American theologies start with analyzing religious knowledge from the sociohistorical experiences of black folks of African descent, and then test the validity of their religious beliefs that threaten their agency, freedom, survival, and quality of life. African American methodologies include (1) correlation—that is, relating black experience to a particular religious experience, exploring blackness and identity; (2) the use of symbols and themes that locate the self, culture, and society within an epistemic framework; and (3) the use of sources and resources that reflect the African American experience. In the academy, Ware sees three paradigms: the hermeneutical school employs biblical and theological interpretation of faith and black struggles for liberation; the philosophical school engages scholars who use philosophy within black theology; and the human sciences school uses cultural studies of black theology. Womanist theologians have engaged these paradigms to explore the multidimensional oppression experienced by "the least of these," reflected in the lives of poor, black women.

African American Judaism

In addition to exploring God and philosophy, many modern Jewish theologians focus on the characterization of Jewish people and the right to exist as an autonomous community. Traditionally, Jewish theology studies the nature and acts of God in the Hebrew Scriptures, rabbinical reflections and textual commentaries, within communal worship. Authority within the written law (Torah) is divine inspiration; oral law (rabbinic tradition) is fallible. Little scholarship exists on African American Judaic methodologies. Judaic sources do not make distinctions based on race. Judaism focuses on adherence to its principles.

African American Christianity

In the African American Christian tradition, Old Testament prophets, New Testament disciples/apostles, and contemporary pastors are all proclaimers of God's law, will, and biblical tenets for human guidance. These spokespersons, often referred to as "preachers," are divinely called: for example, a burning bush speaking to Moses (Exodus); Paul blinded and hearing the voice of Christ (Acts). In worship, greater divine intimacy occurs with the proclamation of texts, through which congregants better understand God and God's relationship to humanity. Through God's revelation of God's self, proclamation, prayerful reflection, and adoration, God's self-revelation in biblical narratives expresses ideals of the divine for humanity. Embracing these ideals develops one's personal engagement with God and enhances the spiritual, ethical, and moral state of others. Liberation occurs when revelation, proclamation, and human execution intersect.

Within the academy, studying history, theology, doctrine, and ethics of the faith provides a fuller, liberative understanding of African American Christian identity. The first Black Theology Project (one of eight projects in Theology in the Americas [1977]), involved academics, street and church folk, nationalists, and Marxists. The founding of the Society for the Study of Black Religion (1970) and of EATWOT (Ecumenical Association of Third World Theologians), an association of men and women committed to the struggle for the liberation of Third World peoples, provided new models of theology for religious pluralism, social justice, and peace. Formal liberative theologies emerged in Africa, Asia, Latin America, and African America. Faith seeks understanding through engagement with doctrine and text, and aims to create a religious context and community that reflect the liberating Christian deity.

African American Muslims

Most Black Muslims, except those who follow Elijah Muhammad's theology, subscribe to the foundational Five Pillars of Islam. These entail life, prayer, concern for the needy, self-purification, and pilgrimage. They are (1) *shahadah*, declaring there is no god except God, and Muhammad is God's messenger; (2) *salat*, ritual prayer five times a day; (3) *zakat*, giving 2.5 percent of one's savings to the poor and needy; (4) *sawm*, fasting and self-control during the holy month of Ramadan; and (5) *hajj*, pilgrimage to Mecca at least once in a lifetime if one can. An essential part of the faith tradition has to do with diet, humility, and dress, considering the person's entire well-being, which is important to the liberating nature of theology because the person reflects God. Persons abstain from alcohol, tobacco, premarital sex, and foods such as pork. The body must be healthy to do the work of Islam. To cause harm to the body is to destroy the temple and hinder personal and communal development.

There are many different groups of Black Muslims, including NOI. Shi'a and Sunni adopt most of the same principles, though they call them by different names and differ on beliefs regarding Muhammad's rightful successor. The faith of Black Muslims and their dedication to the development of self and race are crucial to understanding their place among African American liberative theologies. Their focus on liberation concerns their dedication to God, a connection with their lineage as African descendants, and the mandate for racial equality that is characteristic of all African American liberative theology.

Leading Scholars and Figures

While the list of scholars and figures below is not exhaustive, it represents persons who have made significant contributions to African American religious thought, to liberation and transformation, and have influenced religious thought and theology through the years in the African American context.

W. E. B. DuBois (1868–1963) was a sociologist, economist, and historian who did liberative pioneering work on the development of race, education, and the need for racial equality. He developed the theory of double consciousness, which recognizes the sociopsychological and spiritual challenge of reconciling an African heritage with a European-dominant context, as one must reconcile the two cultures that compose one's identity amidst an oppressive irreconcilable context of oppression: black folk must survive in a white world while whites have no idea or need to know what it means to be black. His seminal work is *The Souls of Black Folk*.

Vincent Harding (1931–2014) was a historian, theologian, and nonviolent activist. Harding cofounded the Mennonite House, an interracial service center and gathering place, assisted antisegregation campaigns for several protest organizations, including the Southern Christian Leadership Conference, and was an aide/speechwriter for Martin Luther King, Jr.

C. Eric Lincoln (1924–2000) was the founding president of the Black Academy of Letters. Lincoln did groundbreaking research on African American Islam and on understanding the African American church and mosque cultures, reflected in his classic works *Black Muslims in America* and *The Black Church in the African American Experience* (with Larry Mamiya).

Martin L. King, Jr. (1929–68), was a Baptist minister, pastor, social activist, author, humanitarian, and major leader in the U.S. civil rights movement (1950s–'60s). King was a visionary leader of the Southern Christian Leadership Conference, won the Nobel Peace Prize (1964), helped orchestrate the historic Montgomery Bus Boycott, and used the thought of Gandhi to help the disenfranchised use nonviolent direct action for protest.

Gayraud Wilmore, recognized as a scholar, theologian, ethicist, educator, and historian, did seminal work on the history of the African American church and the African American religious experience, notably through his collaboration with James H. Cone.

James H. Cone is recognized globally as the founder of black liberation theology. He is a mentor to numerous black scholars whose work has had an impact on the academy and the church.

Delores S. Williams, intent on liberating the voices of black and poor women, played a decisive role in the development of womanist theology. Her work has centered on historical and present testimonies of black women and the African American religious experience.

Kelly Brown Douglas is a leading voice in the development of womanist theology, especially her groundbreaking work that champions sexuality and the black church as it intersects faith and praxis.

M. Shawn Copeland has done groundbreaking work on theological and philosophical anthropology and political theology, in African and African-derived religious, cultural, and intellectual history, and has pioneered liberative theology, merging womanist and Catholic theologies.

Cheryl A. Kirk-Duggan is a womanist interdisciplinary scholar who has expanded the womanist liberative conversation to include systematic theology, ethics, history, women's studies, music, literature, and the Hebrew Bible.

Ben Ammi (Ben Carter) is an African Israelite founder and leader who led about four hundred

Howard Thurman (1899–1981), undoubtedly one of the greatest minds of the twentieth century, grew to become an educator, pastor, theologian, renowned mystic, and dean of Howard University's chapel. He was a man of great faith and prophetic insight. Thurman believed that there was an unsearchable depth to God where we all can find ourselves enraptured. While we can never know the depths of God, it is essential for us to continue in the quest of this God to gain wisdom. Thurman founded the Church for the Fellowship of All Peoples, which reflects his desire of inclusivity and seeking to delve into the deep parts of God. Thurman believed that we must analyze and question evil's existence, and honor the place of Spirit within all humankind. When we fight against Spirit (the God consciousness), evil becomes manifest.

Black Hebrews to Liberia for purification, then to Israel (1969). Though not accepted by Israeli authorities as biblical Jews entitled to citizenship under the "Right of Return" law, they received residency (2004), but not full citizenship.

Robert E. Hood (1936–94) is a theologian and a historian of religion, race, and culture who did groundbreaking work on exposing the demonization of blackness, and the mythic roots of racial prejudice in Western attitudes.

Dwight Hopkins has furthered the academic conversation on contemporary models of theology and global liberation using multidisciplinary academic approaches.

J. Deotis Roberts is a peacemaker and pioneer of black theology and modern American theology who has done critical work on forgiveness and reconciliation, amidst the black power movement and student activism.

Wallace Fard (1877/1891 [birthdate uncertain]–1934) was an Islamic minister and founder of the Nation of Islam; he established the Temple of Islam in Detroit and the University of Islam. His "theology" generally ignored traditional Islam and focused on an elaborate myth in which Yakub, a renegade black scientist, created the white race as both curse and test for the black master race.

Charles Buchanan Copher (1913–2003) was the first dean of the Interdenominational Theological Center, a consortium of black divinity schools, and was a progenitor of African American biblical hermeneutics. He pioneered addressing race and ethnicity in ancient texts and contemporary interpretation.

Miseducation: Carter G. Woodson, African American historian, author, and journalist, explored miseducation in his *Miseducation of the Negro* (1933). He critiqued educational and religious establishments because they failed to present authentic black history and culture to African American school children. Miseducation, for Grammy winner Lauryn Hill, is the displaced allegiance to an "other" outside of oneself that negates history, denies and silences oneself, and sabotages excellence. The transformation of miseducation requires dealing with power and authorities that perpetuate oppression, create myths of inferiority, and serve as catalysts that maintain white supremacy.

Trends

Amid the horrific events of the twentieth and twenty-first centuries, from genocide and the targeting of civilians in wars to terrorist attacks and the collapse of entire nation-states and societies, all of us have had to rethink what it means to be human, to be free, given the obvious evidence that we can easily destroy ourselves and the planet. Most recently in the United States, the disrespect and disregard for the office of the president after the election of

President Barack H. Obama remind us that we live in a world of power-mongers and of those willing to oppress, scapegoat, and disregard people deemed different or "other." Corrie ten Boone, a Holocaust survivor, states, "to forgive is to set a prisoner free and discover that the prisoner was you." In the wake of the recent senseless murders of African American young men by the police and their peers, the fear-based tactics around immigration and the gutting of public education, one thing becomes clear: to employ liberation theology, we have to explore the complexities of our society, expose the misuse of power, reiterate the need for confession and claiming responsibility, and recognize that all who are a part of oppressive systems are prisoners first. Then we can reckon with the forgiveness of the oppressor by the oppressed. We must not rush to forgiveness before dealing with the pain and costs. Conscientization must occur, so that acknowledgment and acceptance of wrongs committed can occur, which can then lead to forgiveness and reconciliation, tenets at the heart of liberative theology.

African American Judaism

African American Jewish trends involve the intersection of African American connectivity to Judaism and Jewish texts, and historical contacts of Judaism/ Jews in ancient times with African peoples. Common themes and diverse histories converge in diverse black Jewish lives and complex Jewish identities. Through a variety of religious encounters, some black African societies adopted or rediscovered a Judaic religious identity. As these groups continue to develop, they will need to continue to engage Jews in general and black Jews in particular, dealing with identity, how they relate to the state of Israel, and the capacity for listening to one another, embracing differences with mutuality amidst a varied history, including the Holocaust and the ***Maafa,*** or Middle Passage (enslavement), twenty-first-century anti-Semitism, and hatred of black folk. Ultimately, what does it mean to be African, American, and Jewish, wherein one can experience rejection on multiple levels, and wrestle with these tensions while being faithful to their sacred texts and traditions?

***Maafa*:** a Kiswahili term for "terrible occurrence" or "great disaster," which refers to the Black Holocaust, when millions of Africans died during the journey of captivity from the west coast of Africa to the shores of the Americas—also known as the Middle Passage.

African American Christianity

The African American church and African American liberation theologies have undergone huge changes in the past decade. Christianity in the African American context has long focused on the congregant's spirituality, on social justice, education, and economic inequality. Yet youth and young adult believers know less about biblical narratives than ever before, and some churches have become places to garner their attention rather than places that emphasize transformation through Spirit. Some churches feel like empty, disconnected arenas that have no personal contact with the pastor; others offer an abundance of pastoral care and outreach. In some respects and in some areas of the African American Christian church, a sense of liberative theology is being lost. While a social gospel is being preached and great rhetoric speaks to the ills of society, little transition from theory to praxis occurs.

Previously, the liberative theologies of the African American church were reflected in the seriousness of education for persons only a few generations out of slavery. Education was essential, and the pulpiteer would be prepared to share with the people. In this age, many have access to education, but often gain credentials without utilizing the fullness of the educational experience for personal growth and congregational development. Many in our society are yet enslaved, imprisoned in mind and body. Authentic African American liberative theology speaks truth to power, takes needed action, and empowers people to love God and God's people through compassionate action.

Undoubtedly, shifts have occurred from slave religion and the dedicated but unlearned preacher to generations in which theological education became accessible and highly regarded among African American congregations, to the age of T. D. Jakes and the megachurches. Jakes is not seminary educated but is a world-renowned pastor, author, motivational speaker, and entrepreneur. His conferences on life issues related to African American liberative theology draw thousands. The twenty-first century and the black church have also seen the dawning of political change with the first African American U.S. president, and the ministry of Jeremiah Wright, Barack Obama's former pastor. Known for years as a well-respected pastor, evangelist, and liberation theologian, Rev. Wright's solid grounding in African American liberative theology, love for the church universal, and critical analytical assessment of the human condition allow his voice to be criticized yet respected.

In discussing trends in African American Christianity, we must also mention Cyprian Davis, noted as the father of African American Catholicism. His caretaking of the history of African American Catholicism in the United States has shaped both the Catholic Church and African American theology.

From the time of lined hymns to the gospel traditions of Thomas A.

Dorsey and Kirk Franklin, to a generation that has interwoven hip-hop and gospel liturgical dance and mime to speak to an unchurched generation in a way that is meaningful, valuable, and relevant, music has long shaped protest and proclamation. This is the power of African American liberative theology in the Christian context: ever changing, fluid, and momentous. Clearly it is without boundaries and cannot fully be defined and is highly contextualized, and it is such that it is deemed to be liberating.

African American Islam

Many different sects of Islam, particularly Black Muslim expressions, are emerging every day. As we see new forms of Islam, we see also a loss of some major tenets reflecting traditional Islam: NOI, a prominent Black Muslim group, exemplifies this crucial transition from traditional Islamic faith. Some of the Nation's ministers utilize Christian scriptures rather than quoting from the Qur'an, seemingly interweaving Christianity and Islam. Some would argue that this is noteworthy, especially for those who work with theology focused on ecumenical pluralism and interreligious dialogue. The dress of some Black Muslims has also changed. Traditional Islam has clear expectations regarding the dress of men and women. However, one can see some practicing Muslims wearing attire that is much like that of secular culture. This may be due to the liberating nature of faith that focuses on the lifestyle and internal state of the person rather than outer apparel.

Some expressions of traditional Islam, including some Black Muslim expressions, show little desire for interaction with persons outside of the faith and a profound dislike for Anglo-Americans. Strong language is sometimes employed to describe individuals of European descent, although this militancy is often not as strong as in earlier times.

Study Questions

1. What does it mean to be of African descent and a person of faith?
2. What are the significant movements and persons that shape African American liberative theologies?
3. How does the twenty-first-century African American church embrace an authentic liberative theology that suggests a sense of inclusivity?
4. Is there a way for black Jews, Muslims, and Christians to develop a liberative theology that can meet the needs of each of these groups regardless of the particular tenets of their faith systems?
5. Is a theology of liberation ever inclusive of all people or is it still reflective solely of the particular group that feels a sense of social oppression?

Suggested Reading

Appiah, Kwame Anthony, and Henry Louis Gates, Jr., eds. *Africana: The Encyclopedia of the African and African American Experience.* Philadelphia: Running Press, 2003.

Bruder, Edith. *African Zion: Studies in Black Judaism.* Cambridge, MA: Cambridge Scholars Publishing, 2012.

Cannon, Katie G., and Anthony Pinn, eds. *The Oxford Handbook of African American Theology.* New York: Oxford University Press, 2014.

Carter, J. Kameron. *Race: A Theological Account.* Oxford: Oxford University Press, 2008.

Cone, James H., and Gayraud Wilmore, eds. *Black Theology: A Documentary History,* I: *1966–1979;* II: *1980–1992.* Maryknoll, NY: Orbis Books, 1993.

Douglas, Kelly Brown. *Sexuality and the Black Church: A Womanist Perspective.* Maryknoll, NY: Orbis Books, 1999.

Hopkins, Dwight. *Introducing Black Theology of Liberation.* Maryknoll, NY: Orbis Books, 2006.

Jackson, Sherman A. *Islam & the Problem of Black Suffering.* New York: Oxford University Press, 2009.

Jennings, Willie James. *The Christian Imagination: Theology and the Origins of Race.* New Haven, CT: Yale University Press, 2010.

Landing, James. *Black Judaism: Story of an American Movement.* Durham, NC: Carolina Academic Press, 2002.

Lincoln, C. Eric. *The Black Muslims in America.* 3rd edition. Trenton, NJ: William B. Eerdmans, 1994.

Marable, Manning. *Malcolm X: A Life of Reinvention.* New York: Penguin Books, 2011.

Parfitt, Tudor. *Black Jews in Africa and the Americas* (The Nathan I. Huggins Lectures). Cambridge, MA: Harvard University Press, 2012 (eBook).

Sanders, Cheryl J. *Empowerment Ethics for a Liberated People.* Minneapolis: Fortress Press, 1995.

7

Asian American Liberative Theologies

Grace Ji-Sun Kim

Asian Americans are the silent immigrants in North America, seen but not heard. There is a long history of Asian immigration to the United States, but much of it is not integrated into the institutional memory of the country. The history of Asian immigration is glossed over as insignificant or unimportant. They are the forgotten people whose history is characterized by rejection from immigrant officials and numerous hardships. Much of their history is tarnished by racism, prejudice, and white privilege, all of which inhibited Asian American growth within the community, society, and country.

Basic Tenets

Asian American theology is shaped and distinguished by several contextual, social, and religious determinants. The Asian American immigrant's particular experience of interstitiality, marginality, and hybridity all mold and determine the course of their theology. According to some scholars such as Kwok Pui Lan, the terms "Asian" and "Asian American" are social and cultural constructs, not a homogenized identity, and the high degree of diversity within the peoples comprising this group should be recognized. Asian Americans include peoples coming from China, Korea, Japan, India, Myanmar, and the Philippines, all of whom speak different languages with diverse cultural backgrounds and social histories. They also worship in different faiths, such as Buddhism, Islam, Taoism, Hinduism, Shamanism, and Christianity. Asian Americans, generally speaking, share a solidarity with the struggles and problems of Asian immigrants who bear a colonial history, multiple religious traditions, diverse cultures, and a long history of patriarchal control.

Ancestor worship is a common Asian practice that venerates deceased ancestors. Ancestors are still believed to be part of the family and are able to intervene in the affairs of the living on earth. It has become a religious practice that includes prayers and offerings to the dead ancestors.

For theology to be liberative and to have meaning within an Asian American context, it must address some of the problems faced by Asian immigrants, such as racism, stereotyping, and sexism. The history of Asian immigration to the United States reveals that this has often not been the case. To begin understanding the basic tenets that form an Asian American liberative theology, it is important to know the history of Asians in America.

Asian Americans have a long history of immigration to the United States, beginning in the mid-1800s. The annexation of California in 1846 by the United States opened the door to Asian laborers, with a significant Chinese immigration occurring during the California Gold Rush from 1848 to 1855. At the beginning of the gold rush, the Chinese were tolerated. But as soon as it became more difficult to find gold, tension toward the Chinese grew. Eventually they were pushed out of the gold mines, resulting in many taking low-wage employment in restaurants and laundries. Since Asians were generally viewed as a commodity, many Chinese laborers were imported for the construction of the Transcontinental Railroad. Asian immigrant lives were often seen as expendable, and they were made to participate in the most dangerous work, such as setting and detonating dynamite during the building of the railroads. Other Asians, including Japanese (1880s), Filipinos (1890s), Koreans (1900s), and East Indians (1900s) also immigrated in response to the need for laborers in the building of America. Asians also immigrated to Hawaii, working long, difficult hours and enduring backbreaking work in the sugar cane industry.

The War Brides Act: This act, enacted on December 28, 1945, allowed the non-Asian spouses, natural children, and adopted children of U.S. military personnel to enter the United States after World War II. Due to this act, about 100,000 were allowed to enter the United States before the act expired in December 1948.

Many Asians immigrated with the understanding that they would return home rich after making enough money in the United States. However, the harsh reality was that even though they worked long, difficult hours, their pay was very low, not enough for even the return passage. Though most of the early Asian immigrants were male, Asian women, motivated by a desire for freedom from poverty and patriarchy, sometimes made the decision to immigrate. Other times men arranged for the migration of Asian women for profit and exploitation. Many women were used to feed, wash, and clean for the men. Others who worked in the fields for wages spent a full day under the sun, perhaps with babies strapped to their backs, before returning home to fix dinner for their husbands or other male workers. Asian American women suffered in silence within a culture in which their roles were defined by Asian men.

A series of restrictive laws against Asians were enacted which limited life within the United States. In 1870, Congress passed a law that made Asian immigrants the only racial group barred from naturalization to United States citizenship. In 1882, the Chinese Exclusion Act suspended the immigration of Chinese laborers for ten years. This was then extended indefinitely and was finally lifted in 1943. The 1917 Immigration Act further limited Asian immigration, banning immigration from all countries in the Asia Pacific region except for the Philippines, a U.S. territory at the time, and Japan. Japanese immigration, however, was subsequently limited by the 1924 Exclusionary Immigration Act, which brought an end to all immigration from Asia. Those who did migrate were segregated in public facilities such as schools and were subject to heavy taxation, prohibition of land ownership, and prohibition of intermarriage with whites.

On February 19, 1942, President Franklin D. Roosevelt signed an Executive Order 9066 that prescribed certain areas in the United States as military zones. This consequently led to the deportation of Japanese Americans to internment camps. The conditions of these camps were akin to camps for migrant workers. The walls of the buildings were made of tar paper, which provided little insulation from the elements, thus making winters and summers difficult to bear. The camps were guarded by armed soldiers, and the compounds were surrounded by a barbed-wire fence. These conditions were accompanied by racism and prejudice, including other discriminatory laws that existed before

Chinese Exclusion Act: This was a United States federal law that was signed by President Chester A. Arthur on May 6, 1882. This law prevented the immigration of Chinese laborers into the United States. This act was supposed to last for only ten years, but was renewed in 1892 and was made permanent in 1902. This act lasted until December 17, 1943, when it was repealed by the Magnuson Act.

1924 Exclusionary Immigration Act: This act was a United States federal law that limited the annual number of immigrants who could be admitted from any country. This law was put in place to put restrictions on the immigration of Southern Europeans, Eastern Europeans, Jews, Arabs, East Asians, and Indians, and to preserve the "whiteness" of America.

the beginning of the war, such as the prohibition of Asian Americans from owning land in certain areas. It is also important to recognize that while Japanese Americans were interned, Italian Americans and German Americans were never placed in camps during the war. It was not until the passage of civil rights legislation in 1965 that state-supported discrimination officially ended; however, World War II and the American alliance with China began the trend toward integration for Asian Americans, especially in the armed services, when President Truman ended racial discrimination in the U.S. Army.

A Religious Response

Many Asian immigrants brought their own religious traditions such as Buddhism, Taoism, and Shintoism as they came across the Pacific Ocean. Many Korean American immigrants were already Christians because American missionaries had long before succeeded in planting Christianity in Korea. Though many Koreans were reluctant to immigrate to the United States, American missionaries encouraged Koreans to migrate, claiming that America was a Christian land and that it would be a good place for them to live.

As Asian immigrants experienced difficulties with the dominant culture, their different faith traditions provided substance and kept the community together. Worshiping in temples and churches in their own Asian communities was more than a faith act; it was a social and cultural practice through which many Asian Americans learned to cope with the racism and prejudice of the dominant culture. They found comfort in communion with fellow Asians in a space in which they were able to communicate and understand one another's sorrow and pain. For many of the Asian community, but especially for Korean American communities, the churches became a place of solace, survival, and salvation. They were able to eat together food typical of the homeland, share their stories of pain, find out cultural survival techniques, and socialize with other immigrants from their country. Religion continued to nurture their community and livelihood.

Hsiao (filial piety) is a term within Confucian philosophy that describes a virtue of respect for one's parents and ancestors. It was understood that to have a good and healthy society, one needed to incorporate *hsiao*. Filial piety is considered a very important virtue within Chinese culture.

The hardships experienced by Asian Americans are often overshadowed by experiences of racism by other racial minority groups. Nevertheless, these difficulties are not a thing of the past; they continue even today. Fourth- and fifth-generation Asian Americans living in the United States often believe that they will never find "home" in this land, where they are viewed as the perpetual foreigner because they will never look white, no matter how well they speak English or how successfully they have inculturated into the dominant culture. Due to their physical appearance, specifically their skin hue and eye shape, many Asian Americans believe they will be forever viewed as the other or as foreigners.

Asian American theology was still in its nascent stage in the 1970s when Asian American theologians began to undertake theological discourse from their own cultural, historical, and religious perspectives. Some of the pioneering Asian theologians are C. S. Song, Peter Phan, Fumitaka Matsuoka, Jung Young Lee, and Kwok Pui Lan. They all brought their cultural identities to the process of developing and constructing a theology that spoke to their own communities and religious groups. They each developed space within the overall theological discourse that began to take seriously their Asian-based religious heritage. Their voices contributed to Christian theology, including within the field of liberation theology. Their work contributed distinct features to the discourse and helped construct a theology that distanced itself from European and American academic theology.

Perpetual foreigners: Asian Americans have been depicted as "perpetual foreigners," "unassimilatable," and by many other stereotypes that reveal the historic and persistent racism experienced by this racial/ethnic group. Almost every Asian in America has been afflicted with the "perpetual foreigner" syndrome. Questions such as "Where are you really from?" which I will call the "really question," differ from the usual "Where are you from?" The "really" question figuratively and literally transports the Asian American respondent to Asia, because the assumption behind the question, even if the questioner is oblivious to it, is that Asian Americans cannot be "real" Americans.

Need for Liberation

Asian Americans find themselves in need of liberation from racism, stereotypes, and colonialism. These external factors are threats to the preservation of Asian American ways of life as well as threats to Asian American religious and cultural identity.

Racism

Asian Americans suffer from institutional racism, the "model minority" myth, and white privilege. By Fumitaka Matsuoka's definition, racism is a system that promotes domination of the vulnerable by a privileged group in the economic, social, and cultural spheres. Asian American liberative theology attempts to dismantle inequality by decentering the center and white hegemony, calling attention to white privilege and the discrimination employed against Asian Americans who are relegated to the margins of society. Asian American liberative theology attempts to construct an understanding of a God who welcomes the marginalized and the oppressed: a Spirit God who lives in the margins of society and empowers the outcasts, the subordinated, and the dominated peoples of society. Asian American liberative theology searches its own rich religious and cultural heritages and finds what is liberative within them. These elements are then adapted or reconstructed into a theology that can be liberative for all Asian Americans.

Asian American males have long had to endure stereotypes in American life. It is difficult to find an Asian American man in a leading role in a major Hollywood movie or television program. They are often depicted as the cleaner, factory worker, or the "sidekick." Asian American male identity is negatively impacted by how they are stereotypically cast. They usually play feminine roles, often stereotyped as having long braided hair, ugly protruding teeth, small squinty eyes, and dressed in traditional Asian clothing. This is exemplified in the character of I. Y. Yunioshi played by Mickey Rooney in the 1961 movie *Breakfast at Tiffany's*. Asian American women, on the other hand, are portrayed as hyper-sexualized feminine bodies, as in the play *Miss Saigon* or in the movie *Memoirs of a Geisha*. In reality, many of these early immigrant women were trapped into prostitution or massage parlors, having to use their bodies to sexually gratify white male clients. They are portrayed as docile, subordinate, subjugated, and obedient to men. Not surprisingly, they often are treated as infantile, unable to make decisions on their own, and needing to be told what to do.

Colonialism

Colonialism's negative impact on the Asian American community begins even before they arrive in the United States. For example, Koreans, colonized by the Japanese, attempted to decolonize themselves by immigrating to the United States but then became subject to American imperialism within their Asian American context. This is an ongoing struggle for Asian Americans. In my book *Colonialism, Han, and the Transformative Spirit*, I recognize the deep-seated colonialism experienced in the lives of Asians and Asian Americans.

Colonized people lose their land, identity, family, culture, religion, and politics. This loss of self affects not only those who are colonized but also their descendants, regardless if they stay in their home country or migrate. In the United States, the colonization of Asian Americans is compounded by how Americans view them. Many Asian Americans not only lose their rich heritage but also have come to despise their own culture, ancestry, and history. In effect, they learn to see themselves through white eyes, viewing their Asian heritage as unimportant, embarrassing, or a detriment to their lives within the United States. Rather than welcoming and embracing their heritage, they discard it as "backward" and primitive. These problems and the consequences of colonialism require acknowledgment and understanding if the community seeks to help Asian Americans rebuild their sense of selves.

Model Minority and Honorific Whites

Asian Americans are easily overlooked in the binary divide between whites and African Americans in American racial and ethnic politics. Since Asian Americans do not have a history of slavery within the United States, their experiences of racism are frequently ignored or pushed aside as imaginary. Their experience of discrimination within the larger society is seldom viewed as true discrimination because they are seen as "almost white" people. They are viewed as not engaging in civil rights issues nor having any racial problems within the dominant society. Thus, the dominant culture and news media do not view injustices endured by Asian Americans as cases of racial crimes.

This myth is easily debunked by the story of Vincent Chen's brutal murder. Vincent Chen was a Chinese American who was severely beaten with a baseball bat in Detroit, leading to his death on June 23, 1982. The attackers were a Chrysler plant superintendent and his stepson, both upset with the layoffs in the auto industry because of an increase in sales of Japanese-made vehicles within the United States. The initial charges brought against Chen's murderers were reduced to manslaughter, with no jail time to be served. The killers were given three years' probation, fined $3,000, and ordered to pay $780 in court costs. Although the Civil Rights Act of 1968 provided for prosecution of acts committed against people based on race, the added sentencing for "hate crimes" was not enacted by Congress until the Violent Crime Control and Law Enforcement Act of 1994. This verdict angered the Asian American community; however, there was not an equal uproar from other racial groups. The inability to see Vincent Chen's death as a hate crime because he was Chinese illustrates the problem of Asian Americans being seen as a privileged ethnic group.

Asian Americans are often viewed by mainstream American culture as hard, smart workers. They get into Ivy League colleges and excel in the workforce. However, in reality, this model minority imagery further stereotypes Asian Americans, diminishing the daily racism many experience within society, work, and school. Since many Asian Americans do work hard and have succeeded, it is believed they have not suffered the difficulties or hardships of racism, prejudice, and stereotyping to the extent of other ethnic communities.

Asian American liberative theology counters the racist effects of the model minority and honorific white stigma by recognizing the marginality of Jesus and the hybridity of the Spirit, which we will discuss later in the next section. Jesus lived on the margins of society as a poor, marginalized Jew. His identity was questioned by many: people questioned the identity of his father, and some even wondered about his knowledge of the Torah. The marginalized Jesus is simpatico with the difficulties of the Asian American struggle to emerge from a marginalized identity.

Hybridity

Asian American liberative theology tackles the issue of hybridity and uses this concept to formulate its own discourse and theology. According to Robert Young, hybridity means a mixture of two elements to create new spaces and places of discourse. Homi Bhabha extends this notion of hybridity by including forms of counter-authority, a "third space." It is in this particular third space that creativity can arise so that new ways of articulating faith, beliefs, and theology can emerge.

Asian American liberative theology incorporates hybridity as it challenges the dominant white theology, reexamining the traditional theology that limits and can be suffocating to colonized people. Asian American liberative theology seeks to find this site of articulation within the hybridity of beliefs and practices between Christianity and indigenous religions such as Shamanism. The decolonizing practices are accompanied by a willingness to embrace and rearticulate indigenous religious and cultural worldviews. Asian American liberative theology tries to bring together two entities, indigenous religion(s) and Christianity, and to make them into one shared space.

Important also in this view is the hyphenated reality of Jesus Christ. The hyphenated reality shows that Jesus can be juxtaposed with other adjectives such as wisdom, Christ, and Spirit. Because Jesus can be understood in many realities, each community must answer the question posed by Jesus, "Who do you say that I am?" The Holy Spirit also resides in the margins and in the difficult places where Asian Americans find themselves. The Spirit also recognizes its own hybridity as it lives in the in-between spaces, giving encouragement and empowerment to the disenfranchised.

As immigrants or the descendants of immigrants, Asian Americans are trying to understand and come to terms with their bicultural identity of being both Asian and being American. This identity is complicated, for many do not feel fully Asian nor fully American. Many are beginning to identify themselves as hybrid, as they view themselves as a mixture of Asian heritage as well as American identity.

Sexuality

In part because of the long history of **Confucianism** in Asia, patriarchy has a strong hold on the Asian American psyche. The consequences of patriarchy are enormous for Asian women, who have endured subordination, abuse, violence, and subjugation, including the harmful effects of **footbinding**, female infanticide, and a long history of being concubines or second, third, and fourth wives. This long history of patriarchy affects how one views one's self, world, and God. Patriarchy's negative effects are also found in the church, where many women cannot occupy positions of leadership nor be ordained.

Patriarchy is damning not only for women; it also negatively affects men. Rita Nakashima Brock states that men are socialized and reinforced in their behaviors and attitudes through a hyper-masculine culture. Men are encouraged to control and even sexually exploit women. In many cases, women are objectified and eroticized to justify male control over and against women. This sense of domination and entitlement encourages the culture to diminish the humanity of women. Many women lose control over their own lives and live under the duress of patriarchal expectations and obligations.

Confucianism is a philosophical system that is often described as a religion, developed from Confucius, a Chinese philosopher (551–479 BCE). Confucianism emphasizes the primacy of the family and believes that human beings are teachable and perfectible.

Footbinding in China was a painful, oppressive, and inhumane practice among certain classes and ethnicities of Chinese women. It was a way to make them dependent on men and to keep them within the household, as after footbinding it is very difficult to walk. Although Chinese women were viewed as weak, timid, and sexually available, they were also believed to be dangerous, powerful, and sexually insatiable. These acts of footbinding were instilled in part to further oppress them and keep them subjugated to men.

Orientalism: The Other

While European immigrants can often easily assimilate into North American culture and society, Asian Americans find the task of assimilation more difficult. They continue to be regarded as "exotic" foreigners, reinforcing their marginalization within the wider society. Seeing Asian Americans through the lens of the exotic reinforces an inferior status vis-à-vis Euro-Americans. Edward Said believes that the concept of Orientalism has been used by Europeans and North Americans to subjugate the East, creating for the West a self-appointed power. European culture creates its power over and against the East by contrasting itself against the Orient. The Orient is made feminine by Europeans as a way to further reinforce the West's own "masculine" power. Hence, the Orient is viewed as weaker, exotic, sensual, and less intelligent than the West, which is self-defined as superior.

Within this Western-based dualist model, as objects and people become feminized, there develops a further progression of domination over women. Both Asian American women and their homelands become romanticized and understood as the weaker subject who exists only for the master. This concept of orientalism has placed Asia in a subordinate position, as if it can be conquered and dominated by the masculine hand of the West. Orientalism, as constructed by white Euro-American power, must be dismantled if the Asian American community is to be "saved." Recognizing this, Asian American liberative theology attempts to bring salvation, to bring liberation, to the community by struggling to "decenter" the power held by white Euro-Americans.

Asian American liberative theology arises in response to problems of racism, subordination, and prejudice, challenging the centered, dominant Eurocentric theology. Introducing unsettling perplexities capable of displacing the dominant Western thought, Asians American liberative theology reintroduces a mixing of concepts, forms, and religions. Hybridity generates this "third space" (Bhabha), where creativity is possible. This third space, as mentioned earlier, can be the site from which theology is done with the potential to empower and liberate.

Asian immigrants experience a betwixt-and-between predicament, which, while a source of much soul searching and suffering, can also become an incentive and resource for a creative rethinking of both cultural traditions, native and foreign. Being in between is being neither this nor that, but also being both this and that. Immigrants belong fully to neither their native culture nor to the host culture but exist rather in between the two cultures. A space to articulate and communicate an unapologetic Asian American theology can be created within this in-betweenness, constructing a site for creativity and empowerment where disenfranchised people can speak and articulate their faith. An important task of Asian American liberative theology, especially for those who are Christians, will be to reread biblical texts with an eye toward postcolonial concerns. Specifically, a biblical interpretation that interacts with and reflects on postcolonial concepts such as hybridity and in-betweenness becomes important in Asian American liberative thought.

Marginality

Asian American liberative theology creates multiple theological centers so that the marginalized can move away from the margins. Traditionally, the "center" of theology has been dominated by Western, male Eurocentric theology. That center is being displaced, as Asian biblical scholars such as R. S. Sugirtharajah, in his book *Voices from the Margins,* illustrates. Sugirtharajah provides a methodology by which Asian and other Third World people interpret and reinterpret biblical passages apart from the dominant Western norm. These readings help replace the traditional center so that multiple centers of creativity, importance, authority, knowledge, and theology can exist.

For example, the story of the foreign women in Ezra 9 can be interpreted through the lens of Asian American women, who also experience foreignness in their new adopted land. In Ezra 9, the foreign women are all asked to leave. They are to leave their families, their children, and the land. This particular passage of the expulsion of the foreign women holds much meaning for foreigners living in the United States, particularly Asian American women, who, due to their "Asian features," continue to be viewed as foreigners even after generations of living in the United States. Many find it difficult to assimilate or be welcomed into American society or culture. Reading this particular passage from the viewpoint of the "foreigners" who are treated poorly allows us to recognize the historical and religious roots of that marginalized and expelled community.

Some Main Themes and Methodologies

Among the leading scholars and figures in Asian American theology is Peter Phan, a noted Catholic scholar. Born in Vietnam, he immigrated to the United States in 1975 as a refugee of the Vietnam War. He has written prolifically on Asian American theology, religion, and Asian American Catholic theology. Phan recognizes the value and importance of theological pluralism and therefore incorporates different Asian religions into his work on global theology. Acknowledging and asserting that much wisdom and truth lies in Asia becomes a theological move to decenter white Euro-theology and move toward a global theology that embraces Asian tradition and heritage. He understands that Christianity can be viewed through various global lenses, including those of other world religious traditions, thus contributing to a fuller understanding of God.

Choan-Seng Song is a Taiwanese American theologian who has written extensively on Asian theology, Christology, church, and faith. He critiques individualistic Western theology and recognizes the redemptive nature of worldwide religions. He incorporates Asian cultural concepts, ideas, religions, and dimensions into his theological discourse to help articulate an Asian American theology that embraces Asian tradition, religion, and culture. Much of Song's theology is rooted in "story theology." He believes that before there were texts, there were stories. Stories are important because they pass on truth to the next generation. His unique contribution is the idea of a "Third-Eye" theology, derived from Zen Buddhism. Within Zen Buddhism, there is an understanding that there is an unheard-of region that is not shown to believers because of their own ignorance. Accordingly, theology should not only be seen from a Western-European perspective but from multiple eyes, such as Chinese, African, and Latin American eyes. In other words, it must accept theological pluralism.

Kwok Pui Lan, a theologian from Hong Kong, has produced a large body of work that explores Asian American feminist theology through postcolonial theory. She has written extensively on Chinese women and Christianity as well as on Asian American feminist theology. She recognizes the value of her Chinese tradition, religion, and ancestry as she weaves them into her theological views and development. Kwok recognizes that her Asian tradition contains wisdom and a wealth of understanding about God, humanity, and creation. Kwok's feminist approach critiques some Chinese patriarchal practices and therefore attempts to retrieve only those aspects that are liberating and empowering for women. She uses her own Asian religious heritage to help articulate a theology that seeks to liberate Asian and Asian American women. She recognizes the evil and devastation of empire and the way colonialism has subjugated her people and people around the world.

Andrew Sung Park teaches and writes in the areas of systematic theology, global theology, cross-cultural theology, Asian American theology, mysticism, and the intersection of religion and science. He has written several books on Asian American theology and the concept of *han*. His theological endeavors use Korean concepts to help recognize the problems of Asian Americans that are inherent in North American society. *Han* is an important Korean concept that captures the essence of immense pain caused by unjust suffering. His Asian American theological contributions are important because his theology works toward racial conflict resolution and healing. With this recognition, Park develops an Asian American theology that empowers the subordinated and racialized peoples.

Liberative Theology in Action: The Issue of Suffering and *Han*

Koreans have used the term *han* to articulate a response and state of being to the tragic situation of the oppressed. In terms of its etymology, *han* is a psychological term that denotes repressed feelings of suffering, through the oppression of others or through natural calamities or illness. Sometimes translated as "just indignation," *han* is deep spiritual pain that rises out of the unjust experience of the people. *Han* appears inevitably in the biographical stories of Asian American women. Asian American people embody this *han* in their lives. They experience *han* through the various oppressions and sufferings in their daily lives. *Han* can be understood as a suppressed experience of oppression. It affects one's being and dampens and diminishes one's spirit.

Han exemplifies brokenheartedness but also the raw energy for the struggle for liberation. *Han* has emotive and transrational aspects and becomes a useful term within theological discourse to help understand some of the struggles, pain, and suffering.

Han has three different levels: individual, collective, and structural. At the individual level, *han* is the will to avenge and to resign. It makes one become bitter and helpless in the oppressive situation. It becomes a reaction to individualistic oppression, which is not isolated but is often attached to communal and structural oppression. At the second level, *han* is the collective consciousness and unconsciousness of victims. For example, there is the experience of cultural inferiority, racial resentment, physical inadequacy, and national shame. These collective *han* can make the community experience great despair and anguish. Finally, at the structural level, sin is unjust and evil systems feed racism, sexism, exclusiveness, and domination. All these levels of *han* are undesirable and something that many try to eliminate from their lives.

Possible Future Trends

Among several trends developing in Asian American theology is a growing tendency among theologians to work toward a global understanding of theology, one that incorporates religious traditions from around the globe, including Asian religious traditions, to help articulate a liberative theology. C. S. Song, in many of his books, such as *Tracing the Footsteps of God*, recognizes that we are all children of God and all need to be welcomed to the table. We cannot live isolated lives but must welcome and integrate theology from around the globe. In my own book, *The Grace of Sophia,* I introduce the different understandings of wisdom within Buddhism, Shamanism, and Confucianism. There are many similarities, for example, between the Wisdom literature found within Christianity and that found around the world in other traditions. As I argue, theology should take seriously the wisdom and truth from these cultures and be able to embrace them within theological discourse.

Along the same lines, Asian American liberative theology engages in interreligious dialogue with other faith traditions, as outlined by Peter C. Phan in his book *Being Religious Interreligiously.* Asian American liberative theology has engaged with its own religious heritage to find deeper meaning within Christian theology. It has retrieved some religious aspects of its own tradition and has incorporated it within its developing theology. However, it has not yet fully engaged in interfaith dialogue with world religions. This engagement may help Asian American theologians find deeper truths within their own theological development.

Asian American liberative theology also should take seriously both the struggles of Asians in the United States (i.e., ethnic studies) and the role that religion plays in the lives of Asian Americans. One example of how this is done is Joseph Cheah, in his book *Race and Religion in American Buddhism,* where he examines the struggles of the residents of Burma as well as those living in the United States. The Burmese face economic and internal cultural struggles that are different from the struggles of Burmese Americans. The fact that the majority of Asian Americans are foreign born means we cannot understand the identity and experience of Asian Americans without attending to what takes place in their homelands. The political, social, and cultural context of Asia needs to be taken seriously when developing Asian American liberative theology. The economic landscape is slowly changing in Asia; in particular, East Asia has seen unprecedented economic growth in the last thirty years. This reality will impact Asian Americans in North America.

The various struggles Asian Americans face daily require closer examination. Because many Asian Americans worship in their own communities, few are interacting religiously with other ethnic groups or with the dominant white society. These exclusive worshiping and faith-practicing communities may prove unable to sustain themselves, especially when we consider that the next generation of Asian Americans is probably not willing to continue to participate solely in exclusively Asian faith communities.

Furthermore, Asian American liberative theology will need to continue tackling its own patriarchal structure, which exists deep within its own culture, history, and religion. For example, Kwok Pui Lan's book *Chinese Women and Christianity, 1860–1927* examines the patriarchy embedded in

Chinese culture. Patriarchy continues to exist within Asian American liberative theologies, and it is important to continuously dismantle it and work toward a liberative theology for both men and women. We need to reread scripture and reexamine our faith practices that continue to oppress women.

Another concern requiring more attention revolves around LGBTQ issues. Human sexuality and sexual orientation are difficult topics to discuss within Asian American communities, not only within religious discourse but also in cultural and social discourses. However, support groups within Asian American communities are emerging and addressing LGBTQ issues. Patrick S. Cheng discusses these concerns in his book *Rainbow Theology: Bridging Race, Sexuality, and Spirit.* It is long overdue for the church and Asian American theology to address this important trend.

Further research within Asian American liberative theology is also required in the engagement of postcolonial theory. Much of Asia has experienced colonization. This has had damaging effects on the region's history, religion, and culture. Understanding these consequences and working toward liberation is a key trend among many Asian Americans who also feel like colonial subjects living here in North America. Postcolonial theology offers a new language in helping Asian Americans communicate their own discrimination, pain, and suffering, recognizing that empire has played an important role in defining and redefining culture, religion, and society. Since colonialism has defined empire and religion, it is important to unpack the impact of colonialism on Christianity and its implications for Asian Americans, as Kwok Pui Lan is doing in her recent book, *Postcolonial Imagination and Feminist Theology.* Such scholarship will help in further developing an Asian American liberative theology that will work toward liberating colonialized minds.

The notion of hybridity also needs further research. While hybridity is a tool that Asian American theologians are using to help create new spaces and places for discourse, it is also significant to remember that Christianity, emerging from subjugated Palestine, where Judaism intersected with Greco-Roman cultures, has been hybrid and syncretistic from its origins. Throughout church history, Christians have adopted and assimilated cultures and practices from their neighbors and surrounding communities. A pristine, unmixed Christianity has never existed. In the same way, Asian American understandings of interstitiality and hybridity can play a crucial role in how they understand Christ, Spirit, and God.

Study Questions

1. How can the composition of American society be more inclusive of Asian Americans?

2. How do the significant tenets of Asian American theology differ from Eurocentric thought? What can the latter learn from the former?
3. How can we all work together to dismantle racism, sexism, and colonialism within our theological discourse?
4. How does Asian American liberative theology impact your own personal theology?
5. What aspect of Asian American liberative theology works within your own unique community?

Suggested Reading

Brock, Rita Nakashima. *Journeys by Heart: A Christology of Erotic Power.* New York: Crossroad, 1998.

Cheng, Patrick. *Rainbow Theology: Bridging Race, Sexuality, and Spirit.* New York: Seabury Books, 2013.

Kim, Grace Ji-Sun. *The Grace of Sophia: A Korean North American Women's Christology.* Cleveland, OH: Pilgrim Press, 2002.

———. *The Holy Spirit, Chi, and the Other: A Model of Global and Intercultural Pneumatology.* New York: Palgrave Macmillan, 2011.

Kwok, Pui Lan. *Discovering the Bible in the Non-Biblical World.* Eugene, OR: Wipf & Stock Publishers, 2003.

———. *Introducing Asian Feminist Theology.* Cleveland, OH: Pilgrim Press, 2000.

Lee, Jung Young. *Marginality: The Key to Multicultural Theology.* Minneapolis: Fortress Press, 1995.

———. *The Trinity in Asian Perspective.* Nashville, TN: Abingdon Press, 1996.

Lee, Sang Hyun. *From a Liminal Place: An Asian American Theology.* Minneapolis: Fortress Press, 2010.

Matsuoka, Fumitaka. *Out of Silence: Emerging Themes in Asian American Churches.* Eugene, OR: Wipf & Stock Publishers, 2009.

Park, Andrew Sung. *Triune Atonement: Christ's Healing for Sinners, Victims, and the Whole Creation.* Louisville, KY: Westminster John Knox Press, 2009.

———. *The Wounded Heart of God: The Asian Concept of Han and the Christian Doctrine of Sin.* Nashville, TN: Abingdon Press, 1993.

Phan, Peter C. *Christianity in Asia.* Oxford: Blackwell Publishing, 2011.

———. *In Our Own Tongues: Perspectives from Asia on Mission and Inculturation.* Maryknoll, NY: Orbis Books, 2003.

———. *Vietnamese-American Catholics.* Mahwah, NJ: Paulist Press, 2005.

Song, C. S. *Third-Eye Theology: Theology in Formation in Asian Settings.* Maryknoll, NY: Orbis Books, 1979.

———. *Theology from the Womb of Asia.* New York: Orbis Books, 1986.

Tan, Jonathon Y. *Introducing Asian American Theologies.* Maryknoll, NY: Orbis Books, 2008.

8

Liberative Theologies of Poverty and Class

Joerg Rieger

Liberative theologies that address matters of poverty and class have various origins and histories. Representatives include the social gospel in the United States, Latin American liberation theologies, and more recent efforts to understand the problems of religion and class at a deeper level. Concerns for poverty and class are also deeply rooted in many religious traditions. In the traditions of the exodus from Egypt, which are shared by Jews, Christians, and Muslims, God takes the side of the Hebrew slaves and calls Moses and Aaron to lead them to freedom. The traditions of the prophets pick up God's concern for the poor (Isa. 58:6-12). Jesus picks up these ancient traditions in his own ways, preaching good news to the poor and liberation of the oppressed (Matt. 11:4-5; Luke 4:18-19). Mary, the mother of Jesus, and the Apostle Paul proclaim a God who is not only concerned for the poor and the lowly but who challenges the rich. The God who lifts up the lowly pushes the powerful from their thrones (Luke 1:46-55). And the God who elects the foolish and the weak does so in order to shame the wise and the strong (1 Cor. 1:26-29).

Class, as the term is used here and in a recently published work on religion, theology, and class, addresses the relations between classes. The poor, for instance, do not exist in isolation, as is often assumed. Poverty exists in relation to wealth and needs to be seen in this context. The relationship between classes is marked not only by differentials of wealth but also by differentials of power, which put some classes in positions of power over other classes, able to use them for their own benefits. Low-wage workers, for example, contribute to the wealth of the stockholders of the corporations for which they work, as workers generally produce substantially more than the value of their salaries. Notions of class that speak about

Throughout history, religious communities and their theologians have picked up concerns related to poverty and class, including the Franciscans in the Middle Ages, the Left Wing of the

Reformation in the sixteenth century, and the eighteenth-century Methodist movement. John Wesley, the founder of Methodism, was not only concerned for the well-being of the poor and working people of his time, but he also sensed their theological significance. Religion, he felt, should not go from the greatest to the least but the other way around. In "The General Spread of the Gospel," he wrote, "'They shall all know *me*,' saith the Lord, not from the greatest to the least (this is that wisdom of the world which is foolishness with God) but 'from the least to the greatest,' that the praise may not be of men, but of God."

Matters of poverty and class are, therefore, not merely social concerns; they are the concerns of God, as described in core religious traditions. This insight is at the heart of contemporary theological approaches to poverty and class, despite many other differences. Latin American liberation theologians have formulated what has become known as the "**preferential option for the poor**." This option, according to Gustavo Gutiérrez, one of the founders of this approach, is based on God's own option for the poor as demonstrated throughout the Bible. The option for the poor, according to Gutiérrez, is grounded not in the goodness of the poor but in the goodness of God. Those who are not poor are not excluded here but are invited into God's concern for the "least of these." In the words of the Apostle Paul, "if one member suffers, all suffer together with it" (1 Cor. 12:26).

"Preferential option for the poor"—a term derived from Latin American liberation theology. It refers to a theological and political commitment to the poor, as demonstrated by God and religious communities throughout the Bible, and to the methods and analyses necessary for clarifying and transforming the conditions that produce poverty.

---

social stratification, usually in terms of different income levels, are insufficient because they usually fail to reflect on the relationship between the strata. When class is understood in terms of relationship, class struggle becomes a reality that exists by virtue of the various power relations. In the current situation, class struggle is waged mostly from the top down, as there is a trend to reduce salaries and benefits and to make employees contingent so that they can be more easily hired and fired. This increases both the wealth and the power of the employers. Currently new efforts are under way to understand the relation of religion and class. Even though religion has often supported the ruling class, the support of religion for the lower classes is being reclaimed, and there is new awareness that such support is deeply rooted in the Abrahamic traditions: Judaism, Christianity, and Islam.

The origins of Latin American liberation theology in the 1970s are linked to the concern for the liberation of the poor, as poverty is widespread in many Latin American countries, with large peasant populations that are not able to make ends meet, staggering unemployment rates, and increasing urban poverty. These theologies, however, were concerned not merely about poverty but about the ways in which poverty was addressed. Poverty in the Latin America of the 1950s and '60s was supposed to be fought through so-called development, which meant efforts to bring underdeveloped nations up to the levels of developed nations. Liberation theologians cautioned that this approach overlooked the fact that the so-called developed nations gained their fortunes on the back of the so-called underdeveloped nations. The problem was, therefore, not underdevelopment but exploitation.

Beginning with the Spanish Conquest in the sixteenth century, gold from Latin America helped build cathedrals and banks in Europe, and from the nineteenth century on the United States benefitted from the export of raw materials and the cheaper labor available in Latin America. As a result, foreign investment took out much more from Latin America than what was put in so that the wealth of wealthier nations kept growing at the expense of the poorer nations. This problem was described by the so-called dependency theories of previous decades, which identified the problem as a relation of dependency, in which the North kept the South dependent. These theories provided some insights for the early Latin American liberation theologians. When seen in this light, it is clear that nothing will change without addressing the persisting structures of **dependency** exploitation.

Dependency theory—a theory of economic development that emerged in Latin America to analyze the global economic relations between the Global North and the Global South. This theory claims that the rich nations of the North exploit those of the South, and that the resources and cheap labor of the South are used to produce enormous amounts of wealth for the rich.

Later generations of liberation theologians in both North and South America have developed these critiques further by pointing out that the conflict is not only between the nations of the North and the South but can be found within the respective hemispheres themselves, as both concentrations of great wealth and of dire poverty exist in each. While the earlier critiques focused on nations, now the role of large transnational corporations is being considered as well. In recent years, the language of empire has helped to understand the more complex problems that produce poverty, as empire can take on various forms. Today, empire is frequently embodied in the softer forms of power promoted by global capitalism. In sum, theologies addressing poverty and class developed by addressing economic issues, in particular contexts where poor and lower-class people live.

Liberative Theology in Action: The Issue of Labor

When Americans think of poor people, they often think of people who are homeless or unemployed. Nevertheless, the majority of the poor are people who are employed and hold down jobs. The so-called working poor are working low-wage jobs in the fast-food industry, in service-related jobs, or at big-box retailers like Walmart, which is the largest private employer in the world. With wages below the poverty level, many of these working people hold down more than one job, often still not able to make ends meet. Since many of these jobs do not offer benefits or health care, bankruptcy is never far away, and it affects not only individuals but also whole families. Households headed by single mothers are especially vulnerable, and homeless families are not uncommon in the United States. Merely decreasing unemployment is, therefore, not enough to fight poverty. In many other industrialized countries, workers are organized in unions, which are designed to increase their power in negotiations over salaries (called "collective bargaining") and which support the voice of workers at the workplace. In the late nineteenth and early twentieth centuries in the United States, labor unions and the concerns of workers were frequently supported by religious communities. The Methodist Social Creed of 1908, which was also adopted by the National Council of Churches in the United States, called for shorter workdays and the general support of workers. In the history of the United States, poverty was fought most effectively by organized working people, who became the agents that were able to produce a better life for all. Research has shown that when organized workers negotiate better working conditions and salaries, other workers in the same field benefit as well, so that the accomplishments of the labor movement are multiplied beyond its immediate members. Many Americans today take the gains of the labor movement for granted without remembering the struggles that led to weekends off work, eight-hour workdays, pension and health-care plans. Moreover, many faith communities have forgotten about their historical support for working people, so that religion today is rarely seen as an ally of working people, despite many churches' official support of collective bargaining and economic justice. At the same time, new alliances of religion and labor are emerging, embodied in organizations such as Interfaith Worker Justice (IWJ),

Clergy and Laity United for Economic Justice (CLUE), and Jobs with Justice (JWJ). The concerns of labor and economic justice are taking on new life with younger generations of Christians, who share a greater awareness of the concerns of working people and who are disproportionately affected by poverty. The topics of labor and poverty are also enjoying new attention in the teaching and research of the theological academy.

As with the option for the poor, the notion of development has been picked up elsewhere in a more positive fashion. South African theologians such as the late Steve de Gruchy, for instance, have talked about development in terms of the agency of the common people rather than the outside agency of privileged nations and corporations. The agency of the people is always agency under pressure, which poses challenges to dominant agency because it seeks to shift more power to the people. In this approach to development, poverty and class exploitation are overcome not by the generosity of wealthy and powerful nations or corporations but through organized peoples' movements that, not only in South Africa, often include the labor movement.

In Asia, *minjung* theology in Korea picked up the concerns of the suffering masses, not only in terms of their struggles but also in terms of their agency. The Korean word *minjung* draws on the Greek New Testament word *ochlos*. According to Korean New Testament scholar Ahn Byung Mu, the *ochlos* can be translated as "crowd, multitude, the common people." Those are the people with whom Jesus surrounded himself and who were exploited by the rulers of the day. The Roman Empire was built on the backs of lower-class people; yet they are also the ones to whom Jesus's message gives support, and they are the ones whom he calls to a new life and whom he organizes accordingly. In Korea, those were the people who were not benefiting from the economic and political system in the 1970s. Despite efforts to do away with this theology later, it is being reclaimed again today in various ways.

In the United States, the theologies of the so-called social gospel have addressed matters of poverty and class in the context of industrialization and the related abuse of working people in the late nineteenth and early twentieth centuries. The Social Creed of 1908, first developed by the Methodist Episcopal Church and then adopted by many other churches, supports the abolition of child labor, the protection of workers, and the reduction of work hours "to the lowest practical point." Subsequent versions of the creed develop a deeper appreciation for the agency of workers. The current Social Creed of the United Methodist Church, for instance, promotes workers' rights to collective bargaining and it speaks about the elimination of economic and social distress. Although this is hard to imagine today, at the time of the Great Depression in the late 1920s, many of the churches were taking the side of poor and working people. In the 1932 version of the Social Creed a statement was added that called for the "just participation by the worker in the profits of the industry in which he or she is engaged."

The most important factor in the development of theologies that address issues of poverty and social class is the agency of the poor and of exploited classes themselves, as the place where God is found at work. Although this has often been overlooked, it is true even for the social gospel, as Ken Estey has demonstrated in his recent research on its early leaders such as Walter Rauschenbusch.

Need for Liberation from Specific Structures

Today, at a time when the rich are getting richer, poverty and class exploitation are experienced by billions of people around the globe. According to a March 25, 2014, *Forbes* magazine article, just sixty-seven individuals own as much as half of the world's population (3.5 billion people). Poverty affects growing numbers of the population not only in the Global South but also in the Global North. In the United States, one of the wealthiest countries of the world, a record 15 percent of the population lives below the poverty line, while the poverty rate for children is even higher at 21.8 percent. According to the National Center of Law and Economic Justice, 9.7 percent of the white population of the United States (18.9 million) in 2012 were living in poverty, while over 25 percent of Hispanics (13.6 million) and 27.2 percent of African Americans (10.9 million) were living in poverty. In the city of Dallas, Texas, according to U.S. data statistics, a full 39 percent of inhabitants were considered to be financially insecure in 2012. Contrary to common misperceptions, theologies that deal with poverty are therefore not limited to certain areas of the world.

Matters of poverty and class cannot easily be separated from matters of race, ethnicity, and gender, as these are often linked. In the United States, white women earn merely 77 cents for every dollar men earn; for African American women this number is at 64 cents, and for Latina women it is 56 cents. **Intersectionality**—the coming together of various forms of oppression—is an integral part of the problems of poverty and class. Womanist theologians—African American feminist theologians—have been among the most outspoken advocates for keeping together issues of race, gender, and class. At the same time, in terms of sheer numbers, the majority of the poor in the United States continue to be white, which means that various other forms of privilege will have to be rethought along the lines of poverty and class, providing new challenges to theology that have not yet been sufficiently addressed. White privilege and male privilege, for instance, shape up differently for poor and lower-class people—a fact that the dominant powers seek to suppress in order to keep those poor who are white and male in line with the dominant status quo. If a white worker identifies with his white employer rather than with his African American or Latina coworkers, the system has won.

Intersectionality—a term used to refer to the intersection of myriad forms of oppression along the lines of race, gender, sexuality, class, etc.

A major factor that is often overlooked is that poverty and class are not just about money but also about power. Those who are poor and lower class are forced to survive on very little money; they also hold very little power in most areas of life, including not only economics and politics (where the lack of power is more obvious) but also culture and even religion. In many religious communities, the wealthier members have a disproportionate influence both on programs and on matters of faith. For this reason, the poor are sometimes called the "invisible ones," and they belong to the so-called subaltern, whose voices are rarely taken seriously.

Poverty is, therefore, not a phenomenon that can be considered in isolation from wealth. Poverty is located in a relational network where the poor are related to the rest of society, including the wealthiest members of society. This relational network is best described by the term "class," which is perhaps one of the most misunderstood notions of our time. If the term class is used today, it often refers to social stratification, according to which each class is defined in isolation from other classes, related to respective income levels. A more adequate understanding of class needs to reflect the particular relationships of exploitation in which the poor find themselves. As Latin American dependency theory realized, poverty is not a natural phenomenon but part of the production of wealth by the select few. This relationship between poverty and wealth exists even when the poor have become the excluded ones, that is, the ones who appear to be no longer needed by the economy, like the long-term unemployed, whose numbers are on the rise around the globe.

When reflecting on matters of poverty and class, it is also important to keep in mind that there is a class that is benefiting from the economic status quo, not only in the United States but globally. In the United States, not since the Great Depression has there been such a severe polarization between the classes than at present. This polarization of the classes is considerably greater than it was even in the days of the Roman Empire. In ancient Rome, the top 1 percent controlled 16 percent of society's wealth, compared to the 1 percent controlling 40 percent of all wealth in the contemporary United

States, according to Jillian Berman's *Huffington Post* article "U.S. Income Inequality Higher than Roman Empire's Levels: Study." Ironically, while many believe that class is less a hurdle in the United States than elsewhere, the opposite is the case. The option to move up the ladder—the so-called American dream—is less and less an option, although many people hold on to it. In these matters, the United States is behind England, hardly a country known for its pride in social mobility. *New York Times* journalists Janny Scott and David Leonhardt report in *Class Matters* that in 2005 more people believed in the American dream than ever before, although studies show that social mobility is less and less an option. They quote economist David I. Levine: "Being born in the elite in the U.S. gives you a constellation of privileges that very few people in the world have ever experienced," while "being born poor in the U.S. gives you disadvantages unlike anything in Western Europe and Japan and Canada."

In terms of income inequality, the United States ranks behind any of the other wealthy nations, slightly ahead of Hong Kong and Singapore. Unemployment is at record levels and affects even those in the middle class who had assumed their positions to be secure; minority groups are even more deeply affected. According to the official data, which underestimate the real numbers, in July 2012 unemployment was at 7.4 percent for whites, 14.4 percent for African Americans, and 11 percent for Latinos and Latinas. In addition, the income gap between young and old was at its highest level ever.

Issues and Questions

Poverty and class relations are serious matters. Ultimately, they must be considered matters of life and death. Every day, 25,000 children die around the globe from preventable causes. This number does not even reflect the thousands of others who are dying as well, but even these numbers are only the tip of the iceberg. As Latin American theologians in the 1970s have pointed out, the poor are the ones who die before their time. The deeper problem is that poverty and exploitation along the class lines kill and destroy the lives of many millions of people, their families, and their communities. The consequences of this destruction are not limited to those directly affected by them, because the community as a whole suffers and even the lives of the privileged are distorted. The theological dilemma raised in this context is not the abstract discussion whether there is a God or not, but "Where is God in the midst of all this suffering?"

Even though many of the poor may not be starving to death, their life expectancies are much lower. This is due to factors that include lack of healthy and nutritious food, precarious living arrangements that expose people to extreme heat or cold or wet conditions, and conditions of hard labor in perpetuity. Contrary to widespread belief, often supported by religious people, poor people have to work harder than anyone else in order to make ends meet. This includes working several low-paying jobs at once, back-breaking menial labor, dangerous working conditions with little protection, and the endless scavenging by which homeless people are forced to survive.

Lack of adequate health care is also a significant cause of people dying before their time, even in the United States. In the United States, tens of thousands of people die every year behind closed doors, while many religious communities do not even allow an open discussion concerning health care for all. Additionally, poor people experience greater exposure to pressures of all kinds. Ecological pressures such as global warming, for instance, disproportionately affect those who cannot protect themselves from them. Poor communities, because they have fewer means to fight back, are often located in places where landfills and toxic factories are put. Political pressures derive from the fact that members of the lower classes have less political representation because political representatives are often forced to follow the money.

Another issue has to do with power in all shapes or forms, not only economic and political but also cultural and religious. The "power of the poor" (to reference a famous book title by Gustavo Gutiérrez) is restricted by many factors. There are active efforts to reduce the political power of the lower classes through the redistricting of voting areas and the introduction of voter ID laws, which discriminate against people with fewer means. As a result, democracy is curtailed and diminished.

While political democracy is on people's minds, **economic democracy** is not commonly discussed. Economic pressures are substantial, not merely because of severe inequalities in distribution, which are easier to see, but also because of severe inequalities in how productive capacities of people are valued. While it has been argued that low-wage workers are paid according to the laws of the market, the truth is that salaries are kept artificially low, for instance by eliminating the collective power of workers gained by organizing labor unions. While the churches in the past often supported labor unions and the right to organize, this is less common today, although new religion and labor coalitions are emerging in many places. When corporations have all the power, worker salaries and benefits are cut even when profit is made at the top. Even better-paid workers take home ever smaller fractions of what their labor is actually worth.

Economic democracy—a way of organizing both economic activity and everyday life around the power of the people and in a way that focuses on how the work of the worker is valued.

Restricting the power of the poor along the lines of politics and economics goes hand in hand with restricting their cultural and religious power as well. Cultural pressures are produced, for instance, by aggressive marketing of certain consumer goods in lower-class communities, including alcohol. Religious pressures should not be overlooked, because the poor are often preyed upon by religious enterprises that seek to build megachurches or media churches. Where poor and lower-class people are pressured to tithe or donate extra sums of money, additional burdens are placed on their lives that do not affect those who can afford to give more. It is often overlooked that when billionaires donate millions to causes, they retain both funds and power that are thousands of times greater than those of the average person.

Dominant culture and religion, despite increasing diversity, continue to be shaped by the interests of the wealthy and powerful. The location of God in all of this is therefore seen at the top, with the wealthy and the powerful, rather than at the bottom, with poor and working people. Theologies addressing poverty and class, in conversation with time-honored religious traditions, have made valiant efforts to turn this misperception around.

The good news is that the power of the poor continues to be a factor that is to be reckoned with, not only in politics and economics but also in culture and religion. This is one of the deepest insights of liberation theology. The power of the poor cannot be repressed indefinitely, as people's movements throughout history have shown. This is not a utopian idea but a reality that has changed history in the past and continues to change it today. This power shapes up differently from dominant power, because it is not held by individuals but by collectives, and this is a power that needs to be organized. This experience has led to new understandings of Jesus as more than a radical preacher. What made Jesus particularly challenging to the dominant power of the Roman Empire was that he organized the power of the people by making disciples and connecting to social movements in his own time.

Main Themes and Methodologies

One of the main insights of theologies that address matters of poverty and class is that we are dealing with structural realities. This is perhaps the most significant insight, as too often the poor and lower classes are blamed for their misfortune. Such blame is doled out in various ways. Conservatives, both in politics and religion, often blame the poor directly because they believe that people are poor because they do not work hard enough, are lazy or otherwise deficient. Liberals, both in politics and religion, blame the poor indirectly when they seek to devise ways of reintegrating them into the current system through welfare and education. Here, the poor are not blamed as individuals, but systematic deficiencies are identified as the problems of the poor. With both conservatives and liberals, the task is seen as reintegrating the poor into the economic system of capitalism, which is assumed to work. As a result, the structures that produce poverty and that place people in lower classes are either not questioned at all or questioned insufficiently. God is identified as on the side of this system, if only by default.

The preferential option for the poor, introduced above, addresses both the plight and the potential of the poor and members of the lower classes at a deeper level. If the poor and the lower classes are not exclusively at fault for their condition, what are the problems that keep reproducing poverty and class oppression? And how does this understanding change our understanding of God?

The current capitalist economic system works by producing the structures that lead to dire and long-term misery. There is an underbelly of low-wage workers and unemployed people that is not only taken for granted but assumed to be necessary for the flourishing of the system. While common economic opinion in the United States once put the desirable unemployment rate at 5 percent, that number has now been adjusted to 6 percent. The real unemployment numbers are much higher, because in the United States the long-term unemployed and people who have given up on the job market are not counted. If unemployment sinks too low, the common economic opinion goes, labor becomes too expensive and workers will gain too much power.

Latin American liberation theologians have indicted as sinful the structures that keep producing and reproducing poverty. This is a substantial contribution to theology, particularly since sin is often either defined too narrowly as a personal problem or too broadly as a universal metaphysical distortion. Structural sin that produces poverty and class exploitation cannot be overcome by religious rituals or by well-meaning attempts to help the poor. Praying for forgiveness is important, but structural sin requires a more complex response that includes a change of life. A deeper understanding of sin is also missing in the old adage that it is better to teach people to fish than to give them a fish. If the misery of the poor is primarily linked not to their inability to fish (or to work) but to a sinful condition where large corporations took all the fish or where private interests built fences around rivers and lakes so that people have no access, we need to rethink what we mean by salvation.

Salvation in this context needs to address how such **structural sin**, which includes the structural violence that is exerted by the system, can be overcome. Salvation thus includes the broader horizon of social reality, which means that working for justice for the poor and oppressed classes is not just social service (as is commonly assumed) but a concern that is linked to the very identity of Christianity. There can be no salvation that does not include social salvation at the same time. Looking at salvation in this broader horizon does not exclude personal images of salvation, although this is a common accusation against it.

Structural sin—a way of identifying sin in the structures of society. This idea links salvation and justice to the overcoming of structures and systems that reproduce and maintain inequality and poverty.

Salvation is a common concern of theologies that focus on poverty and class. John Wesley, father of the Methodist movement and of holiness movements, made it clear that salvation is not primarily a matter of going to heaven but of what is happening in people's lives here and now ("The Scripture Way of Salvation"). Salvation as going to heaven does not need to be rejected but it needs to be put where it belongs: after a discussion of salvation as what makes a difference here and now. In other words, the question whether there is life after death can only be answered after we have addressed the question whether there might be life before death that includes the poorest of the poor.

Salvation is, therefore, not just something that happens to the poor but with the poor and, to some degree, even by the poor. Latin American liberation theologian Jon Sobrino has rephrased the old motto of "no salvation outside of the church" to "no salvation outside of the poor." In this model, the poor are not saved by others, but they are integrated into God's history of salvation in Jesus Christ. The poor are no longer recipients of charity, but they then become agents of salvation that, as the apostle Paul encouraged the Philippians, "work out [their] own salvation with fear and trembling" (2:12). This does not mean that the poor assume

Individualism is an ideology that is applied in various ways to the tensions of poverty and class. It claims that people are able to determine their lives and that they are responsible both for their fortunes and misfortunes. The tenets of individualism are often used to blame the poor and working people when they fall on hard times, challenging them to work harder. The tenets of individualism are also used to praise the rich, because it assumes that they produced their wealth through their own abilities and skill. Expressions such as "pulling oneself up by one's own bootstraps" or talk of the "self-made man" show how deeply entrenched individualism is in the popular mind. The truth is, however, that there are no self-made people. Great wealth and success are for the most part produced through networks and, sometimes unconsciously, on the backs of others. Vice versa, misfortune such as unemployment or low-wage work has frequently nothing to do with individual failure but with structures that interfere with people's lives. Individualism is an ideology that serves the wealthy and the powerful. Such individualism cannot be fought by challenging individualism as if it were real—a common effort of religious communities that blame individualism. Individualism needs to be fought by telling the truth about how we are all connected in relationships that are often exploitative. No one is wealthy in isolation, and no one is poor in isolation.

the place of God, but they become participants in the work of God. Recall that the problem of poverty and class exploitation was not just a lack of assets but also a lack of power, broadly conceived. Those who are not poor are not excluded but are invited to join this emerging community and work alongside the poor.

Many liberation theologies have thus emphasized "orthopraxis" (right action) in addition to a more common emphasis on orthodoxy (right belief). But what has often appeared to be a turn to social ethics is really a turn to a more complex and a fuller understanding of religion. Religion is not just what affects and transforms people's minds but also people's lives and their communities. Politics is not an add-on in these theological approaches but something that is an integral part of religion at all times. When the role of politics in religion is not realized, politics does not disappear but is merely taken for granted, which explains why religion has too often supported the status quo.

Theologian Frederick Herzog, a white North American theologian at work in the second half of the twentieth century, has emphasized God's agency as the basis of any human agency. Herzog thus talked about "Theopraxis," "Christopraxis," and "Spiritpraxis" as the foundation of orthopraxis. Here, the circle comes to a close as human action and divine action are seen in relation to each other. One of the basic insights of many theologies concerned with poverty and class is that we need a reversal of the relation of theory and practice: practice is not a second step, after theory, but is an integral part of theory and reflection. In other words, we will understand God only when we begin to participate in God's own work. This understanding reflects a time-honored experience, all the way back to the disciples of Jesus.

Theology that addresses the issues of poverty and class must not be considered a passing fad. As long as we are confronted with dire poverty and class exploitation, which are matters of life and death, theology cannot afford to return to business as usual. Moreover, if poverty and class are relational and if the poor and the rich are thus connected, theology that focuses on poverty and class cannot be considered a matter of special interest. All of us are implicated, even those who feel safe in the middle, as the matter will not go away if we choose to ignore it.

Future trends will have to take into account that things are worsening rather than improving, as the poor are getting poorer and the rich are getting richer, which is particularly odd at a time of unprecedented wealth. While this growing gap should be common knowledge by now, the truth is still rarely admitted in public. Since 2006, Warren Buffett, one of the wealthiest persons in the world, has repeatedly pointed out that there is indeed a class struggle being waged in the United States and that his class is winning. Nevertheless, Buffett's remark has not found much of an echo among his peers or in the American mainstream. In June 2014, Lloyd Blankfein, the CEO of Goldman Sachs, admitted that inequality was indeed a problem in America. This might begin a new debate, but Blankfein was quick to add that there is nothing that can be done about it. This stance reflects a widespread opinion in the United States and hardens positions.

In the history of the United States and of many other countries, social movements have been able to change history. Not surprisingly, theologies concerned with poverty and class have often been in tune with social movements. The social movements of recent history have provided some hope that things may be changing again. The Occupy Wall Street movement, for instance, has reintroduced the discussion of class into the public debate by differentiating between the 99 percent—people who have to work for a living—and the 1 percent—people who can afford to live off their investments. This is a major breakthrough that has found a profound resonance with some theologians. The intersectionality of class with issues of race, ethnicity, gender, and sexuality is, of course, part of this newly developing discourse. While this is one of the challenges for the future, it was part of the past as well. After all, Martin Luther King, Jr., was killed not when he tried to integrate lunch counters but when he supported the striking sanitation workers in Memphis. King himself wondered, "What does it profit a man to be able to eat at an integrated lunch counter if he doesn't earn enough money to buy a hamburger and a cup of coffee?"

A new sense of the growing differentials of class also affects the middle class. Contrary to common assumptions, this is not the class that rests in relative safety, but this is the battleground where the tensions are often worked out. Defining a poverty line does not necessarily mean that people above this line are doing okay. In fact, members of the middle class are increasingly experiencing similar pressures to the ones experienced by the lower classes, as benefits are reduced or cut, salaries frozen, job security is vanishing, and both economic and political power disappear. Even the benefits of the middle class that are not available to the poor, such as pension plans, homeownership, and modest investments, are no longer as secure as once thought. The so-called Great Recession of 2007–2009 reshuffled the playing field. The younger generation of the middle class is no longer able to expect that it will be doing better than the older generations, and the older generations of the middle class increasingly depend on the support of the younger generations.

One of the most important developments in relation to religion and class, which has been reflected in theology, has to do with those who are not considered poor. This has caused a transition from a conventional idea of solidarity as the support of the privileged for the underprivileged to what I have called "**deep solidarity**" (*Occupy Religion*). Those in the middle class who seek to be in solidarity with the poor and the lower class are beginning to realize that they find themselves in the same boat, despite all the obvious differences that remain. While the middle class has traditionally oriented itself in terms of the upper class—assuming that it, too, would have the opportunity to rise up, if only in the next generation—now some members of the middle class are beginning to realize their actual affinity with the lower classes. This realization changes not only how relationships are viewed but how they are lived, with deep implications for religious communities and for theology. Members of the 1 percent are not excluded here, as they are at liberty of putting themselves on the side of the 99 percent and in so doing are able not only to embark on new encounters with the majority of humanity but also with God.

Solidarity is one of the principles of organizing poor and working people. It grows out of the recognition that the poor and working people are not able to change the situation as individuals but need the support of extended communities. Historically, working people have formed their own organizations in the form of labor unions and sometimes in religious communities. Religious communities are also places where the poor are finding some support and, in certain cases, where the poor are organized to speak out and to gain a voice. Solidarity is, therefore, not merely a principle but a practice that can be found throughout history. Nevertheless, religious communities have sometimes practiced solidarity as if it were a matter of the privileged helping the underprivileged. This attitude has created certain problems, including a lack of communication and patronizing attitudes. In order to address these problems, I have suggested the term deep solidarity (*Occupy Religion*), which serves as a reminder that even people who consider themselves privileged or

---

Deep solidarity—a way of reconceiving the relationship between the middle classes and lower classes that emphasizes their affinity. Deep solidarity moves beyond solidarity as the support of the underprivileged by the privileged and toward recognition that the vast majority of people lack the wealth and power of the 1 percent. Deep solidarity is the recognition that we are all "in the same boat," without neglecting differences.

One of the most important religious consequences of this shift is that images of God are changing in the process. The theological question is whether these changing images of God might correspond better with the many traditional images both in the Old and the New Testament that see God not at the top but in proximity to, and in deep solidarity with, the people. An increasing number of theologians and members of religious communities are waking up to this possibility. These are exciting times.

in the middle class are among the 99 percent who are not benefiting from capitalism as much as they used to. Members of the 1 percent are invited to put themselves on the side of poor and working people as well.

Study Questions

1. How does focusing on the power of the poor transform how we conceive political power and political action?
2. What are the possible gains and problems of discussing intersectionality through the lens of poverty and class?
3. What are some examples of religious images and language that reflect the status quo and need to be reconsidered?
4. What are the implications of salvation "here and now" for your community? What movements or organizations might you consider being a part of?
5. How do the issues of class and poverty affect how we discern the work of God in the world?

Suggested Reading

Bock, Kim Yong, ed. *Minjung Theology: People as the Subjects of History.* Singapore: The Commission of Theological Concerns, Christian Conference of Asia, 1981.

Cochrane, James R., Elias Bongmba, Isabel Phiri, and Des van der Water, eds. *Living on the Edge: Essays in Honour of Steve de Gruchy, Activist and Theologian.* Pietermaritzburg, South Africa: Cluster Publications, 2012.

De La Torre, Miguel A. *Doing Christian Ethics from the Margins,* 2nd ed. Maryknoll, NY: Orbis Books, 2014.

Groody, Daniel G., and Gustavo Gutiérrez, eds. *The Preferential Option for the Poor beyond Theology.* Notre Dame, IN: University of Notre Dame Press, 2013.

Gutiérrez, Gustavo. *The Power of the Poor in History.* Eugene, OR: Wipf & Stock Publishers, 1983.

Rieger, Joerg. *No Rising Tide: Theology, Economics, and the Future*. Minneapolis: Fortress Press, 2009.

Rieger, Joerg, ed. *Religion, Theology, and Class: Fresh Engagements after Long Silence*. New Approaches to Religion and Power. New York: Palgrave Macmillan, 2013.

Rieger, Joerg, and Kwok, Pui Lan. *Occupy Religion: Theology of the Multitude*. Religion in the Modern World. Lanham, MD: Rowman & Littlefield Publishers, 2013.

Williams, Delores. *Sisters in the Wilderness*. Maryknoll, NY: Orbis Books, 1993.

Part III

The U.S. Gender and Sexual-Identity Context

9

Feminist Liberative Theologies

Rebecca Chabot and Sarah Neeley

Most people know Elizabeth Cady Stanton's name because of the women's suffrage movement in the United States. Fewer know that earning women the right to vote was just one part of Stanton's work. She also was an abolitionist and a critic of the way theology, especially the Bible, was used in Christianity to subjugate and exploit women. In 1848, Stanton was an outspoken critic of Christianity's treatment of women at the Seneca Falls Convention, and in 1895/1898, she published *The Woman's Bible*. The book caused many to view her as a radical, but the book was written in consultation with twenty-six other women, and, despite being denounced by the National American Woman Suffrage Association, it enjoyed a broad popular audience.

What Stanton and the others who worked on *The Woman's Bible* did would help to lay the groundwork for the rise of theological reflection explicitly by and for women during the women's movement several decades later. Though none who worked on the book were trained in biblical studies, they were concerned with the way that certain passages were interpreted and the very real consequences those passages had on women and their lives. Bible scholars were not interested in discussing **sexism**, misogyny, or the creation of a canon that disproportionately told the stories of men and either ignored or omitted completely those of women. As feminism began to gain its footing in the academy, biblical scholars such as Letty Russell and Phyllis Trible came to do their work through an explicitly feminist lens.

Sexism: Systematic discrimination against women because of their sex.

Misogyny: Mistreatment and, at times, hatred of women based solely on the fact that they are women.

Feminism: Feminism is the belief that women should be treated as equal to men in all spheres of life, public and private.

Building on the work that was, in part, started by Stanton and her compatriots, feminist scholars in the 1960s and '70s began to question the entire construction of the canon, asking what it meant for women to be outside the process of its creation, what it meant that questions had previously been asked and answered solely from the perspective of males. Many early feminists focused solely on gender, failing to take into account the diversity of womankind and how those who are not white and middle or upper class experience many of these same issues differently. Just as there were multiple waves of feminism, there have been multiple waves of feminist theologies, each one critically reflecting on that which had preceded it and attempting to resolve the issues voiced by critics while pushing the movement as a whole forward.

Feminist theologies are, like all liberative theologies, concerned with freedom from structures of oppression and freedom for human flourishing. There are many different oppressive structures that impact women around the world. In this section, we will examine some of the structures from which liberation is needed: the devaluing of women's experiences, exclusive religious language, patriarchal relationships, and sexist texts. We will also look at several other areas of concern for feminist theologians: the emphasis on the maleness of Christ, sexuality, and ecology.

Women's Experiences

Just as history is written by the victors, theology has long been a reflective exercise available, at least formally and academically, to those with power, namely white men of a certain level of power and privilege. This is not to say that theological reflection was done solely by white males, but that their experience was the lens through which theology was presented, and it was assumed that it was the only way of doing theology. One of the first issues raised by feminist theologians was the lack of women's experiences represented in or understood by theology. This quickly led to a rediscovery of women's experiences that had, at one point, been part of the tradition and had been removed, deleted, or otherwise obliterated over the years. The problem of the lack of women's experience is thus twofold: women's lives and experiences were removed or missing from the tradition and the tradition was not something that women saw themselves in or to which they were able to relate.

As feminist theologians began doing theological reflection from within their own experiences, they also did the important work of recovering the stories of their foremothers and foresisters. One example of the importance of this recovery is Elisabeth Schüssler Fiorenza's *In Memory of Her*, which takes its name from the biblical story of the woman who anoints Jesus. In the passage, Jesus responds to criticism of the woman by his disciples by saying, "Truly I tell you, wherever the good news is proclaimed in the whole world, what she has done will be told in remembrance of her" (Mark 14:9). Notice that the redactor of Mark failed to include the name of the woman, despite Jesus's lavish praise of her actions. How exactly is what she has done to be remembered throughout the tradition if she was not deemed important enough to name?

**Liberative Theology in Action:
The Issue of End-of-Life Care for Pregnant Women**

The Marlise Munoz case brought issues of end-of-life care for pregnant women to national attention in recent years. Munoz was a young Texas woman, fourteen weeks pregnant with her second child. The day before Thanksgiving, she went to get a bottle for her toddler son in her kitchen. Later, her husband found her unresponsive on the kitchen floor. According to Munoz's family, they were told a couple of days later that she was brain dead. Munoz and her husband, Erick, were both paramedics and had discussed their advanced directives (legal documents expressing their wishes in the event that they are medically unable to do so themselves) with each other. Erick Munoz asked the hospital to remove the ventilator (the machine that breathes for a patient, commonly referred to as life support) from his wife's body to follow her end-of-life wishes. His request was denied.

The hospital refused to remove the ventilator due to the Texas law that states that life-sustaining treatment cannot be removed from a pregnant woman regardless of her advanced directive. This law is not unique to Texas. At least thirty-one states have laws that restrict the removal of life-sustaining treatment. As problematic as such laws are for many women's rights groups, the Munoz case was unique in that she had been declared brain dead. Texas is also one of the many states that has legal definitions of death that include brain death. This means that Munoz was legally and medically dead. Ventilators offer the ability to provide life-sustaining treatment in the hopes of giving physicians time to provide curative treatment that prevents cardiac or brain death. Life-sustaining treatment cannot be provided to a dead body. It was on these grounds that Erick Munoz won a lawsuit against the hospital and received a court order for all machines to be removed from his wife's body.

There are several important issues that arise in this case. First, given that Munoz was legally and medically dead, it seems safe to assume that the life-sustaining treatment was for the fetus in the hopes that it would survive long enough to attempt a viable delivery at a minimum of at least twenty-four-weeks gestation. Obviously, this case was watched by advocates on both sides of the abortion debate. Munoz was a dead body serving as an incubator for a very young fetus. Although "human incubator" has become a buzz phrase in feminist theology and women's rights in general, it is not an uncommon medical practice. Dead bodies of adults and children serve as incubators for organs in the event of organ donation. They remain on a ventilator until medical teams arrive for each organ going to a recipient. However, organ donation is always performed at the express wishes of the patient before death, or at the wishes of the patient's family. That was not the case with Munoz. The law and actions of the hospital imply that the purpose of a woman's life and body is to bear children. It did not matter that she was dead. It did not matter that all of the things that had made her who she was had ended. It did not matter that she had decided, based on her extensive medical background as a paramedic, that she did not want to be on a ventilator long term.

It could be argued in this case that physicians have an ethical obligation to advocate for the fetus. Physicians do not, however, argue so fervently for organ donation and the possibility of life that each organ represents. Actually, the government has clear guidelines for conversations requesting organ donation. In order for hospitals to continue receiving money from Medicare and Medicaid, physicians or other hospital representatives cannot be aggressive when approaching families for organ donation and must respect the family's decision.

Regardless of one's views on abortion, who has the responsibility and right to make decisions for the fetus? Many supporters of abortion advocate for women to have choices over their own bodies. What about after a woman has died? Munoz was fourteen weeks pregnant, and although she still had another six weeks to opt for a legal abortion in Texas, there was never any indication that she had not planned to carry her fetus to term before suddenly collapsing and becoming unconscious. Should it now be the place of the fetus's father, physicians, or the state to decide? Should the answer to that question change the language and conversation around women's rights?

Many who are against abortion support laws such as the one in Texas that prevents the removal of life-sustaining treatment of pregnant women. However, is it the state's place to make decisions for the fetus? If the fetus survived an attempt at delivery, the father is the baby's legal next of kin and has the responsibility of making all medical decisions, including the use of a ventilator, which would be needed for the baby after birth while it continued to develop. Why is the father not allowed to make decisions for the use of a ventilator for a fetus when he would be expected to make such decisions after birth?

Many of the themes of feminist theology come up in this case. What do you think should have been done in Munoz's case? What should be done in the future? Should laws that prevent the removal of life-sustaining treatment of pregnant women be changed? Do you think these laws are influenced by religion-based concepts of morality? What theological claims do these laws make?

Sexist Texts

Many feminist theologians have been quick to point out that one of the issues that prevents liberation is the fact that, many times, our texts are sexist. Although the Bible is the most widely accepted text, many denominations have additional texts; many of these texts are either sexist in content and/or sexist in their very construction, as the process used to compile the canon and to record events had few, if any, women involved. The exclusion of women's experience from these texts means that they are inherently problematic for a good deal of feminist theologians. Some feminist theologians reject the use of the tradition, or sacred texts, altogether; most, however, are more interested in doing the critical reflective work to name the problems inherent in these sexist texts and to acknowledge the good that does exist within the tradition despite its troubles.

One need only look at the cycle of the lectionary to see how the construction of the Christian **canon** can pose problems: certain readings, often involving women, are omitted completely; others are optional readings that are included or excluded at the discretion of the liturgist in charge. With the exclusion of women from the

Mary Magdalene: One of the most important recoveries of women's experiences throughout the tradition is the renewed interest in Mary Magdalene. One of the few women in the New Testament who is not named in relation to a husband or children (like Mary, mother of James and Salome, or Mary of Bethany, sister to Lazarus and Martha), the idea of Mary Magdalene as a reformed prostitute became popular over the centuries, despite the complete lack of support for that notion from either history or the tradition. How did the woman whom Augustine called "the apostle to the apostles" come to be known as a whore? Because of a homily by

Pope Gregory I, wherein he conflated Mary Magdalene with both Mary of Bethany and the unnamed woman in Mark 14, causing three different women with different experiences to be lumped into one. Feminist theologians have helped to trace the misunderstanding and to help rebuild the image of a woman who had been brave enough to witness the crucifixion and to go to the tomb, while her male counterparts were in hiding.

construction of the lectionary calendar, it is not surprising that there was not a particular concern for the inclusion of women and women's experiences within the **lectionary**. This is not to say that the women of the early church did not have experiences, write about those experiences, or have stories written about them; for numerous reasons, they were overlooked, omitted, or consolidated over time.

Canon: The collection of official texts that are part of a religious tradition or a type of literature.

Lectionary: The three-year cycle of readings used by the Catholic Church, the Orthodox Church, and many mainline Protestant denominations that is the basis for the structure of the liturgical year. Readings are organized according to liturgical season.

Exclusive Religious Language

Another closely related issue that feminist theologians have attempted to tackle is the problem of exclusive religious language, especially the use of gendered language when referring to all people and to God. One does not need to look very hard or very far to find examples of gender-exclusive language: Catholic documents are addressed to "all men of Good Will," and the Southern Baptist Convention uses language that reads, "God is all powerful and all knowing; and His perfect knowledge extends to all things, past, present, and future, including the future decisions of His free creatures. To Him we owe the highest love, reverence, and obedience." Gender-exclusive language is both a horizontal problem in Christianity, in which it complicates relationships between people, and a vertical one: the use of solely masculine pronouns to refer to God leaves half of the world's population to wonder if they were indeed made in the image and likeness of God. If both men and women are made in God's image, the gendering of God is problematic. Feminist theologians have helped to demonstrate that, sometimes, our language does not line up with our theology.

To that end, some feminist theologians have begun creating new language and terms, or reappropriating and redefining terms to use when doing theological reflection. This is in addition to refusing to gender God, which is a practice that several mainline Protestant denominations (including the ELCA and the United Methodist Church on their official websites and teachings) have already adopted. Some thinkers have appropriated terms like ***shekhinah*** or other terms found in the Hebrew Bible and adapted them for modern interpretations; others have actually constructed words, like proponents of ecofeminism, to address current concerns. **Ecofeminists** connect the domination of women with the domination of the earth and animals. They find that these two forms of domination are parallel and reinforce each other. Ecofeminist liberative theologians believe that justice for women cannot be achieved apart from ecojustice for all nonhuman life.

***Skekhinah*:** The English transliteration of the grammatically feminine Hebrew name of God.

Ecofeminism: The philosophy that connects the exploitation and domination of women to that of the environment.

Patriarchal Relationships

Patriarchy has an enormous impact on relationships between people. It creates and sustains imbalances of power, sets up oppressors and people to be oppressed, and creates the illusion that everything is black and white, an either/or choice. Patriarchy perpetuates the idea of women (that is, those who are physically female) being lesser, the denial of access to the public sphere. These relationships happen at social, religious, and personal levels. One of the predominant themes of patriarchal relationships is essentialism and its consequence, complementarity. Essentialism is the belief that biology dictates one's place or role in society, with only certain roles being available to an individual. Having a body that does not have a penis precludes full participation in all spheres of society.

Gender, sex, orientation: Often, people conflate gender and sex. Sex refers to the particular sexual organs with which a person is born. Gender refers to the way a person identifies. While both are often presented as a binary, the reality is that intersex births are not uncommon, and many people do not identify as either male or female. Orientation adds another level of complexity, as there are a variety of ways that people identify to explain their sexual orientation. Put simply, sex is about what is in a person's pants; gender is how a person's mind is wired, and orientation is about how a person's heart is wired.

Patriarchy: A system of society or government in which men hold the power and women are largely excluded from it.

Women and those who fall outside the binary presented by the patriarchal system and relationships are kept from positions of power and influence. One of the side effects of this is the emergence of notions of complementarity, the argument that the sex-based roles assigned to men and women in society are separate in order for them to complement each other. Many scholars have argued that this position, based in essentialism, is used by the Catholic Church to justify its all-male priesthood and is used by many other denominations to reserve ministry to males. Essentialism constructs a world where roles are assigned according to a person's sex, and there is no room for individual vocation, creativity, or challenging established norms.

Letty Russell, one of the earliest feminist theologians, argued for "a new focus of relationship in which there is continuing commitment and common struggle in interaction with a wider community context." She spoke in terms of relationship and human relationality, something that is never static, but always growing and changing. Relationships can be described, but the description is always changing and growing, and describing the relationship can impact the relationship. She saw people as partners with God and with one another; human existence is marked by the partnership that all share with others and with God. In partnership, power moves from one person or group to another, changing and flowing based on circumstances and not on an obfuscated understanding of natural law. This understanding is based on the servanthood of Jesus. Before Russell's death, she began speaking about hospitality as another way of understanding how relationships and partnerships should work.

Liberative Theology in Action: The Issue of Sex Trafficking

It is not often that one sees the words "nuns" and "human trafficking" in the same sentence, but the Sisters of Mercy of the Americas are on the frontline of the battle against sex trafficking. In partnership with Mercy Investment Services, the socially responsible investment arm of the Sisters of Mercy and their ministries, and other organizations, the Mercy Sisters have been actively combating sex trafficking around one of the biggest sporting events in the world, the Super Bowl, since 2012. The Super Bowl usually occurs in January, which is National Human Trafficking Awareness Month in the United States. Major events like the Super Bowl result in the demand for prostitutes and escorts, so the choice of the Super Bowl goes beyond just a coincidence with the month dedicated to raising awareness about the 27 million people who are trafficked each year.

As Sister Jeanne Christensen explains in a piece for Faith and Public Life's blog:

> 80% are women; 15% are children; and 5% are men. In the U.S. 82% of the incidents involved sex trafficking, of these 98% are women & girls. Ninety-five percent of the victims experienced physical or sexual violence during trafficking and the majority of trafficking victims are between 18 and 24 years of age. In the U.S. alone, 100,000 U.S. children are commercially sexually exploited every year and the number may be as high as 300,000. The Internet is a major source for predators' hunting, recruitment and trapping unsuspecting and/or innocent victims.

And where do these people who are trafficked end up? "They can be found in sweatshops, forced prostitution, domestic servitude, restaurants, agriculture, construction, and in hotel/motel cleaning services to name a few." Part of the Sisters' work involves educating and training hotel staff, helping them to learn what signs to look for. They also provide resources for people attending the event to learn more about how to spot survivors and to get them the help they might need. One of the resources was a letter that was designed to be printed and given to the hotel on check-in, a way to remind the hotel of their responsibility to combat trafficking.

So how did the Sisters of Mercy come to be involved in this fight? They have a long history of social engagement, from their foundress, Catherine McCauley, who founded the institute as a way to serve the poor and those pushed to the margins of society, up to the present day. McCauley knew that women committed to addressing the needs of those on the margins could and would make a difference. Over their nearly two hundred years as a religious order, the Sisters have always been keenly aware of the dangers and oppression that women face. They still run many high schools and colleges dedicated to educating young women, and striving to respond to changing times by identifying the areas of greatest need. Thus, given the sheer number of women who are impacted by the global human sex trade and other forms of human trafficking, and given their concern for all whom society pushes to the margins, the Sisters of Mercy have chosen this as one of their ministries: the chance to raise awareness, and by raising awareness, help to provide hope and opportunities for safety for those who have been trafficked.

Maleness of Jesus

Just as the gendering of God and the use of exclusive language are practices from which feminist theologians seek liberation, the maleness of Jesus, specifically the traditional emphasis on the maleness of Jesus, is an issue on which many theologians have written and that continues to be a topic of conversation and research today. The focus on Jesus's maleness has been used to keep women out of the public sphere and, importantly, ministry. The Nicene Creed, used by the Catholic Church, the Eastern Orthodox, the Anglican Communion, and a variety of Protestant denominations, includes the phrase "and became man" (*homo factus est*). Some denominations and churches substitute "and became human," but the use of "man" remains the official translation. While it is likely that the men responsible for constructing the creed intended "man" to mean "human," it nevertheless remains a problematic usage.

Feminist theologians such as Elizabeth Johnson have raised important questions about the emphasis on "man." What really matters? That Jesus was human, or the fact that Jesus was a man? If it is the former, substitution of either "human" or "flesh" for "man" makes sense; if it is the latter, then can women truly be saved if they are, in the words of Thomas Aquinas, simply "misbegotten males"? The challenge of these questions helps to push the church back to what really matters and helps to recover what is really at the heart of Christianity rather than simply accepting things as they have been handed down.

Liberative Theology in Action: The Issue of Violence

On April 24, 2014, a mass shooting took place in Isla Vista, California. The shooter was a young man who, in a series of videos posted online and a 140-page manifesto, made it clear that women, on the whole, were to blame for his lack of success with them and that he would get revenge against them. Though not all of the victims were women, it was clear that misogyny was one of the motivating factors, if not the sole motivating factor, in the attacks.

In response to those who tried to downplay the reality and impact of misogyny on women each and every day, Twitter user @gildedspine tweeted that she was going to be tweeting under the hashtag #YesAll Women and invited others to share examples and experiences of the pervasive nature of misogyny, especially in how it leaves men believing that women's time, bodies, attention, and even smiles are something to which they are entitled. The hashtag quickly started to trend, with up to 51,000 tweets per hour at its high point, as women shared their experiences and male allies called on their brothers to stop being defensive, to stop trying to hijack the hashtag, and to simply listen to the experiences of women.

Many feminist writers, including Rachel Held Evans, helped to draw attention to the hashtag and added their own stories. Held Evans, best known for writing a book about a year in which she tried to live out every verse in the Bible directed to or about women, has become one of the loudest voices for gender equality in the Evangelical Christian tradition in the United States. Her blog and speaking engagements regularly attend to matters of sexism, misogyny, and discrimination in the church, which has made her the target of those who disagree with her. Helping to underscore many of the stories in #YesAllWomen, Held Evans and others who speak out on these issues have received death threats, rape threats, and a whole variety of other threats against their persons and bodies.

Some Main Themes and Methodologies

In the previous section, we considered some of the major concerns in feminist theology. Each of these concerns has been explored and developed by feminist theologians in different ways. Feminist theology can be thought of as having three major methodologies or approaches. In this section we will look at each of these approaches and some of the liberative themes important within each of these traditions.

Reformist or biblical feminist theologians accept the basic core tenets of traditional Christian teaching. They often use scripture or Jesus Christ as their point of departure to call for inclusive religious language and the just treatment of women in families, churches, and society. Because they test their theological thought against the Bible, this group of scholars is often called "biblical feminists." Biblical scholar Phyllis Trible uses the experience of women in the biblical text to offer a theological and literary account of the terror imposed on women to counter the **chauvinism** in Christian communities. She insists that stories of violence against women in the biblical text should not be ignored; rather, believers have the responsibility to study the stories to remember the victims, ask questions about why violence happens in the stories, and advocate for the end of such violence against women.

Chauvinism: The attitude that members of one's own sex are better than the opposite sex.

Trible and theologian Sallie McFague have used biblical texts to explore female divine metaphors and imagery as a critique of the sexist language used to talk about God. For example, McFague offers a theological exploration and recovery of the metaphor of God as mother in the biblical text. She advocates for the use of both father and mother language to talk about God in order to move beyond thinking about God as male or female without losing the androcentric metaphors and pronouns that provide theological truths about the divine.

Revisionist or reconstructivist feminists, often called "liberation feminist theologians," believe that the reformist approach does not go far enough and that other sources are needed outside of the biblical text. They believe that allowing women in the leadership of the church is an important goal but is not enough to provide justice for women. Feminists using this approach use their own and other women's experiences of God as a source in addition to sacred texts and theological writings. Using women's experiences is methodologically necessary in this approach, since sacred texts and theological writings have most often been written by men and reflect the patriarchy of their culture. Since revisionist feminists are concerned with particular experiences of women as a source for theology, they are equally concerned with liberative action resulting from their theological writings. They want concrete applications of their theological work that provide justice to the wrongs experienced by women.

Rosemary Radford Ruether is a leading revisionist feminist theologian. Ruether is a pioneer in feminist reinterpretations of Christian symbols. She draws from a variety of resources, including the recovery of understandings of the divine suppressed by Hebrew monotheism, to argue that God is found in the world, rather than the dominating God of the sky found in ancient Western religious systems, and is the source of the ongoing renewal of creation. This image of the divine is the basis for Ruether's call for liberative action to confront injustices against women and the earth. Carter Heyward is another example of this tradition. She is best known for her work on lesbian feminist Christology. Heyward's understanding of Christ is closely related to her understanding of God and the divine in all of us. Thus, one's understanding of God is found in one's relationships, and a fuller knowledge of God and Christ requires inclusive relationships with all humanity and creation.

It is important to note that these approaches are helpful in understanding the scope of liberative feminist theologies, but that they are not isolated from one another. Scholars often fall somewhere in between these approaches, move from one approach to another in their research trajectories, and are in conversation with scholars from approaches they do not use. Elisabeth Schüssler Fiorenza is an example of a scholar who falls in between the biblical and revisionist categories. She is a biblical scholar, like Trible, whose work explores theological themes and is widely influential among feminist theologians. Since she is a biblical scholar, the biblical text is her point of departure. However, she uses a variety of sources, such as the Sophia/wisdom tradition, when writing about Jesus. Mary Daly is an example of a scholar who started out as a revisionist feminist and became the leading rejectionist feminist in her later writings. We will turn to that approach next.

The rejectionist or radical feminist theology is the third major approach in feminist theology. Scholars using this approach are often considered post-Christian because they reject the church, Bible, and traditional Christian teachings as embedded in patriarchy and, therefore, unable to speak to or provide justice for women. Many of them were once a part of Christian churches but have rejected Christianity as patriarchal. Some of the scholars in this tradition opt for the **worship of goddess** instead.

Thealogy: The study of goddesses.

Mary Daly is a pioneer in feminist theology and the leading figure in rejectionist feminist theology. Her early works cite lengthy examples of patriarchy in her own tradition, Catholicism, and in religion in general, with the hope for liberative action within the context of religion. However, her later works reject Christianity because it is the result of patriarchy and, thus, cannot be separated from patriarchal oppression. She claimed that a male Christ cannot save women and labeled herself post-Christian. She advocated for women-centered culture and claimed that women should rule over men.

Carol P. Christ is another example of the rejectionist approach. She developed thealogy,

Sophia/Gaia: Feminist scholars often use feminine expressions of the divine to explore theological themes. Two of the most common in Christian feminist theology are Sophia and Gaia. Sophia is the personification of wisdom and is associated with divine wisdom in the biblical text. Gaia is the personification of the earth and is often used as a theological concept by feminists concerned with ecological justice.

Hampson/Ruether debate: In May 1986, Daphne Hampson and Rosemary Radford Ruether held a public discussion on the question "Is there a place for feminism in the Christian Church?" Hampson, who considers herself a post-Christian, answered no. Christianity, according to Hampson, cannot be moral because it is inherently sexist. She said that instead of wanting to change actors in a play, she wants a different kind of play. Ruether criticized Hampson for seeing Christianity as a closed system, set in the past. Ruether argues that revelation is not solely a past event and thus Christianity is open to development. Although Christianity has been expressed as a culture of denomination, it also includes deeply rooted themes of liberation. For Ruether, there is room for feminist liberation in the church in efforts for churches to become vehicles of hope that bring about a new human future.

Kyriarchy: Kyriarchy is a term coined by Elisabeth Schüssler Fiorenza to denote complex sys-

primarily based on Greek goddesses, as a way of finding new interpretations of history and culture outside of the patriarchal traditions. For Christ, the goddess provides the power of intelligent embodied love to understand one's place in the world and live ethically in it.

As demonstrated by the three methodologies and examples provided, feminist theology is a broad label for a variety of approaches addressing issues arising from patriarchy, sexism, and women's experience. Regardless of the approach taken, feminist theology attempts to make practical applications of theological questions that are liberative for women, men, institutions, and the earth.

Possible Future Trends

Recent political debates regarding the war on women and related issues around religion and the public sphere will ensure the need and relevance of feminist liberative theology. In the future, feminist theology will likely continue to develop by including more voices and a greater plurality. It will be more intentionally intersectional, meaning that it will examine how gender oppression intersects with race, class, ethnic, and postcolonial oppressions. Feminism needs to take seriously the critiques from people of color and postcolonial scholars. It is only through listening to a multiplicity of voices that white women can begin to see their own oppression and impositions in the name of feminism.

Along similar lines, liberative feminist theology will become more interreligious. For the past several decades, a number of Christian and Jewish feminist theologians have worked closely together, and we are beginning to see the inclusion of Muslim feminist voices in U.S. feminist theology. However, to remain relevant and to be mindful of the perils of a Euro-American and Christian dominance, feminist theology needs to include voices and insights from all religious and spiritual traditions.

In a world that considers labels such as post-modern, post-Christian, and post-secular, feminist theology, like all theology, will need to continue to consider the relevance of theological themes. Feminist theology, which has been concerned with practical applications since its earliest beginnings, will continue to develop theology in the context of current experiences. One example of this is developing a theology around issues of body image, self-understanding, and public perception of women.

Feminist theology is still needed in the world. The oppression of women is still present in homes, churches, and societies. Yet, feminist theology, as a truly liberative discourse and call to action in this world, has a future only when it is in conversation with other liberative theologies and when feminist theologians consider the experience of other oppressed groups, many of whom are represented in other chapters in this book. If feminist theologians fail to take these other experiences into account, it becomes a force of oppression through complicity and loses its future as a liberative theology. Feminist liberative theologians who consider the experiences of those affected by forms of oppression different from their own will be able to work more effectively toward a reimagined human future.

tems of domination and subordination. The word comes from the Greek words *kyrios*, meaning "lord," and *archia*, meaning "rule or government." It means the rule of the emperor/master/lord/father/husband over his subordinates. This word is used to recognize that there are multiple, intersecting forms of oppression in the world, not just the oppression of men over women.

Study Questions

1. If you were writing a book about feminist theologies, what kinds of stories would you choose to include? Why?
2. Which of the methodologies resonates with you? Why?
3. Which of the methodologies is the most difficult for you to accept? Why?
4. How would you respond to the question, "Is there a place for feminism in the church?"
5. What kinds of issues do you think feminist theologians should talk about that are not included in this chapter?

Suggested Reading

Christ, Carol P. *Odyssey with the Goddess: A Spiritual Quest in Crete.* New York: Continuum, 1995.

Christ, Carol P., and Judith Plaskow, eds. *Womanspirit Rising.* New York: Harper & Row, 1979.

Fulkerson, Mary McClintock. *Changing the Subject: Women's Discourses and Feminist Theology.* Minneapolis: Augsburg Fortress Press, 1994.

Fulkerson, Mary McClintock, and Sheila Briggs, eds. *The Oxford Handbook of Feminist Theology.* Oxford: Oxford University Press, 2011.

Hampson, Daphne, and Rosemary Radford Ruether. "Is There a Place for Feminists in a Christian Church?" *New Blackfriars* 68 (1987): 7-24.

Heyward, Carter. *Our Passion for Justice: Images of Power, Sexuality, and Liberation.* New York: Pilgrim Press, 1984.

Hopkins, Julie. *Toward a Feminist Christology: Jesus of Nazareth, European Women and the Christological Crisis.* London: Society for Promoting Christian Knowledge, 1995.

Isherwood, Lisa. *The Fat Jesus: Christianity and Body Image.* New York: Seabury, 2008.

Isherwood, Lisa, and Elizabeth Stuart. *Introducing Body Theology.* Sheffield: Sheffield Academic Press, 1998.

Johnson, Elizabeth A. *She Who Is: The Mystery of God in Feminist Theological Discourse.* New York: Crossroad Publishing Company, 2002.

Jones, Serene. *Feminist Theory and Christian Theology.* Minneapolis: Augsburg Fortress Press, 2000.

McFague, Sallie. *Models of God: Theology for an Ecological, Nuclear Age.* Philadelphia: Fortress Press, 1987.

Ruether, Rosemary Radford. *Sexism and God-Talk: Toward a Feminist Theology.* Boston: Beacon Press, 1993.

Russell, Letty. *Household of Freedom: Authority in Feminist Theology.* Philadelphia: Westminster Press, 1987.

———. *Human Liberation in a Feminist Perspective.* Philadelphia: Westminster Press, 1974.

Schüssler Fiorenza, Elisabeth. *In Memory of Her: A Feminist Theological Reconstruction of Christian Origins.* New York: Crossroad Publishing Company, 1994.

Stanton, Elizabeth Cady. *The Woman's Bible.* Mineola, NY: Dover Publications, 2010 [1895, 1898].

Tatum, Lucy. *Knowledge That Matters: A Feminist Theological Paradigm and Epistemology.* Sheffield: Sheffield Academic Press, 2002.

Trible, Phyllis. *Texts of Terror: Literary Feminist Readings of Biblical Narratives.* Minneapolis: Fortress Press, 1984.

10

Women of Color Liberative Theologies

Andrea Smith

The genealogy of women of color liberative theologies begins with a genealogy of the term "women of color" itself. Often, "women of color" is defined solely on the basis of identity: it is a category that includes African American, Native American, Arab American, Latinas and Asian American women. However, as Loretta Ross and Aurora Morales have noted, "women of color" is primarily a political category. Loretta Ross recounts the political history of the term "women of color." In 1977, a group of black women developed a Black Women's Agenda for the National Women's Conference, which had been funded by then President Jimmy Carter. This agenda was developed in response to a "Minority Women's Plank" that had been written by the white women's conference organizers. However, once the conference began, nonblack women with racial minority status wanted to join the effort. In response, the term "women of color" was developed through their negotiations. As Ross states, these women did not see "women of color" as a biological designation, "but it is a solidarity definition, a commitment to work in collaboration with other oppressed women of color who have been 'minoritized.'"

Aurora Morales similarly defines women of color: "This tribe called 'Women of Color' is not an ethnicity. It is one of the inventions of solidarity, an alliance, a political necessity that is not the given name of every female with dark skin and a colonized tongue, but rather a choice about how to resist and with whom." Thus, as her definition implies, not all women who are racially minoritized will identify as women of color. Women of color indicates a political identity chosen to act in solidarity with all women who have been racially minoritized.

With the rise of liberal multiculturalism, "women of color" is often extracted from its radical political history to connote a biologically designated melting pot of women of African American, Native American, Latina, Asian American and Arab American descent. Such deradicalized women of color projects focus a political of identity representation that do not necessarily

Postcolonialism: a term that is often meant to signify the end of formal colonialism. Consequently, there has been a reluctance by indigenous scholars in particular to engage postcolonial theory since indigenous nations are still undergoing active colonialism. In fact, this term comes from Frantz Fanon; it signifies the radical rupture in history created at the colonial moment. Thus the "post" signifies everything that happens in history after the colonial moment. This suggests that there is no return to a "precolonial" state. So, for instance, appeals within oppressed communities to go back to "traditional" ways are problematic in that the very understanding of tradition is unalterably shaped by current colonial conditions. Thus, postcolonialism signifies what the terrain of struggle looks like, knowing that we cannot pretend colonialism never happened.

challenge the logics of white supremacy, **settler colonialism,** and patriarchy. Women of color politics that are not radical tend to focus on representing the interest of their groups rather than dismantling systems of oppression that structure the world. It is in this context that women of color theologians have sought to remember this radical history by focusing on political praxis. Women of color politics does not necessarily dismiss identity, but structures inquiry around the logics of race, colonialism, capitalism, gender, and sexuality as they shape the world, not only for women of color but for everyone. As Robin D. Kelley stated about women of color politics in *Yo' Mama's Disfunktional!*: "A careful examination of the movements dismissed as particularistic shows that they are often 'radical Humanist' at their core and potentially emancipatory for all of us. We need to seriously rethink some of these movements, shifting our perspective from the margins to the center. We must look beyond wedge issues or 'minority issues' and begin to pay attention to what these movements are advocating, imagining, building. After all, the analysis, theories and visions . . . may just free us all" (124).

Settler Colonialism: Colonialism in which colonialists attempt not simply to control territory but to replace the indigenous population of that territory with the colonial population.

Thus, an account of women of color liberative theologies would not be an account of the separate trajectories of black feminist/womanist, Latina feminist/*mujerista,* native/indigenous, Asian American feminist theologies. Indeed there may be strands within each of these theologies that would not properly be called "women of color." For instance, many black and indigenous women of color reject the term because they do not think "women of color" addresses the specificities of **anti-blackness** or settler colonialism. Rather, women of color theology is an account of how these theologies intersect and what these intersections tell us about not just women of color but politics and theology as a whole. Thus in this section, I will not be detailing all the separate trajectories of identity-based theologies. Rather, I will focus on those theological strains that indicate a broader commitment to solidarity work across identity lines as they emerge from distinct trajectories. This is not to say that identity-specific theologies are not important. The term "women of color," again, is not a catch-all term that erases the specificity of black, Native, Latina, and Asian American histories. Rather it is a political complement to these histories that imagines theological and political politics that focus on how the distinct racialization of diverse women of color intersect to structure the world.

Anti-blackness: Signifies the fact that white supremacy does not operate just by positioning whiteness as superior to all those who are racialized, but by positioning blackness as inferior to all others from whom nonblack racialized groups will seek to distance themselves.

Just as "women of color" does not simply signify the aggregate of all women who have been racialized, the term also does not signify a simple politic of adding race to gender or vice versa. Rather, women of color analysis emerged out of the need to engage in what Kimberle Crenshaw would later describe as **intersectional** politics. As an example, women of color have been targeted by racist reproductive policies such as sterilization. Often, male-dominated racial-justice groups and white-dominated gender-justice groups have not organized around this issue. Since men were not being sterilized, they saw this issue as a gender issue that did not impact them, whereas white women, who were also not being sterilized, saw it as a racial issue that also did not impact them. As women of color were consistently marginalized from both racial- and gender-justice organizing, they began to articulate an intersectional analysis that would organize around how gender and racial oppression mutually enable each other.

Intersectionality is a term coined by Kimberle Crenshaw to mean that oppressions transform one another when they intersect. So, for instance, women of color do not simply face race and gender oppression, but their gender oppression is shaped by race, and their racial oppression is transformed by gender.

Furthermore, this intersectional analysis has political implications beyond that which impacts women of color specifically. An example of that can be seen in the rise of Incite! Women of Color against Violence as well as in other radical feminist of color antiviolence organizations. These organizations began not because women of color were often marginalized by mainstream antiviolence organizations but because their marginalization negatively impacted the politics of these organizations. In particular, women of color activists realized that they are just as impacted by state violence (in its many forms, such as border violence, the prison industrial complex, Native boarding schools, militarism, etc.) as they are by interpersonal gender violence. Thus, they needed a strategy for addressing state violence and interpersonal violence simultaneously. Mainstream antiviolence organizations by contrast worked primarily with the criminal justice system as the solution to gender violence without critiquing the violence of the criminal justice system itself. They invested in what is now described as a "carceral feminist" strategy. Victoria Law describes carceral feminism as "an approach that sees increased policing, prosecution, and imprisonment as the primary solution to violence against women." Carceral feminist strategies certainly negatively impact women of color, but they also negatively impact everyone because militarism, the prison industrial complex, and anti-immigration policies create a society that furthers violence against all. Thus, having an intersectional analysis as developed by women of color is politically transformative for all of society.

Liberative Theology in Action: The Issue of Gender Violence

Many feminist theologies have developed in reaction to gender violence. The epidemic of gender violence *within* faith communities has belied the promise that faith can create "safe" spaces from worldly oppression. However, the white-dominated feminist movement has often failed to address the reality of state-based racial violence in its strategies for ending gender violence. Communities of color are often portrayed by the media and political class as violent. Within the mainstream antiviolence movement in the United States, women of color who survive sexual or domestic abuse are often told that they must pit themselves against their communities to begin the healing process. Meanwhile, communities of color often advocate that women keep silent about sexual and domestic violence in order to maintain a united front against racism. Likewise, mainstream remedies for addressing sexual and domestic violence here in the United States have proven to be inadequate in general, but particularly for addressing violence against women of color. The problem is not simply an issue of providing multicultural services to survivors of violence. Gender violence has not simply been a tool of patriarchal control, but, in the days since Adam and Eve, has snowballed and served as a tool of structural racism itself, as well as of economic oppression and even colonialism. The implications are significant. Colonial relationships, as well as race and class relations, are themselves gendered and sexualized. Consider the history of sexual colonization of Native women, the sexual slavery of African American women, and the sexual exploitation of immigrant women's labor. As such, we must understand the state, then, rather than being the solution to ending violence against women as a primary perpetrator of violence. Consequently, strategies designed to combat sexual and domestic violence *within* our pews must be linked to strategies that combat violence directed *against* communities represented in our pews, including state violence (e.g., police brutality, prisons, militarism, racism, colonialism, and economic exploitation). To the extent that feminist movements within churches do address state violence, they often focus on state violence committed in other countries. To borrow from Gayatri Spivak, they concern themselves with saving brown women from brown men, without looking at the role of the U.S. imperial state in furthering violence globally. For instance, many feminist movements supported the U.S. war in Afghanistan in order to "save" women from the Taliban, without questioning why bombing women would somehow save them. Thus, theologies for ending gender violence cannot simply limit themselves either to solving intra-community by the state or to engaging in imperial ventures designed to save Third World women without centrally addressing the role of violence in constituting the U.S. state itself.

This impulse has also informed the various strands of women of color theologies. Women of color theologians have found that if you intersect race and gender, you transform the theological project. One such example would be the critique of **substitutory atonement** that is prevalent among many (although not shared by all) women of color theologians. This critique emerges from black feminist/womanist theologians who note the manner in which the suffering of black women becomes naturalized under patriarchal white supremacy. On the one hand, black women are to be the servants of white women. As Saidiya Hartman describes in *Scenes of Subjection*, in the afterlife of slavery,

Womanism: A term coined by Alice Walker in her book *In Search of Our Mother's Gardens.* It was later taken as a distinct theological formation that centered on the experiences of black women by scholars such as Delores Williams, Katie Cannon, Stacey Floyd-Thomas, Monica Coleman, and many others. Alice Walker defined womanism as follows: "1. From womanish. (Opp. of 'girlish,' i.e. frivolous, irresponsible, not serious.) A black feminist or feminist of color. From the black folk expression of mothers to female children, 'you acting womanish,' i.e., like a woman. Usually referring to outrageous, audacious, courageous or willful behavior. Wanting to know more and in greater depth than is considered 'good' for one. Interested in grown up doings. Acting grown up. Being grown up. Interchangeable with another black folk expression: 'You trying to be grown.' Responsible. In charge. Serious. 2. Also: A woman who loves other women, sexually and/or nonsexually. Appreciates and prefers women's culture, women's emotional flexibility (values tears as natural counterbalance of laughter), and women's strength. Sometimes loves individual men, sexually and/or nonsexually. Committed to survival and wholeness of entire people, male and female. Not a separatist, except periodically, for health. Traditionally a universalist, as in: 'Mama, why are we brown, pink, and yellow, and our cousins are white, beige

black women's suffering under racialized gender violence is completely illegible and unacknowledged. At the same time, black women are to remain silent in the face of violence *within* black communities in order to maintain a united front against racism. The simultaneous centrality and invisibility of black women's suffering was the focus of womanist theologian Emilie Townes's anthology *A Troubling in My Soul*. In this collection, Frances Wood notes that "Idealization and romanticization of Black women's suffering is as insidious a habit in the African-American community as it has been historically in the dominant society. Elevating women's suffering to a form of martyrdom for the cause (of others) virtually guarantees that it will remain unexamined" (39). She asks, "*Must women bear the yoke alone, and all the men go free?*" (46). Jacqueline Grant (also in this collection) concurs: "For women of color, the sin is not the lack of service, but too much service" (215). In this context, Delores Williams critiques the valorization of suffering by the idea of substitutory atonement. Beginning with the biblical story of Hagar in *Sisters in the Wilderness*, Williams argues that black women have historically been forced to play the role of the "surrogate" whereby they are forced to take on roles that belong to someone else (such as the role of the caretaker for white women's children). How can the doctrine that Jesus suffered for the well-being of others (essentially acting as the surrogate to be punished for the sins of others) be salvific when black women are always supposed to suffer for others? Joanne Terrell challenges Williams in *Power in the Blood?* by suggesting that while suffering should not be seen as redemptive, the cross can be a powerful sign that there can indeed be life and survival after death and suffering.

Substitutory atonement is a Christian doctrine that claims that humans required punishment from God because of the original sin of Adam and Eve and our own sinful nature, and that Jesus died on the cross in our stead, as a substitute for us.

and black?' Ans. 'Well, you know the colored race is just like a flower garden, with every color flower represented.' Traditionally capable, as in: 'Mama, I'm walking to Canada and I'm taking you and a bunch of other slaves with me.' Reply: 'It wouldn't be the first time.' 3. Loves music. Loves dance. Loves the moon. Loves the Spirit. Loves love and food and roundness. Loves struggle. Loves the Folk. Loves herself. Regardless. 4. Womanist is to feminist as purple is to lavender."

Similarly, Rita Nakashima Brock (with Rebecca Parker) elaborates on this critique by contending in *Saving Paradise* that the centrality of death found in substitutory atonement is not fundamental to Christianity—the centrality of the cross in Christian theology coincides with the rise of Christian conquest and imperialism. In particular, as Christianity embarked on the Crusades, the spread of Christianity became increasingly tied to the death of others that enabled the life of Christendom. The "life" of Christendom thrived through the mass extermination of indigenous peoples, Crusades against Muslim peoples, and the enslavement of Africans. The resurrection of Christ symbolizes the life of European Christianity at the expense of religious/racial others left at the cross.

This women of color theological engagement with substitutory atonement is an example of intersectional analysis. When one focuses on how the logics of race and gender intersect in the theological enterprise, one begins to more fundamentally challenge the theological assumptions undergirding that enterprise. Thus, a seemingly gender- and race-neutral concept such as substitutory atonement becomes revealed as a gendered and racial project from the perspective of women of color.

Thus, women-of color-theologies are not simply an add-on to male-dominated liberation theologies or white-dominated feminist theologies. They fundamentally challenge the presuppositions of both. For instance, Native feminist theologies challenge Native theologies by arguing that colonization is fundamentally gendered. My own work (as seen in *Conquest*) analyzes how colonization was effected through sexual violence. Sexual violence was a strategy by which Native bodies (both male and female) were rendered inherently rapable, and by extension their lands inherently open to invasion and their resources inherently extractable. Thus, it is not possible to

Decolonization: Native feminist theologies have focused primarily on decolonization as their framework of liberation. Waziyatawin and Michael Yellow Bird have contended that decolonization actually requires a dismantling of the current settler state and its economic system. In their book *For Indigenous Eyes Only,* they encourage critical thinking skills and community action. Decolonization is the intelligent, calculated, and active resistance to the forces of colonialism that perpetuate the subjugation and/or exploitation of minds, bodies, and lands, and it is engaged for the ultimate purpose of overturning the colonial structure and realizing indigenous liberation. But make no mistake: decolonization ultimately requires the overturning of the colonial structure. It is not about tweaking the existing colonial system to make it more indigenous friendly or a little less oppressive. The existing system is fundamentally and irreparably flawed. Other scholars have conceptualized decolonization less in terms of promoting radical changes to the current political and eco-

decolonize without addressing how gender violence enables settler colonialism. Meanwhile, it is also not possible to end gender violence without examining how the biggest perpetrator of gender violence is the state (as can be seen in the state's role in imposing gender violence in Native communities through state-mandated boarding schools and other policies). In the germinal collection on Asian and Asian American women's theology, *Off the Menu*, several authors in this collection point to how an intersecting analysis transforms theological paradigms. Jung Ha Kim notes that the concept of religion itself is often based on an orientalizing strategy by which Western religions define themselves over and against a mystified notion of Eastern spirituality. Kwok Pui Lan challenges the manner in which white feminist theologians appropriate romanticized notions of Eastern traditions without any in-depth engagement with their political, social, and historical context. Such appropriations then make invisible feminist movements *within* Asian religious/spiritual traditions. And Wonhee Anne Joh analyzes how racialization structures theological inquiry itself by positioning a white subject that is radically distant from and unconnected to other subjects in order to enable its claims to objective analysis.

In fact, Monica Coleman, building on the work of black womanist/feminist scholarship in her collection *Ain't I a Womanist Too?* proposes that womanist theology is a practice that is less about identity representation and more about a commitment to theological praxis that focuses on the intersections of deconstructing anti-black racism and patriarchy. "That is, a hallmark of third wave womanist religious thought is that it is more of an ideology politic, than an identity politic. . . . To put it more constructively, if womanist religious thought relinquishes a sense of ownership around membership identity and consciously notes the connections among white feminism, black feminisms, women of color feminisms, global and Third World feminisms, it has the potential to link to various types of struggles and form unlikely but fruitful alliances in pursuit of social transformation" (18). Similarly, Ada María Isasi-Díaz (with Eduardo Mendieta) note in the collection *Decolonizing Epistemologies* that Latino(a) theology requires more than the representation of Latinas within theology—it requires decolonizing Western epistemology itself. "To survive and thrive, we must decolonize ourselves. Our confrontation with the 'coloniality of power' . . . requires a relentless and ceaseless struggle to value our past as our peoples experienced it and not as the West has written it. . . . Our decolonizing enterprise to free subjugated knowledges is a creative process" (6). Stacey Floyd-Thomas, in *Deeper Shades of Purple*, contends that womanist theology is a revolutionary epistemological project that challenges the very basis by which we claim theological truth.

nomic system and more in terms of centering indigenous thought within Native studies. Linda Tuhiwai Smith says that decolonization "is about centering our concerns and world views and then coming to know and understand theory and research from our own perspectives and for our own purposes." Thus decolonization requires not just the dismantling of colonial structures but decolonizing the ideologies and theologies that shape what we think to be true.

Thus women of color theologies go beyond a simple identity politics, of which they are sometimes accused. Rather, they challenge how all identities (including normative white and male identities) are constructed through patriarchy and racialization. They seek less to be included in mainstream theologies and instead ask how theology has been developed through normative whiteness and maleness. And finally they ask, what would theology look like if it focused on the lives, histories, and experiences of women of color?

Need for Liberation

Women of color theologies develop not just out of the need to be liberated from the structures that oppress them but from the liberation struggles designed purportedly to free them. That is, women of color are often represented within racial- or gender-justice struggles that claim to fight for their liberation, and yet these movements continue to engage in practices or utilize frameworks that continue to oppress them. As Delores Williams argued in *Sisters in the Wilderness,* black theologies often romanticized a "black church" without regard for the gender violence and oppression faced by black women in the church. At the same time, a feminist theology must take into account the manner in which black women have been historically and continue today to be oppressed by other women. Similarly, given the context in which black women were slaves of white women and the fact that "emancipation meant slavery without chains" such that "the abolition of slavery left intact the basic relationship between Black women and White women," Jacqueline Grant argued in *White Women's Christ and Black Women's Jesus* that to talk of sisterhood between black and white women is a "crude joke" (196-97).

Thus, women of color theologies that reflected on how liberation struggles that claim to represent them have actually excluded them have generally called for a theological praxis that is directed to all structures of oppression. According to Katie Cannon in *Black Womanist Ethics*, "the cumulative effect of womanist scholarship is that it moves us toward a fundamental reconceptualization of all ethics with the experience of Black women at center stage" (305). Consequently, she charges womanist ethicists with the responsibility of challenging the traditional paradigms for understanding ethics that do not take into account race, class, and gender. Womanist ethics should also analyze how black women resist, survive, and sometimes are complicit in their own oppression. Analysis of the political and economic forces that undergird systemic oppression in this country is crucial for womanist theory. Similarly, Native feminist theology has called for the abolition of all forms of oppression, with a particular focus on the settler state and its attendant gender violence that oppresses not only indigenous peoples but everyone.

This commitment to ending all forms of oppression has contributed to a commitment to self-criticism: how do even women of color liberative theologies exclude and marginalize? For instance, Marcia Riggs's *Awake, Arise and Act* calls on black feminist/womanist theologians to be more attentive to class. She argues that it is not enough for middle-class black women to be concerned with the underclass. Rather, they must renounce privilege so that they can act in true partnership with the poor to achieve liberation. She states, "Renunciation might . . . mean re-organizing the structure of an institution to include those who have not traditionally held positions of power" (95).

Renee Hill and Kelly Brown Douglas have critiqued womanist theologians for their complicity in homophobia and heteronormativity. In *Sexuality and the Black Church,* Douglas describes homophobia as "a sin and betrayal of Black faith" (126). She contends that homophobia and a reluctance to address sexuality is the result of white supremacist assaults on black sexuality. Similarly, Chris Finley, in *Queer Indigenous Studies,* critiques Native feminists for their silence on sexuality and calls on them to "bring sexy back" to Native studies. She as well as many other scholars traces the imposition of a heteronormative, gender binary system in Native communities to settler colonialism. Kwok Pui Lan calls on women of color to "queer" theology itself—to assess how theology is itself constructed through heteronormativity.

In addition, many women of color scholars have critiqued women of color theologies for their Christian supremacism. Dianne Stewart, for instance, argues that Christianity must be recognized as an oppressing rather than a liberating religion. Native feminist scholars such as Paula Gunn Allen as well often reject Christianity as a colonial tradition, particularly given the way Christianization and missionization were used to instill patriarchy into Native communities. Similarly, Kwok Pui Lan calls on feminist theologians to more fully engage postcolonial theory in order to thoroughly assess the colonial and imperial assumptions that undergird even liberative Christian theological projects.

Thus, women of color theologies engage a praxis of liberation through self-reflection. They do not position women of color in the position of innocence from oppression. Frances Wood has argued that rather than see God as being on the side of the oppressed, we should see God as standing against oppression, no matter who commits it. Rita Nakashima Brock has similarly written that analysis of oppression should not presume innocence on the part of the oppressed.

> Moral high ground goes to innocent victims. There is danger, however, in this structure of morality and victims. If a victimized group can be proven to lack innocence, the implication is that the group no longer deserves justice. Any hint of moral ambiguity, or the possession of power and agency, throws a shadow across one's moral spotlight. Maintaining one's status as victim becomes crucial for being acknowledged and given credibility. This tendency to identify with innocent victims, and to avoid discussions of the moral ambiguities of life, continues to place responsibility for abuse on the victims of the system. Abuse is wrong not because victims are innocent, but because abuse, even by good people for a good cause, dehumanizes the abuser and abused. Hence, we need to focus not on innocence, but on what is wrong with abusive behavior. (*Violence against Women and Children: A Christian Theological Sourcebook*, 80-81)

Women of color theologies thus do not presume that women of color themselves are not complicit in oppression. Rather, they focus a women of color analytic as a means of examining intersecting forms of oppression in which all are complicit.

While women of color theologies strive for a holistic framework for liberation, certainly strands of these theologies have focused on particular structures of oppression. And, consequently, sometimes there are tensions among these strands. For instance, *mujerista*, or Latina feminist, theologies have often focused on the violence created by borders. This includes not only the

***Mujerista* theology:** A term coined by Ada María Isasi-Díaz. She defines a *mujerista* as a "Hispanic Woman who struggles to liberate herself not as an individual but as a member of a Hispanic community" (*En la Lucha*, 4). Isasi-Diaz's methodology was consistent with her community framework. She relied primarily on ethnography in order to discern the theological concerns of Latina/Hispanic women. *Mujerista* theology did not gain as wide circulation outside of the works of Isasi-Díaz as womanist theology did among African American women theologians. Michelle Gonzalez, for instance, uses that term solely to signify the work of Isasi-Díaz.

violence of a repressive U.S. immigration policy, but the identities created through the violence of the borders. Ada María Isasi-Díaz, in *En la Lucha*, describes *meztizaje* as resulting from the mixture of "religious traditions brought to Latin America and the Caribbean by African slaves, and the Amerindian traditions bequeathed by the great Aztec, Maya, and Inca civilizations, as well as other Amerindian cultures, such as Taino, Siboney, Caribe, Aruaucona. The mingling of sixteenth-century Spanish Catholicism with religious understandings and beliefs from the African and Amerindian religions in these religions is what has given birth to Latino popular religiosity" (47). Maria Pilar Aquino transcends borders in her formulation of Latina feminist theology. She does not draw a line between U.S. Latina and Latin American feminist theologies but suggests that such theologies should identify with social political movements for change on a hemispheric level.

Native feminist theologians, by contrast, have focused on the disappearance created by the settler states. Indigenous feminists tend to more specifically focus on the settler state; they are less likely to call for more democratic inclusion within U.S. polity since the very existence of the United States is dependent on the genocide of indigenous peoples. This focus on genocide has caught the attention of scholars such as Laura Donaldson and Ines Hernandez-Avila, who have critiqued *mestizaje* as a colonial discourse that positions indigenous identity as a primitive precursor to a more evolved *mestizo* identity. At the same time, Latina theologians have critiqued Native theologians for allowing the U.S./Mexico border to demarcate who is and who is not indigenous. Thus, indigenous peoples south of the border suddenly become Latinos rather than indigenous. Coya Hope Artichoker has made an internal critique of this phenomenon in a "Love Letter to Our Mestizo Brothers and Sisters," calling on indigenous peoples in the United States to stop allowing the U.S./Mexico border to define who is and who is not indigenous. Furthermore, as Leeanne Simpson argues in "I Am Not a Nation-State," an indigenous critique of settler colonialism goes beyond critiquing the United States to questioning the presumption that governance should happen through nation-states at all. This suggests that rather than vie for recognition from the nation-state, decolonization requires decolonizing our relationship to the land so that we do not see land as a commodity that can be bought, owned, and controlled by one group of people. If we decolonize our relationship to the land, we can completely recast the issue of immigration because the very term "immigrant" implies that someone only rightfully belongs in one place, and if she moves, she is now out of place and an immigrant.

Asian American feminist theologians have furthered this discussion on place by focusing on the centrality of U.S. imperialism, which makes militarized violence as something happening "over there" and hence not of concern to people in the United States. Kwok Pui Lan, in *Off the Menu*, argues that racism against Asian Americans in the United States cannot be analyzed separately from U.S. militarism and imperialism in Asia. She argues that Asian American feminist theologies "point to the necessity of a transnational analysis of the intersections of race, labor, state, and gender in the age of global capital" (5).

Womanist/black feminist theologians have also focused on what Saidiya Hartmann calls the fungibility of the black body. That is, anti-blackness is not simply about the valorization of whiteness but the positioning of blackness as the bottom of the racial hierarchy. This reality requires nonblack women of color to address their complicities in anti-blackness. This discussion can be seen over the discussion of the use of the term "womanist." The American Academy of Religion, for example, once organized a discussion on whether nonblack women of color could use the term "womanist," given its particular association with black women. On the one hand, Alice Walker's definition itself describes a womanist as a "Black feminist or a feminist of color." On the other hand, part of the legacy of anti-blackness is to position black peoples as property. The legacy of anti-black racism is that the black struggle gets deemed the property of all other social-justice struggles. The symbols and tactics of black struggle are deemed the common property of all. Black people are required to show solidarity with other oppressed communities, without other struggles owing solidarity to black communities. Black oppression is always analogized to other forms of oppression in a manner that hides black oppression itself. It is presumed that we already know everything about black oppression, so we can just use it as an empty signifier to explain other oppressions. In this light, Shawn Copeland disagrees that nonblack women of color should be able to use this term. Meanwhile, Monica Coleman has indicated that while she sees no need to police the term based on identity, the politics that should emerge from a "womanist" designation is a commitment to focusing on the experiences of black women in particular.

As I have argued elsewhere, white supremacy operates through multiple logics, such as anti-blackness, settler colonialism, and Orientalism. Thus, a women of color theological praxis requires us to dismantle patriarchal white supremacy in all of its forms. At the same time, since one of the ways white supremacy operates is not only to oppress us but to render us complicit in other logics that support white supremacy, it is not surprising that there would be conflicts, tensions, and disagreements among women of color. The women of color liberative theological project, then, does not presume homogeneity or solidarity among women of color, but a political commitment to working through complicity, disagreements, and tensions in order to build solidarity.

Basic Tenets and Methodologies

Because women of color liberative theologies are diverse and contingent, there are innumerable tenets and methodologies that emerge from them. It is not possible to give an exhaustive account. But I will explore a few as a way to illustrate ways women of color liberative theologies engage with one another.

Relationship to Feminism

Despite the fact that women of color theologies focus on patriarchy (both as imposed by white supremacist structures and as internalized in communities of color), they have maintained a critical distance from white feminism. Whereas many strands of white feminism have insisted that "sisterhood is global," women of color have instead insisted that white supremacy and settler colonialism prevent any true sisterhood between white women and women of color. This, of course, is not to argue that white women do not face gender oppression, but they do not face it in the same way because gender violence is also racialized. For instance, as Andrea Richie notes in her study of police violence against women of color, black women are much more likely to be beaten by the police because they are not seen as "real" women. Thus, it is not a surprise that black feminist theologians have often eschewed the term "feminist" in favor of the term "womanist," as coined by Alice Walker. Such a term allows them to claim a politic opposed to patriarchy without joining these politics to white feminism. For similar reasons, Ada María Isasi-Díaz adopted the term *mujerista* theology to signify a Latina feminist theology.

Unlike womanist and *mujerista* theologians, who have attempted to distance themselves from the term "feminist," many Latina feminist theologies have consciously adopted the term. María Pilar Aquino, Daisy L. Machado, and Jeanette Rodríguez Holguín argue in *A Reader in Latina Feminism: Religion and Justice* that while they recognize the contribution of *mujerista* theology, they prefer the term "feminist" because of its connection to feminist social movements. Similarly, many contemporary Native feminists have claimed the term "feminist" "without apology." Previously, many Native women writers eschewed the term "feminist." One of the most prominent writings on Native American women and feminism is Annette Jaimes Guerrero's early 1990s article "American Indian Women: At the Center of Indigenous Resistance in North America." Here she argues that Native women activists, except for those who are "assimilated," do not consider themselves feminists. Feminism, according to Jaimes, is an imperial project that assumes the givenness of the U.S. colonial stranglehold on indigenous nations. Thus, to support sovereignty, Native women activists reject feminist politics. While many still have this understanding, increasingly more are rejecting the idea that feminism is white and, in fact, argue that feminism is an indigenous concept that white women appropriated from indigenous women. Consequently, there is a growing grassroots indigenous feminist movement that is the foundation for an indigenous feminist politic. Thus, the issue for Native feminist theologians is less around the term "feminist" than it is around the term "theologian." Since most indigenous feminists tend to not identify as Christian, they often do not identify with the term "theologian."

Relationship to Tradition, Culture, and Community

While women of color theologies retain a critical distance to white feminism, they are also critical of the sexism within their own communities. Thus, on the one hand, they look to the traditions and resources within communities of color as a source for liberation, but, on the other hand, they critique how these traditions can be used to support gender oppression.

Within Native feminist theologies, Native traditions are often seen as a source of liberation because they are often not understood to be patriarchal. Many (although not all) Native feminists argue that patriarchy is a colonial imposition. Given the genocidal conditions under which Native peoples live, it is understandable that recovering and remembering tradition plays a significant role in liberative theologies. Nonetheless, Native feminists do critique the politics by which traditions are remembered. For instance, Navajo scholar Jennifer Denetdale's work deconstructs tradition as an origin story, going so far as to argue that Native communities reproduce a **heteronormative**, Christian Right agenda in the name of "tradition." Jennifer Denetdale critically interrogates the gendered politics of remembering "tradition" in her germinal analysis of the office of Miss Navajo Nation. Denetdale notes that this office is strictly monitored by the Navajo nation to ensure that Miss Navajo models "'traditional' Navajo women's purity, mothering and nurturing qualities, and morality [which] are evoked by the Navajo nation to extol Navajo honor and are claimed on behalf of the modernizing project of nationalism." Denetdale notes than "when Miss Navajo Nation does not conform to the dictates of ideal Navajo womanhood, she is subjected to harsh criticism intended to reinforce cultural boundaries. Her body literally becomes a site of surveillance that symbolically conveys notions about racial purity, morality, and chastity."

Heteronormative: The assumption that heterosexuality and its related institutions (such as marriage) is or should be socially normative. One can be heteronormative without being homophobic (fear of or hate for people who identify as lesbian or gay).

Meanwhile male leaders who may be guilty of everything from domestic violence to embezzlement are rarely brought before any tribal committees. Denetdale argues that the ideals that Navajo women are supposed to represent are not simply "traditional" Navajo values but also unacknowledged European Victorian ideals of womanhood. Meanwhile, Lee Maracle contends that "tradition" is itself not a Native tradition. She argues that Native communities have always changed and evolved based on changing circumstances. It is only colonialism that views tradition stopping at 1492 and sees any changes to it now making Native peoples less authentic. And Emma Larocque has argued that traditions should be analyzed from a feminist analytic. Not all traditions are good, and we should abandon the ones that are oppressive.

Within womanist theology, scholars such as Delores Williams focus less on indigenous African traditions, whereas others such as Dianne Stewart contend that it is important to have a less Christian-centric perspective with regard to tradition. For instance, Williams only briefly mentions African influences on black slaves' interpretations of both the Bible and the new culture they found themselves in. She warns womanists not to romanticize their African heritage, thus suggesting that it has limited value as a resource for womanist theology. Dianne Stewart, by contrast, argues in *Three Eyes for the Journey* that womanist theology is limited by its Christocentrism and engages African indigenous traditions only to the extent that they are recognizable within Christian forms. She calls for a theological approach that recognizes Christianity as an oppressor tradition and that views African indigenous traditions as the foundation for liberative theology.

In a more general way, Isasi-Díaz affirms "popular" religion and decries those who see the indigenous and African roots of popular religion as pagan. "Mujerista theology," she notes in *En la Lucha*, "does not shrink from claiming that the fusion of Christian, Amerindian, and African religious strands operative in the lives of Latinas may be good and life-giving" (50). She notes that the syncretism of Greek and Christian thought in the dominant Christian tradition is considered acceptable, even canonical, while the syncretism practiced by Latinos is deemed "pagan"; white Christians tend to decry syncretism only when the hegemony of Christianity's European and classical roots are at stake. Isasi-Díaz continues by stating, "The imperialistic attitude on the part of 'official' churches, particularly vis-à-vis the Amerindian and African strands in popular religiosity, is anticultural, and in this case, anti-Latino" (51). Even so, Isasi-Díaz never mentions specific indigenous traditions; even while maintaining the necessity of criticizing the elements of popular religiosity that may be oppressive to Latinas, she never identifies the particular indigenous or African traditions to which she refers. Chung Hyun Kyung develops this multireligious focus further, identifying herself as both a practicing Christian and a Buddhist and rejecting theological boundaries of religious orthodoxy. Her 1996 address to the World Council of Churches sparked controversy among many conservatives because they claimed she was eroding the theological boundaries of Christianity. Her response was that mainstream Christianity is already syncretic because it has absorbed customs of European traditions. It is only when Christianity intermixes with non-Western traditions that the fear of syncretism arises.

Representation

Another issue related to theological representation and methodology has to do with their foundations. When we make claims about the theological concerns of our communities, what is the basis of our knowledge? Women of color liberative theologians often focus on the experiences of women as a starting point for theology, but here a host of methodological questions arise: Whose experiences are being represented, and by whom? What counts as "accurate" representation? How does the theologian claim to "know" the experience of the collectivity, and what authorizes her to be its voice? *Mujerista* theologian Ada María Isasi-Díaz calls on theologians to account for their methods: Are they rooted in the day-to-day experiences of the people they write about? She writes in *En la Lucha*, "Often we have seen the experiences of other marginalized groups, including Hispanics . . . used as examples to illumine answers to questions determined by those who control the systems, while never allowing the marginalized groups to post the question. . . . *Mujerista* theologians discovered that we needed the voices of Hispanic women themselves to be present in the theological discourse" (63). As the proliferation of black, womanist, *mujerista*, Latina feminist, Asian, etc., theologies indicate, liberation theologians in the United States have often relied on a politics of representation. That is, these theologies seek to represent the theological concerns of the communities from which theologians emerge. As Kwok Pui Lan argues, this strategy is not without its merits in a context where peoples from oppressed communities are denied a voice within mainstream theological discourse. Unfortunately, however, this representational strategy can in turn lend itself to totalizing and essentializing discourses about the communities theologians seek to represent. As Namsoon Kang argues, this "trap of essentialized identity" discursively restricts our political imagination. This politics of recognition does not allow us to look at tensions and oppressive dynamics within communities, particularly homophobia, sexism, ableism, and class oppression. We also often create litmus tests for cultural authenticity that restrict the kinds of intellectual and political creativity we need to challenge the status quo.

At the same time, as queer of color scholars such as Hiram Perez and Jasbir Puar have noted, the claim to go beyond "identity" often results in the disavowal of white identity politics. Within that context, Monica Coleman, as noted previously, calls for a womanist theology that focuses on black women's experience without rigidly guarding who can produce womanist theology. Ada María Isasi-Díaz has similarly argued in *Mujerista Theology* that *mujerista* theology is not a theology just for Latinas, but a theology rooted in the experiences and analyses of Latinas that have implications for all those who engage in liberative theologies.

Sources of Theology

Thus, given these issues of representation, women of color theologians have had to wrestle with identifying the sources of theology. How do we engage broader communities in the production of theology? The methodology of Chung Hyun Kyung provides some insights into uncovering the political voices of indigenous women. Chung looks to Asian women's activism and storytelling—and not just to their Bible stories—as resources for theology. She argues that liberation theologians must engage in, and that their work must reflect, their communities' struggles so that as the gap between religion and politics closes, "the community becomes the theologian." In Chung's estimation, "Doctrinal purity or religious boundaries [are] not of concern. . . . What matter[s] [is] the life-giving power of justice in whatever form it comes."

The methodologies of both womanist and *mujerista* theologians offer possibilities for uncovering Native women's perspectives on spirituality and liberation. As a matter of principle, feminist theologians focus on the experiences of women as a starting point for theology, but here a host of methodological questions arise: Whose experiences are being represented, and by whom? What counts as "accurate" representation? How does the theologian claim to "know" the experience of the collectivity, and what authorizes her to be its voice? In a yet unpublished paper, womanist theologian Dianne Stewart pointedly asks, "How can womanist theologians actually develop a theology that will be informed by, and synthesized with, the religious life of ordinary black women who never read books published by Orbis [Books] and other elite publishing houses?" Consequently, women of color liberative theologies are often creative and flexible in identifying their theological resources.

Many black feminist/womanist and Latina feminist/*mujerista* theologians use stories to represent black and Latina women's voices. Because slaves were not allowed to read the Bible and learned it by word of mouth, black communities have tended to experience the Bible through the flexibility of an oral/aural culture. According to Renita Weems, the protean nature of oral tradition has given black communities the freedom to modify and retell stories from the Bible to suit their changing needs. Williams, for example, uses this freedom to tell the story of Hagar in a manner she thinks will speak to African American women today. But storytelling is not limited to biblical stories. M. Shawn Copeland uses slave narratives to analyze black women's experiences of suffering. In *Black Womanist Ethics*, Katie Cannon claims that black women's literature as a mode of ethical instruction and cultural dissemination provides a crucial link to the oral traditions of the past. She writes, "This literary tradition is the nexus between the real-lived texture of Black life and the oral-aural cultural values implicitly passed on and received from one generation to the next" (5). Gloria Ines Loya similarly describes the literature, music, and art of Latinas as a source for theology, "a mirror of the lived experience of women."

Like African American culture, Native cultures are orally based. Consequently, storytelling is a critical resource for uncovering Native women's experiences. The burgeoning literary tradition of Native women provides a window into how story maintains community. Such literature is generally more accessible and more likely to be written with Native people in mind, unlike theological texts, which are written for a non-Native audience. Consequently, I will look to Native women's literature as well as to the more academic writings of Native women as a resource.

Of course, using storytelling and literature as theological resources does not answer Dianne Stewart's problem with the inaccessibility of Orbis Books to a larger audience. Instead, it raises yet another question about the politics of method. At what point does using literature as a representation of "authentic voices" from the community become a way of ignoring actual people? Isasi-Díaz uses meta-ethnography as a way of including women at a grassroots level in the development of *mujerista* theology. She interviews Latina women from different communities in the United States about their lives and their spiritual practices, and then draws from her interviews generative themes for *mujerista* theology. In this way Isasi-Díaz hopes to undermine the division between theology done in academic circles and that done on the grassroots level. Similarly, Stewart insists that womanist theologians remain connected to the everyday experiences of black women. She writes, "If womanist theologians are committed to understanding and analyzing black women's social and religious experiences, we cannot talk about black women without talking *with* black women." I contend that the limitation of such ethnographies is that most people in communities of color are not actually engaged in the struggle for liberation. Thus it makes sense to do ethnographic work with those who are seeking liberation and to learn from the theologies that emerge from these contexts (even as they may not be formally called "theology").

As mentioned previously, since so few Native feminists identify as theologians, it becomes necessary not only to question what we can identify as theological resources but also to determine who is a theologian. Thus, while there is a shortage of Native feminist theologians, there is not a shortage of Native women who engage in a praxis of liberation from a spiritually grounded framework. Native women involved in liberation struggles often do so from a sense of divine purpose. Whether or not they call themselves Christian, they *are* theologizing because they are articulating what they perceive to be the relationship between spirituality, liberation, and the vision of the world they hope to cocreate. Their theologies may not be concerned with definitive statements about faith and belief, but rather with exploring the *possibilities* about thinking about spirituality in light of our current political context. If we expand our understanding of theology beyond that of an academic discipline, then we can identify some of the theoretical and methodological considerations for developing women of color liberative theologies both inside and outside academia.

Healing and Creativity

As Ada María Isasi-Díaz notes, it is important to articulate not only what we are fighting against but also what are we fighting for. Thus, liberative theologies are not only about critiquing systems of oppression but also about articulating the vision of what liberation may actually look like. For instance, Emilie Townes's collection focuses on hope and transformation because "evil and suffering should never be our last and only word about the nature of humanity and the way in which the divine works in our lives" (xi). She notes that given the manner in which black life is always depicted in mainstream society as grim and hopeless, it is critical to transform the conditions of blackness theology through visions of possibility.

Native feminist theologies are informed by indigenous resistance movements that are about making power. That is, on the one hand, it is necessary to engage in politics that are opposed to corporate and state power (taking power). On the other hand, if we engage only in the politics of taking power, we will replicate the hierarchical structures in our movements. Consequently, it is also important to "make power" by creating those structures within our organizations, movements, and communities that model the world we are trying to create. These "autonomous zones" can be differentiated from the projects of many groups in the United States that often try to create separatist communities based on egalitarian ideals, because people in these "making power" movements do not just create autonomous zones, but they *proliferate* them. The idea is to start building the world we want that will eventually squeeze out the world we live in. Even if the system collapsed today, would we have something better with which to replace it? This emphasis on building the world we want is informed by indigenous spiritual practices that are what Manu Myer calls a "radical remembering of the future."

Native ceremonies can be a place where the present, past, and future become co-present. Native communities prior to colonization were not structured on the basis of hierarchy, oppression, or patriarchy. We will not re-create these communities as they existed prior to colonization because Native nations are and always have been nations that change and adapt to the surrounding circumstances. However, our understanding that it was possible to order society without structures of oppression in the past tells us that our current political and economic system is anything but natural and inevitable. If we lived differently before, we can live differently in the future. Similarly, Cheryl Kirk-Duggan demonstrates the importance of what she calls "black aesthetics," rooted in beauty and joy as a way not only to "exorcise evil" but to celebrate black life. And Michelle Gonzalez calls for the recentering of theological aesthetics from the perspective of the oppressed. She argues against the assumption that a focus on beauty distracts from the struggle to analyze beauty within the context of struggle. She notes, "In the encounter with Beauty, there is the experience of the Divine."

There are innumerable themes within women of color liberative theologies. In fact, the impulse within these theologies is not to assert rigid and dogmatic boundaries around what constitutes women of color theology but to make even the definition itself something to contest and with which to engage. Thus, this discussion should not be seen as any definitive account of women of color liberative theologies but as an invitation to join the discussion.

Study Questions

1. If one bases theology on the experiences and oppression faced by women of color, how would our theologies change?
2. What is the importance of identity in theological reflection?

3. How does one develop a liberative theology from Christianity, given Christianity's complicity in the oppression of many peoples?
4. How are women of color liberative theologies distinct from white feminist theology or male-dominated theologies emerging from communities of color?
5. Does the term "women of color" homogenize and erase the distinct histories and specificities of racial/gender oppression? What is the value (if any) of "women of color" as a political category?

Suggested Reading

Allen, Paula Gunn. *The Sacred Hoop.* Boston: Beacon Press, 1992.

Aquino, María Pilar, Daisy L. Machado, and Jeanette Rodríguez Holguín, eds. *A Reader in Latina Feminism: Religion and Justice.* Austin: University of Texas Press, 2002.

Brock, Rita Nakashima. "Ending Innocence and Nurturing Wilfulness." In *Violence against Women and Children: A Christian Theological Sourcebook,* edited by Carole J. Adams and Marie M. Fortune. New York: Continuum, 1995.

Brock, Rita Nakashima, et al., eds. *Off the Menu.* Louisville, KY: Westminster John Knox Press, 2007.

Brock, Rita Nakashima, and Rebecca Parker. *Saving Paradise.* Boston: Beacon Press, 2008.

Cannon, Katie, *Black Womanist Ethics.* Atlanta: Scholars Press, 2006 [1988].

Coleman, Monica, ed. *Ain't I a Womanist Too?* Minneapolis: Fortress Press, 2013.

Crenshaw, Kimberle. "Mapping the Margins: Intersectionality, Identity Politics, and Violence against Women of Color." In *Critical Race Theory,* edited by Kimberle Crenshaw, Neil Gotanda, Gary Peller, and Kendall Thomas, 357-83. New York: New Press, 1996.

Douglas, Kelly Brown. *Sexuality and the Black Church: A Womanist Perspective.* Maryknoll, NY: Orbis Books, 1999.

Floyd-Thomas, Stacey, ed. *Deeper Shades of Purple: Womanism in Religion and Society.* New York: New York University Press, 2006.

Isasi-Díaz, Ada María. *En la Lucha.* Minneapolis: Augsburg, 1993.

———. *Mujerista Theology.* Maryknoll, NY: Orbis Books, 1996.

———, and Eduardo Mendieta. *Decolonizing Epistemologies.* New York: Fordham University Press, 2012.

Gonzales, Michelle. *Sor Juana.* Maryknoll, NY: Orbis Books, 2003.

Grant, Jacqueline. *White Women's Christ and Black Women's Jesus.* Atlanta: Scholars Press, 1989.

Hartman, Saidiya. *Scenes of Subjection*. Oxford: Oxford University Press, 1997.

Kang, Namsoon, "Who/What Is Asian?" In *Postcolonial Theologies*, edited by Catherine Keller, Michael Nasuner, and Mayra Rivera, 100-117. St. Louis: Chalice, 2004.

Kelley, Robin D. G. *Yo' Mama's Disfunktional!: Fighting the Culture Wars in Urban America*. Boston: Beacon Press, 1997.

Kirk-Duggan, Cheryl. *Exorcising Evil*. Maryknoll, NY: Orbis Books, 1987.

Kwok Pui Lan. *Postcolonial Imagination and Feminist Theology*. Louisville, KY: Westminster John Knox Press, 2005.

Maracle, Lee. *I Am Woman*. Richmond, BC: Raincoast Books, 2002.

Riggs, Marcia Y. *Awake, Arise, and Act: A Womanist Call for Black Liberation*. Cleveland: Pilgrim Press, 1994.

Smith, Andrea. *Conquest*. Cambridge, MA: South End Press, 2005.

———. "Dismantling the Master's Tools with the Master's House: Native Feminist Liberation Theologies." In *Hope Abundant*, edited by Kwok Pui Lan, 72-86. Maryknoll, NY: Orbis Books, 2010.

Stewart, Dianne. *Three Eyes for the Journey*. Oxford: Oxford University Press, 2005.

Terrell, Joanne Marie. *Power in the Blood?* Maryknoll, NY: Orbis Books, 1998.

Townes, Emilie, ed. *Embracing the Spirit*. Maryknoll, NY: Orbis Books, 1997.

———, ed. *A Troubling in My Soul*. Maryknoll, NY: Orbis Books, 1993.

Weems, Renita. *Just a Sister Away*. New York: Warner Books, 1988.

———. "Reading Her Way through the Struggle: African-American Women and the Bible." In *Stony the Road We Trod*, edited by Cain Hope Felder, 57-77. Minneapolis: Augsburg, 1991.

Williams, Delores. *Sisters in the Wilderness*. Maryknoll, NY: Orbis Books, 1994.

11

Queer Liberative Theologies

Hugo Córdova Quero

What does "liberation" mean to queer individuals and communities? How do Christian traditions relate to queer issues and queer believers? This chapter focuses on the emergence of queer liberative theologies, mainly in the Anglo-speaking world, while taking into account issues of geographic location, ethnicity, and cultures that shape the development of these theologies worldwide. However, the complexity of the issues addressed extend beyond this chapter.

Basic Tenets

Queer theologies are intimately connected with queer theory, especially drawing from the works of Judith Butler, Michel Foucault, and Eve Kosofsky Sedgwick, among others. It is from that theory that these theologies draw many insights. At the same time, queer theologies are heir of previous homosexual and gay/LGBTI theologies that emerged in the last seventy years. This heritage is expressed by extending some of the topics discussed by those theologies and by making explicit critiques of them.

According to Annamarie Jagose, the term "queer," originally a degrading word, was recovered in the 1990s as a word of resistance to distort the order of traditional heteropatriarchal dictum. For "queer theory," a term coined by Teresa de Lauretis in 1991, categories of gender identities are multiple and constantly changing in order to reflect the multiple realities that individuals and communities face in our ever-evolving world. Queer theory comprises issues of sexual orientation, bodies, self-identification, and politics.

The term "queer" disrupts the binary "hetero/homo" terminology that marked lesbian and gay movements in the decades of the 1970s and 1980s. The term implies a break with the heteropatriarchal logic that at times seemed to coopt and dominate the struggles and activism of the gay and lesbian movements. This cooptation was observed in the collective treatment of gay and lesbian, bisexual, transgender, intersex, double-spirit, **polyamorous, polygamous,** and like people. For many gay and lesbian people in those days, it was very difficult to recognize, for example, bisexuality as an expression of sexuality. Instead, bisexuality was understood as a "confusion." The term "queer" is preferred to designate these emerging sexual theologies.

To say that someone does queer theology in our times means explicitly to recognize that there are multiple ways in which sexuality is expressed beyond the heteropatriarchal dichotomy "hetero/homo" and that this reflects both the images of the divine as well as the possibilities of expressing gender and sexuality within the diverse array of faith-based communities. Gender and sexuality have been present in theological discourses since the very beginning of Christianity, especially from its Jewish theological heritage. The images of the divine and of humankind in both sacred texts (Hebrew Bible as well as the Christian Scriptures) are tied to sexual and gender elements, such as "God the Father" or the "Virgin Mary." However, to talk about sexuality from a theological point of view entails interrogating how gender-role expectations, the sexual division of labor, the formation of couples and families, the concept of marriage and the performativity of affection, intimacy, and eroticism are produced within the context of each culture and determined beyond a heteropatriarchal hegemony.

Polyamory: The term "polyamory" relates to the fact that one person can love multiple individuals at the same time. The term comes from the joining of two words in different languages. "Poly" comes from the Greek *polus*, which means "multiple," "many," "several"; and "amory" comes from the Latin word *amare*, which is one of the terms for "to love." ***Polygamy:*** The term "polygamy" comes from the Greek *polus gamos*, which means "multiple" or "many" "marriages." It is used to designate a male or a female individual who maintains simultaneous committed relations with different individuals. Traditionally it has been the case of a male who maintains a family unity with two or more females. Females with multiple male spouses have been rare.

On the other hand, to do queer theology in the global context entails that one (re)considers how diversity and transnational movements further complicate those elements in the life of queer individuals and communities regarding race/ethnicity, culture, geographical location, and societal expectations. Queer theologies through these ideas give birth to new ways of thinking and acting theologically that highlight the reality of individuals as receivers of God's love—in other words, to honor all people with their sexual stories, their hopes and their dreams, without disregarding their gender and their sexual identities. These experiences allow us to relate to bodies, senses, and daily experiences as places for divine empowerment. At the same time, queer theologies take into account that daily lived experiences are important and that all individuals are shaped by their culture, their ethnicity, and their various experiences of the divine, and that at those intersections lie the richness and complexity of being human.

History

Many scholars, especially Robert Shore-Goss and André Sidnei Musskopf, divide the history of queer liberative theologies in three stages while recognizing that there are overlaps and continuities in these three phases. The *first stage* encloses *homosexual theologies* that arose around the 1950s. These theologies were apologetic, that is, their purpose was to defend and justify the presence of homosexual individuals within the Christian faith. We need to remember that the term "homosexual" was a product of the medicalization of homoerotic practices into the conformation of a subject and a population in the eighteenth and nineteenth centuries. In the Middle Ages, the construction of the notion of "sodomy" was understood as just a practice deviating from heterosexual norms. However, as Foucault states, "The nineteenth-century homosexual became a personage, a past, a case history, and a childhood, in addition to being a type of life, a life form, and a morphology. . . . [While] the sodomite had been a temporary aberration; the homosexual was now a species." Homosexual theologies took on the task of demanding from the Christian churches the same things that homosexual and homophile groups were demanding in European and North American societies: their inclusion while eliminating the criminalization and the persecution they were suffering. Therefore, as Musskopf affirms, these theologies were a religious discourse "about" homosexuality that challenged heteronormative readings of the sacred texts.

The *second stage* is related to the events in the 1960s, with the many emphases on liberation movements, such as the French "May of 1968" or the revolutionary movements in Third World countries, which influenced the development of an emphasis on liberation within the emerging gay communities in the 1970s, especially after the events of Stonewall in New York in 1969. Therefore, theologians also began to seek liberation within the confines of the Christian churches. The emergence of alliances with feminist movements gave birth to new sexual theologies that Musskopf and Shore-Goss call *gay theologies*. These theologies were also partly influenced by Latin American liberation theology. The emphasis of gay theologies was not only to challenge the heteronormative readings of the sacred texts—a continuity with homosexual theologies—but also to discover the voices of gay individuals within the long history of Christianity while signaling the oppressive mark that these gay individuals have suffered along that history until our present times.

Their emphasis was defined by the emergence of identity politics, as these theologies adopted the acronym LGBTI for the inclusion of lesbian, gay, bisexual, **transgender**, and intersex identities. Prominent academic works such as John Boswell's *Christianity, Social Tolerance, and Homosexuality* (1980) and the work of Gary David Comstock, *Gay Theology without Apology* (1987), give indications that the apologetic tone of the homosexual theologies was being replaced by a more upfront tone in the emerging gay/LGBTI theologies. At the same time, gay theologies took the task of reevaluating the doctrinal aspects of Christianity from a gay perspective.

Transgender: Those who transition from one side of the spectrum to the other (from male to female or from female to male) are called transgender. Of course, transitions can take multiple roads and not necessarily lead to fully embracing either end of the heteronormative binary.

The *third stage* involves the development of *queer theologies*, which in many ways mark a break with previous homosexual and gay/LGBTI theologies. Queer theologies follow the new understanding of activism and alliances among the many sexual groups that arose at the end of the 1980s. The most important distinction is the destabilization of the identity politics promoted by LGBTI movements with their concomitant assimilationism. Many activists understood that the identity-politics movement represented by the terms "gay" and "lesbian" was closely associated with the white middle class, while other ethnic/social groups were not represented by them. Queer movements emphasized the connection among all the nonheteronormative sexualities. Concurrently, queer theologies developed a similar tone. If for homosexual and gay/LGBTI theologies the basic assumption was to be assimilated to the mainstream of Christianity, for queer theologies the task was to challenge the assumption that Christianity has a right to even question the religious experience of queer individuals and communities. Rather than seeking legitimation, and therefore acceptance, queer liberative theologians have emphasized the diversity of humanity and the oppressive devices enacted by mainstream heteronormative theologies to keep their privilege over other sexually diverse groups.

A *fourth stage* should be added to that periodization, namely, the process at the turn of the new century of queer theologies developing in further connection to racial/ethnic, social, and geographic locations. These elements are important because they condition and structure the possibilities for ethnic and regional queer theologies to emerge. In societies that are highly racialized such as the United States, ethnic dynamics and power mechanisms confront queer individuals and communities not only from the dominant and hegemonic ethnic group—Caucasians—but also from the ethnic communities in which heteronormative conceptions of gender and sexuality have been ingrained for decades. However, it should be said that categories of ethnicity, nationality, race, and social class are contextual and depend on particular situations and societal expectations. Therefore, talking about "ethnic queer theologies" in the context of the United States is not only different from addressing queer theologies in other geographical locations, but also from addressing each ethnic community that bears the marks of its own history. On the other hand, regional queer theologies in Africa, Asia, and Latin America represent the latest stage in the history of these theologies together with Asian American, African American, Latina/o, and Native (North) American queer theologies.

Need for Liberation

Emerging from contexts of religious and theological oppression, queer theologies accompany the journey of queer believers amidst their self-understanding of faith experiences and in the process of subverting the institutional order of Christian denominations. Queer theologies constantly address two aspects in order to dismantle the oppression by Christian denominations: (1) the embedded heteropatriarchal ideology that permeates the interpretation of sacred texts, dogmatic beliefs, and religious practices; and (2) the construction and control of bodies, gender, and sexuality. Both issues are interrelated.

With the aid of queer theory, queer theologies show not only that bodies, sexualities, sexual orientations, and the performances of gender have all been colonized by heteropatriarchalism but also that the legitimation to that colonization lies in the interpretation of sacred texts. Bodies have been the *geography* where theological oppression has kept gender and sexuality captive through the colonization of identities. The violence of this process is revealed in the process of *normalization,* namely, to "correct" or "make normal" whatever does not fit into the binary female/male. The way society is structured molds human relations, sexuality, and gender. In other words, bodies are the cartography where social dynamics are inscribed and legitimized through cultural and theological discourse. Thus, bodies need to be liberated from these cultural and theological closets, especially through the deconstruction of the ways through which sacred texts and theological discourses have helped to establish them.

Liberative Theology in Action: The Notion of Heteropatriarchalism

Heteropatriarchalism is an ideology that permeates the whole of society. It is not the exclusive property of heterosexuals. On the contrary, it is an ideology pass onto everyone in every society by means of socialization, education, and cultural or societal norms. Christian churches are particularly involved in passing this ideology because of "divine arguments" based on particular and contextual interpretations of Holy Scriptures, whether Christian or the Hebrew Bible, which traditionally may have a different understanding of gender and sexuality. Heteropatriarchalism constitutes a crucial oppression for queer individuals and communities because it occludes different experiences of sexuality present in humanity since ancient times. Heteropatriarchalism is a reductionism that divides human sexuality in a male/female binary and imposes it on society as *the* only understanding of human sexuality. Culture expressed through education, mass media, and religion, among other institutions, reproduces this ideology. Bodies, sexualities, sexual orientations, the performances of gender have been colonized by heteropatriarchalism and pervade all dimensions of life in a way that oppresses all human beings. Thus, heteropatriarchalism functions through mechanisms of discrimination. The process is a colonization that *normalizes* people into a reductionist category: heterosexuality. That process is based on several facets: *labeling*, *dehumanizing*, *demonizing*, *exoticicizing*, and *stigmatizing*. This also emerges in queer communities when queer communities oppress other queer individuals through different mechanisms shared with broader society: *ableism*, *ageism*, *body fascism*, *racism*, *classism*, and *xenophobia*. Queer the-

Coming out: The issue of coming out is controversial worldwide because it collides with notions of extended family, family obligations, and social networks upon which one's survival in the society may depend. Prominent in Anglo-Saxon cultures, the notion of "coming out" emerged as a contextual and culturally based feature that may not be suitable for other societies or cultures. Based on the work of Eve Kosofsky Sedwick, Hongwei Bao states that "coming out" is a prominent Western feature that requires "visibility" in order to grant "authenticity." However in many parts of the world, both concealment and disclosure do not necessarily imply authenticity but rather social and historical contingencies where being "in" and being "out" refer to particular social settings that depend on personal as well as social possibilities. The Australian author Carolyn Poljski conveys the issues surrounding the notion of "coming out" among female migrants and their particular situations.
By having a same-sex relationship/partner in the host country and

also a family, children, or extended family, these women could suffer the consequences of that action. She suggests that in this context terms such as "coming home" and "inviting people in" would be more appropriate ways of dealing with one's personal situation rather than jeopardizing one's life while "coming out." Therefore, we should be cautious in judging individuals from other societies or cultures who do not have the material possibilities, although they may have the personal desire, to come out. In many ways, "coming out" is more an issue of privilege rather than possibilities.

ologies respond to heteropatriarchalism by dismantling its connection to and transcendental legitimation with the divine. Heteropatriarchalism should not be equated with homophobia, lesbophobia, or transphobia. The latter are the products of fear and hatred toward queer individuals and communities. On the contrary, heteropatriarchal individuals and communities could be queer friendly while considering queer individuals and communities as "abnormal" or "falling short" of heterosexual expectations.

To do queer theology implies that one revisit and deconstruct aspects of the Christian faith that have been taking for granted as "heteronormatively sacred." This section will briefly discuss three aspects: dogmas, God, and Christ.

Queer Experiences and Christian Dogmas

The basic assumption of Christianity is its role as a vehicle for "saving" people from "eternal condemnation." Over the centuries, this key role has been shaped by the systematization of the beliefs or "dogmatics." The Christian churches' preeminent dogma deals with the transformation of the divine into a human body, that is, Jesus's body, through what is known as *incarnation*. Thus, a discourse on bodies, and therefore gender and sexuality, is at the core of the Christian faith. However, while Christian churches place emphasis on the fact that God loves humanity, when it comes to daily life, gays, lesbians, bisexual, transgender, and **intersex** individuals are often ostracized by those who hold these Christian dogmas and, therefore, can be rhetorically removed from the possibility of salvation. It is easy for most Christian churches (with some few exceptions) to see queer individuals as having a "disease" that has to be *cured,* or a "problem" that has to be *corrected.* What supports these traditional perceptions is the negative view propounded by the heteropatriarchal system, which only sees bodies divided into "straight women and men." This seemingly clear-cut divide does not do justice to the life of queer individuals. Worldwide, mainstream Christian churches have historically incorporated that divide into their understanding of ethics, morality, and biblical/theological interpretations as intrinsically part of their dogmas that do not reflect the varied human experiences.

> ***Intersex:*** The term *intersex* is used to replace the previous ambiguous term *hermaphrodite*. It refers to individuals whose biological body is not only at variance with their displayed gender identity, but also in a strictly biological sense, it does not conform to the *either/or* categories of female/male.

Queering God

The ultimate recognition of queer people is when the divine incarnates their experiences and the faithful can express this in their beliefs. Here language has a great part in acknowledging or denying those experiences of gender and sexuality for queer individuals and communities. Some questions come to mind: (1) Can God love gays and lesbians while many Christian churches deny those individuals the possibility to love other individuals of the same sex? (2) Is it possible for God to transition from *god to goddess* or *goddess to god* in the same way that transgender individuals transition from male to female or female to male? (3) How about a God that is neither male nor female and, therefore, is able to relate to some of the experiences of intersex individuals? (4) Can God embrace the experiences of queer people while also remaining a God for heterosexual people and their particular experiences?

In Christianity, God is understood through the doctrine of the Trinity: the Father, the Son, and the Holy Spirit. To *queer* the doctrine of the Trinity requires one to think about what it means to be *human*, because humanity has been molded in the image of God according to Gen. 1:1–2:4 in the Hebrew Bible. Following Foucault, a queer critique is necessary to overcome heteropatriarchal binaries, especially by dismantling the hegemony of the traditional binary of female/male. According to queer theologians, gender metaphors are tools to discover the divine in daily life but are not the ultimate conception of God. Queering the doctrine of the Trinity requires the constant *deconstruction* and *(re)construction* of our metaphors of God in order not to make them new closets for oppressing the divine. This movement allows for diversity and multiple ways of considering the divine closer to every queer experience without making one interpretation or conception superior to another. Despite the predominance of heteropatriarchal tones, to confess God from the point of view of queer theologies implies recognizing a queer God whose divinity is in constant *trans/formation* and *be/coming*.

Queering Christ

While Christian churches place emphasis on the fact that God incarnated in Jesus to save all humanity, the reality is that some humans are considered worthier than others for that salvation. Beyond the pleasant statements of religious declarations, it is difficult for most Christians to think about Jesus Christ existing among queer individuals. This concern also has implications for soteriology, the study of salvation, as feminist theologian Rosemary Radford Ruether cunningly addresses in the question "Can a male savior save women?" This has broader implications for an understanding of Christ from a nonheteronormative perspective and the need to queer this doctrine in order to unpack its relevance for the life of queer believers. As notions of gender, sexuality, and power are conditioned by culture, political environment, economic relations, historical events, and social processes, so too the incarnation of God in Jesus Christ is a particular historical and cultural event.

However, the option of God to incarnate *a* human body is not trivial but rather a sublime act to dignify the beauty of *every single* human body, whether it is straight, gay, transgender, intersex, and the like. Queering Christ not only challenges ideological constructions of gender and sexuality but also uncovers and dismantles power dynamics amidst hegemonic theological structures. In that sense, Jesus would be considered queer, because he constantly denounced the power mechanisms operating at religious/societal levels of his time. For queer theologians, in Christ, God made a distinct act of divine power and opened up a world, a divine world, to all creation, including queer individuals. A queer Christ, Patrick S. Cheng would suggest, is indeed a "rainbow Christ," as Jesus was someone who bridged and united our cosmic diversity in the persona of Christ, a mirror of all humanity without exclusions.

Leading Scholars and Figures

Queer liberative theologies exist in different manifestations and expressions, because they emerged from particular situations, geographies, social contexts, contact with other theologies, or sociological concerns.

North American/European White Queer Theologies

The first wave of queer liberative theologies was represented by *homosexual theologies.* The work of Derek Sherwin Bailey, *Homosexuality and the Western Christian Tradition* (1955), exemplifies these theologies. Bailey was a clergyman of the Church of England (Anglican), and his book reevaluated the connection between homosexuality and Hebrew and Christian Scriptures. His book became so important that it influenced the production of the Wolfenden Report (1957), through which the Parliament of the United Kingdom decriminalized homosexual activities among consenting adults in England and Wales in the 1960s. Robert W. Wood published in 1959 the book *Christ and the Homosexual.* At that time, Wood was a minister in New York and a witness to how lesbians and gays were discriminated against by the Christian churches. His book was the first to make a severe critique of Christian churches' attitudes toward homosexuality by affirming that homosexuality was, in fact, "blessed by God." It should be mentioned that both Bailey and Wood at the time were lonely voices breaking ground for a new Christian understanding toward sexuality. It was in 1976 that John McNeill, who was professor of systematic theology at Union Theological Seminary in New York, published *The Church and the Homosexual*, a book that caused him to be expelled from the Jesuit order. McNeill's book challenged from a moral point of view the traditional Roman Catholic attitudes toward homosexuality, challenging the idea that the Holy Scriptures condemn homosexuality.

However, the second wave of queer liberative theologies, that is, *gay* or *LGBTI theologies*, included more voices seeking liberation from oppressive structures within Christianity. Some of these authors also became the leading writers of *queer theologies*, the third wave of queer liberative theologies, as the emphasis on sexual diversity was included. In fact, there were and continue to be definite differences in the political agenda of both theologies. Robert E. Shore-Goss is one of the most notable queer theologians of our time. A former Jesuit priest, he is currently minister in the Metropolitan Community Church, after being a professor at Webster University (1994–2004). His first book, *Jesus Acted Up: A Gay and Lesbian Manifesto* (1993), began to define the contours of queer liberative theologies by challenging the "imperial" structures of institutionalized Christianity from a liberation point of view based on the radical activism of Jesus Christ. In this work, Shore-Goss related theology to rights activism from his own commitment to the organization ACT-UP.

In *Queering Christ: Beyond Jesus Acted Up* (2002), Shore-Goss explicitly affirms that he did not think his book should be placed on a shelf along with gay and lesbian apologetics. In fact, this work presents an honest autobiographical and academic reflection on the intersections of Christ, the Bible, sexuality, and theology. The issue of biblical passages seemingly condemning homosexuality, commonly known as "texts of terror," is not a minor aspect for queer theologies. In works such as Nancy Wilson's *Our Tribe: Queer Folks, God, Jesus and the Bible* (1995), Robert Shore-Goss and Mona West's *Take Back the Word: A Queer Reading of the Bible* (2000), and Ken Stone's *Practicing Safer Texts: Food, Sex and Bible in Queer Perspective* (2005), queer theologians explore more inclusive ways to understand Sacred Scriptures.

Another leading scholar is Elizabeth Stuart, professor of Christian theology at the University of Winchester. In 1995 she published the book *Just Good Friends: Towards a Lesbian and Gay Theology of Relationships*, in which she explores the image of friendship to describe relationships among lesbians and gays and with the divine. In other words, friendship shows the limitations of our current notions of marriage and sexuality in order to expose the richness and diversity in our relations. In another work, *Gay & Lesbian Theologies: Repetitions with Critical Difference* (2003), Stuart offers a genealogy from LGBTI theologies to queer theologies while focusing on the way that Christian churches have held onto modern constructions of sexual identities and the need to queer that seemingly homogenous paradigm.

Asian American Queer Theologies

In the case of Asian American communities, queer theologians have assumed the task of challenging not only the more Anglo-oriented queer theologies but also the heteronormative tones of Asian American theologies, since Asian American queer people are doubly oppressed both by the American racial formation with its feature of white supremacy and by the gender-role expectations and the sexual division of labor among Asian communities. When we talk about Asian American communities we must recognize that we are placing under one term very diverse and sometimes very distinctive communities with particular cultures, geographical provenance, and linguistic legacies. Therefore, Chinese American theologian Patrick S. Cheng envisions a "rainbow theology" in order to show how diversity intersects faith, sexuality, and ethnicity in the lives of Asian American queer believers. Queer Asian American theologies seek to represent the experience of queer people who wish to embrace their faith, sexuality, and ethnicity in a harmonious and meaningful way.

Another example is Emerging Queer Asian/Pacific Islander Religion Scholars (EQARS), a group of scholars, religious workers, and activists who began meeting regularly online in 2010 to discuss the emerging area of interest that is queer Asian Pacific Islander (API) religions and to engage in a collaborative methodology to further one another's scholarly, religious work and activism. From EQARS also comes the work of Filipino American theologian Michael Sepidoza Campos, whose piece "The *Baklá*: Gendered Religious Performance in Filipino Cultural Spaces" (2011) takes up a contextual performance of queer: the *Baklá*, or the effeminate gay man in the Philippines, as a Christic trickster figure who simultaneously (re)defines and challenges not only heteronormative spiritual assumptions but also the very construction of gender and gender-role expectations.

African American Queer Theologies

Ingrained in the make-up of U.S. society is the colonial past of slavery. This has partitioned the racial line along the binary "black/white," which has permeated every aspect of society. African Americans until today have suffered the consequences of that past. True, the United States has made tremendous progress in terms of racial justice; however, the tensions are far from being overcome. As in the case of other pan-ethnic groups, queer African Americans need to negotiate the labile border between their place in broader society and their particular insertion in African American communities.

Queer African American theologians make the criticism that black liberation theology in the past has failed to address issues of queer believers. Queer African American theologians add another aspect, which is that of religion, to their colonial past. In a clear postcolonial analysis, Horace Griffin writes in his book *Their Own Receive Them Not* (2006) that the negative views on homosexuality in black churches can be traced back to colonial times when African slaves were converted to conservative Christianity by white Christians. In a similar vein, EL Kornegay, Jr., in his article "Queering Black Homophobia" (2004), deconstructs the assumption of a black archetypical identity that is disrupted by the presence of queer individuals, thus leading to the emergence of black homophobia. For Kornegay, black liberation theology was never interested in sexual liberation, and the task for queer theologians today is to focus on forming a black theology as a sexual discourse of transformation, whose proposals he sets forth in his book *A Queering of Black Theology* (2013).

Another aspect denounced is the absence of attention to black lesbian spirituality. In her paper "Black Lesbian Spirituality: Hearing Our Stories" (2012), Elana C. Betts addresses the issue by exploring how race, gender, sexual orientation, and spirituality unfold and intersect in the personal stories of African American lesbians. Specifically, Betts affirms that fluidity not only applied to the sexuality of lesbian believers whom she interviewed but also to their spirituality, priorities in life, and forms of expressing faith. These elements were conclusive for the African American lesbians in her study to achieve spiritual wholeness while integrating faith and sexuality.

Native (North) American Queer Theologies

A reality on the American continent is that Native American nations were conquered from the sixteenth century on by settlers who legitimized their oppression through the Christian faith, whether Roman Catholicism or Protestantism. In the case of Native (North) American people, Protestantism represented for them not only a source of oppression but also of compulsory conversion. Their land was taken, their languages suppressed, and their status as second-class individuals became evident as the emerging United States extended farther to the west. Within this context, to talk about religion implies leaving the confines of Christianity so as to recover the ancestral beliefs ingrained in the identity of every nation.

In this sense, Will Roscoe, in his essay "We'wha and Klah: The American Indian Berdache as Artist and Priest" (1999), focuses on the role that third-gender individuals occupied in the spiritual practices of their nation. Roscoe rescues the stories of We'wha, a *lhamana* among the Zuni nation, and Klah, a *nádleehé* among the Navajo nation in the nineteenth century. Both terms are more appropriate than the term *berdache*. Patrick S. Cheng argues that the latter is an imposition of the conquerors over Native (North) American queer individuals, and that it is a French adaptation of the Arabic term for "male prostitute." In fact, Qwo-Li Driskill, in *his* essay "Doubleweaving Two-Spirit Critiques" (2010), states that the term *two spirit* was chosen in an intertribal agreement to be used in English in order to communicate the different tribal traditions about queer individuals. What Roscoe highlights in his essay is the fact that two-spirit individuals not only invigorated the cultural traits of their people but also assumed spiritual leadership in order to produce communication between the spiritual forces and humans in terms of healing, counseling, and performances of ritual ceremonies.

Paradoxically, much of the anthropological, historical, and cultural research on third gender among two-spirit individuals focuses on individuals born with male genitalia. On this topic, Paula Gunn Allen, the late poet, lesbian activist, and novelist, in her essay "*Hwame, Koshkala*, and the Rest: Lesbians in American Indian Cultures" (1992), exposes the invisible presence of lesbians in Native (North) American cultural and spiritual life, and in doing so, she decenters the dominance of males in two-spirit studies.

Latina/o Queer Theologies

Among the many ethnic queer theologies in the United States, the latest trend comes from Latina/o queer scholars of religion, who are heirs of a double history of oppression and displacement. Latina/o communities share with Asian Americans an immigrant past because many of the ancestors come from a different provenance than the United States. However, Latina/o communities also share with African American and Native (North) American communities a past of oppression, because large portions of Mexico were taken by force and added to the current map of the United States. As in the case of land taken from Native (North) Americans, those territories were in fact inhabited land. Their inhabitants were forced either to assimilate as second-class U.S. citizens or to move outside the new borders.

It is within this historical double history of oppression and displacement that queer theologians denounce a third historical oppression, namely that based on gender and sexuality. It is important to note that Latina/o queer theologians engage their analysis of queer theology at the intersection of race/ethnicity, postcoloniality, and critical theories. For example, Adrian Emmanuel Hernández-Acosta, in his essay "Queer Holiness and Queer Futurity" (2014), argues that queer holiness provides indecent loves, abject practices, and sexually condemned souls with a space in which to rehearse critical hope. His analysis engages José Esteban Muñoz's understanding of queerness as a potentiality, a critical ideality, contending that Marcella Althaus-Reid's queer holiness is a fruitful structure in which to assemble queer relationality to inform the decolonization of sex and theology.

In a similar vein, in his essay "Decolonizing Grace and Incarnation" (2014), Vincent Cervantes argues that Latina/o queers interact, participate, and embody the sexualized incarnational space that Althaus-Reid constructs. Building on the work of Althaus-Reid, Enrique Dussell, and José Esteban Muñoz, he proposes a decolonized theology of bodies and queerness. Cervantes employs the neologism *put@joteria* [queerness] as a new Latina/o language and performance of queerness in light of the decolonization of incarnation, body, and eros in order to resist not only societal oppression but also racial and ethnic contextual oppression. These emerging scholars join long-established scholars such as Luis León, who in his essay "César Chávez, Christian Love, and the Myth of (Anti)Machismo," reinterprets Chavez as a Christic icon who defies "traditional macho masculinity" among Latinas/os. In the same way, Miguel A. De La Torre, in his bilingual book *A la Familia: A Conversation about Our Families, the Bible, Sexual Orientation and Gender* (2011), addresses the issue of sexual orientation from a theological point of view in a work geared toward Latina/o church members. On the other hand, Orlando Espín has edited a series of booklets both in Spanish and English in support of queer Latina/o believers and their families who want to come to terms with queer issues and religion.

Marcella Althaus-Reid: There is a "before" and "after" Althaus-Reid. Born in May 11, 1952, in Rosario, Argentina, early in her life she felt a calling for ordained ministry. However, the Roman Catholic Church does not ordain women. Althaus-Reid then pursued a bachelor's degree in theology at ISEDET University in Buenos Aires. This university is well known for its solid academic formation and for a prestigious faculty, among whom are Jose Míguez Bonino, Severino Croatto, Beatriz Melano Couch, and Alberto Ricciardi, and many others. All of them are key Protestant and Roman Catholic scholars in Latin American liberation theology. Althaus-Reid's views on gender and sexuality and passion for academic work led her to migrate, completing her Ph.D. in theology at the

University of St. Andrews in Scotland. Althaus-Reid was Professor of Contextual Theology at New College, University of Edinburgh. When appointed, she was the only woman professor of theology at a Scottish university and the first woman professor of theology at New College in its 160 years of history. Her areas of expertise included Latin American liberation theology, hermeneutics, feminism, and queer theology. In addition to being the author of academic articles and several chapters for books, she wrote three books and edited six others. Althaus-Reid died on February 20, 2009, in Edinburgh, Scotland, after fighting a long illness.

Asian Queer Theologies

Asian queer theologies have developed in a region marked by a multireligious environment in which Christianity is one among other religions such as Islam, Buddhism, Hinduism, and local religions as well as by its interaction with Confucianism, the Chinese ethical and philosophical system. Given the variety of cultures, languages, and spiritual environments in every country of the region, it would be impossible to describe all of them in this chapter. I will focus on a few cases.

Since the beginning of the twenty-first century the emerging *tongzhi* theology in Hong Kong and Taiwan has become an important contribution. The Chinese term *tongzhi* is translated as "comrade" and originally referred to members of the Chinese Communist Party. However, it has been appropriated by queer people in Sino-speaking contexts in order to designate a more politically oriented queer activism. The purpose of *tongzhi* theology lies in paying attention to the stories of the oppression of individuals and communities as well as to the mechanisms that reify that oppression. The first work on *tongzhi* theology was done by Ng Chin Pang in his master's thesis "Breaking the Silence" (Hong Kong, 2000). In this work Ng not only bridged queer theory with *tongzhi* theology but also took a postcolonial stand that made his work a pioneering piece in the interdisciplinary tone of this emerging theology. Another example is Hong Kong theologian Lai-Shan Yip. In her essay "Listening to the Passion of Catholic *Nu-Tongzhi*" (2011), she focuses particularly on the experience of oppression of *nu-tongzhi* (female *tongzhi*) within the context of the Roman Catholic Church's moral teachings on sexuality and of Hong Kong's *tongzhi* movement, which is strongly oriented toward male's experiences. Yip interrogates the daily lived experience of the *nu-tongzhi*. Particularly in the context of Chinese societies marked by Confucianist moral philosophy, the reality of Roman Catholic *nu-tongzhi* is in itself a hybrid experience. Yet, the Roman Catholic *nu-tongzhi* are able to resist the two mainstream traditions through a creative resynthesis of the traditions that fosters an understanding of their religious experiences and their sexuality by blending and opening up flexible and liberating spaces of agency and negotiation.

Concurrently, other Asian theologians have begun to develop contextual thought and theological praxis in their own contexts in conversation with other religions such as Islam. Joseph N. Goh, in his essay "Transgressive Empowerment: Queering the Spiritualities of the *Mak Nyahs* of PT Foundation" (2014), uses a queer theological framework to investigate lived experiences in the context of Islam, which he calls "Nyah-Islam." He explores the experience of transgender people (male-to-female) in Kuala Lumpur, who are known in Bahasa Malaysia, the official language of Malaysia, as *mak nyahs.* Goh states that *mak nyahs* seek ways in which to actively live their religion, Islam, and to reconcile it with gender and sexuality, thus subverting the oppressive order of institutional Islam while fostering their perspectives and their actions of faith as highly spiritual and creative experiences.

Other theologians seek to address the role of religions in promoting discriminative actions. Juswantori Ichwan, a theologian in Indonesia, in his essay "The Influence of Religion on the Development of Heterosexism in Indonesia" (2014), embarks on the project of delinking homophobia from heterosexism in order to expose its pervasive influences in civil society. For him, while homophobia is based on the fear of sexual diversity, heterosexism is an ideological system that favor heterosexuality over other sexual orientations, thus privileging and empowering the dominance of **cisgender** heterosexual individuals and their societal structures. Ichwan investigates the distinctive forms through which Hinduism, Buddhism, Islam, and Christianity have all contributed to ingrain heterosexism in Indonesian society.

In a similar vein, Yuri Horie, an ordained minister of the United Church of Christ in Japan, brings to light the situation of lesbians in the Christian churches. In her essay "Possibilities and Limitations of 'Lesbian Continuum': The Case of a Protestant Church in Japan" (2006), she analyzes the rendering of lesbians as invisible in a Protestant Christian denomination in the midst of a non-Christian society. She affirms that the exclusion of gay and lesbian individuals from Christian communities is rooted not only in religious teachings but also in the connubiality of those teachings with ideologies of societal background. However, she points out that this situation could be overcome through the activism of queer individuals and their straight allies who, together, can debunk these pervasive theo(ideo)logies.

Cisgender: Since the 1990s, there has been a growing awareness by heterosexual allies that their identities are usually coopted by heteronormativity and used against their queer friends. In order to prevent this, some scholars and activists have adopted the term "cisgender" as a way to break away from that situation. *Cis* is the Latin prefix for "on the same side." It complements *trans*, the prefix for "across" or "over."

Latin American Queer Theologies

Latin American queer theologies challenge us to establish networks with contextual and regional theologies that posit a rapprochement within the paradigm of queer theologies, even when these are not identified as such. Several Latin American scholars have begun to rethink their theology from the intersection of sexuality and Latin American liberation theology. Althaus-Reid was a pioneer in this regard with her book *Indecent Theology* (2000), the title of which also gives the name to her theology. Indecent theology can properly be regarded as a Latin American queer liberation theology that seeks to embody Latino/a flavors, delights, dilemmas, ecclesial hopes, and the change of social reality.

Althaus-Reid's second book, *The Queer God* (2004), proposes to queer the divine as well as both human and divine relationships in order to challenge the heteronormative tone of classical theologies about God. Taking the daily lived experience of queer believers, she also proposes to liberate God from the closet of traditional Christian thought. Similarly, Mario Ribas, in his essay "Liberating Mary, Liberating the Poor" (2006), addresses the Christian iconography about Mary that reflects the heteronormative view vis-à-vis the more queer understanding of Mary and sexuality in daily life experiences. Although Mary is venerated in Latin America as the pristine model of motherhood, the presence of icons of Mary even in brothels or bars reveals a mixture of sacred and profane whose boundaries are difficult, maybe pointless, to determine. Thus, undressing Mary from her sacred heteronormative garments may render the human Mary closer to the experience of poor women in the midst of their daily struggles in Latin America.

As in the context of Asia, Latin America is a diverse region in terms of languages, cultures, spiritualities, and ethnicities. André Sidnei Musskopf, in his essay "A Gap in the Closet: Gay Theology in Latin American Context" (2009), grounds his analysis in the experience of queer believers in Brazil in order to propose a queer theology that dialogues with the multiple religious experiences of the believers. In a predominantly, but not exclusively, Roman Catholic context, multiple religious affiliations—some of which may not be so heteropatriarchal—suggest that the closet of religious experiences may have gaps that allow for third spaces of negotiation and spiritual creativity. Concurrently, in his essay "Cruising (with) Marcella" (2010), Musskopf states that although Althaus-Reid and other queer theologians seem to "sexualize" theology, the truth is that all theologies, in one way or another, are really sexual theologies, thus highlighting the need to acknowledge this fact.

In a different tone, Dario Garcia, in his book *Mundo de las Princesas: Hermenéutica y Teología Queer* [World of princesses: hermeneutics and queer theology] (2011), takes up philosophy and hermeneutics, a term that means "interpretation," in order to examine not only the emergence of queer theologies but also their critique and destabilization of heteronormative theologies in Latin America. Drawing on Martin Heidegger's concept of *Dasein* ("being there"), Garcia points to the process of be/coming as a hermeneutical tool to understand not only the fluidity of sexual diversity but also how this impacts, molds, and enriches the understanding of the divine and the situation of human beings in relation to that divinity.

African Queer Theologies

Kevin Ward, in his essay "Same-Sex Relations in Africa and the Debate on Homosexuality in East African Anglicanism" (2002), has pointed out how current debates on homosexuality in some African countries stemmed from conservative positions passed on by Western missionaries in colonial times. Given this context, emergent queer theologians in Africa have to confront the ingrained societal heteronormativity in African societies as well as the impact of colonialism on views of sexual ethics. Queer theologies in Africa are yet to be fully developed, but traces of this new trend are already present and evolving. Kenneth Hamilton, who has been professor at Notre Dame de Namur University and the Graduate Theological Union, in his essay "Colonial Legacies, Decolonized Spirits: Balboa, Ugandan Martyrs and AIDS Solidarity Today" (2010), offers a decolonizing view in order to propose a queer theology that rescues the historical past in which homoeroticism was not only permitted but also related to the sacred in African lands. Taking the case of the Ugandan martyrs (1886), he denounces the preeminence of Christian conversion as the moment in which homophobia enters the sexual arena in Africa and denies the fluidity of sexuality already present on the continent.

Theologians point out that in colonial-influenced Christianity in Africa, the sacred texts have specifically been misused in ways to promote discrimination. In this light, Jeremy Punt wrote the essay "Using the Bible in Post-Apartheid South Africa: Its Influence and Impact amidst the Gay Debate" (2006), in which he presents the case of the Dutch Reformed Church in South Africa. He reports how a perception of the Bible as a "moral handbook" rather than a "foundational document" for Christians led to decisions that erased the freedom of nonheterosexual Christians within the church, especially the clergy. Punt indicates that the case of the Dutch Reformed

Church parallels a situation greatly extended across Africa in which the sacred texts are used as a mechanism to deny the faith and belonging of queer Christians. A queer perspective is needed to liberate queer Christians from the closets of heteronormative Bible hermeneutics.

Some testimonial cases that clearly resemble the scholarly work of Hamilton and Punt are compiled in the volume edited by Paul Germond and Steve de Gruchy, *Aliens in the Household of God* (1997). These stories tell not only about the struggles of queer believers in the context of South Africa but also about the need for the sacred and sexuality to be recognized in the midst of their life stories. Rather than fighting over the rightness or wrongness of either side of the debate of queerness in South Africa, the authors and the editors have discovered that what united them in this project was a basic, meaningful desire to meet and recognize one another as human beings. This could be an extraordinary theological *locus* from which to develop and enrich the emerging queer theologies in the African context, enlightening not only theological reflection but also a liberating hermeneutics and inclusive ecclesiologies that would welcome straight and queer individuals alike.

Possible Future Trends

Ecclesiology and Christian Rites

One of the most common critiques of queer theologies is done through the question: How does this affect the Sunday churchgoer? The concern is how to translate the sophisticated theological edifice of queer theologies to regular believers who do not have theological training but indeed want to live out their faith in an inclusive way. One could affirm that while many LGBTI theologies from the 1970s and 1980s were concerned with "a place at the Christian table," many queer theologians may not be interested in acknowledging the power symbolized by that table. This is because for queer theologies it is not enough to reform the existing structures of oppression, but new ways must be found to be a community and to live out the rites and religious practices that give meaning to the daily life of believers.

Drawing on the recognition of the strain among sexual theologies, a possible trend in queer theologies would be to seriously address the aforementioned question about the relation between theological thought and the religious practices of the faithful. On the one hand, this entails considering ways to redress ecclesiological concerns related to the way Christian churches understand and live their purpose as places of worship. Specifically, rethinking ecclesiological concerns means offering opportunities for communities to undo centuries of oppression and discrimination against queer individuals and communities while rebuilding spaces that would welcome all humankind regardless of gender, sexuality, or body status.

On the other hand, queer theologies need to examine how the rites and practices of faith relate to queer individuals in situations of worship marked by multiple realities: ethnic, sexual, gender, national, and religious. That is, how can religious practices empower individuals rather than "sanctify" them under the guise of Christian orthodoxy? The common application of the term "sacred" to religious practices often implies that those individuals who do not conform to a certain way of practicing certain rites are not worthy of being "sanctified," that is, accepted into the community of believers. Rather than seeking "sanctification," queer theologians propose practices that would acknowledge the diversity of humanity without labels or unilaterally defined codes of practice.

Queer Liberative Theologies and Religions

A need exists for queer theologies to embrace the encounter of queer issues in religions other than Christianity. In an increasingly changing and globalized world, the intersection of religious and queer studies is vital for understanding the construction of identities. There are elements in all religions that highlight issues of gender, sexuality, partnership, the formation of families, the sexual division of labor, and cultural and societal gender-role expectations. In fact, religions worldwide tend to relate, and many times legitimize, these elements in one way or another. As is the case within the many branches of Christianity, there are queer believers in almost every religion on this planet. Some of those queer believers may be more visible than others, and some may be more oppressed and persecuted than others. However, the reality that queer individuals are present in all human populations leads us to infer that all religions are in need of recognizing the place of queer folks. The main concern is how queer issues impact and challenge the established corpus of beliefs and religious practices surrounding those religions. Sacred Scriptures may highlight the diversity of human sexuality and the construction of bodies, sexuality, families, couples, and affectionate ties that vary according to different times, but they also reveal that heteronormativity is indeed a hegemonic construction that renders diversity as "invisible." When someone adheres to a religion, s/he does so by embracing its internal mechanism of functioning and the place of the Sacred Scriptures in that religion. In this sense, it is valid for queer believers to challenge and revisit the role and the interpretation of Sacred Scriptures in all religions. This is a necessary step in gaining a voice that can subvert the apparently ingrained homophobia present in every religion. However, it is important for queer believers also to challenge the validity of some scriptural elements that do not enforce freedom and respect. Finally, it is important to remember that the term "theology," knowledge or reflection about God, may not be appropriate for reflections about the intersection of queer issues and religious beliefs. That is to say, when speaking about sexuality, religion, gender, and nation, the term "theology" may represent a colonial tone referring to some religious historical past.

Study Questions

1. What are the main differences between the four stages in the history of queer liberative theologies?
2. How would you briefly summarize the importance of the theological issues of queer liberative theologies as exposed in this chapter?
3. How would you describe the elements that interested you about the future trends of queer liberative theologies?
4. What would be some elements necessary in order for us to talk about queer liberative theologies in religions other than Christianity?
5. How would you expand your insights by taking one of the concepts explained in this chapter?

Suggested Reading

Althaus-Reid, Marcella, ed. *Liberation Theology and Sexuality.* Aldershot: Ashgate, 2006.

———, and Lisa Isherwood, eds. *Controversies in Body Theology.* London: SCM Press, 2008.

———. *The Sexual Theologian: Essays on Sex, God and Politics.* London: Continuum, 2004.

Boisvert, Donald L., and Jay Emerson Johnson, eds. *Queer Religion: Homosexuality in Modern Religious History.* Santa Barbara, CA: Praeger, 2011.

Bong, Sharon A. "Negotiating Resistance/Resilience through the Nexus of Spirituality—Sexuality of Same-Sex Partnerships in Malaysia and Singapore." *Marriage and Family Review* 47.8 (2011): 648-65.

Cheng, Patrick S. *From Sin to Amazing Grace: Discovering the Queer Christ.* New York: Seabury Books, 2012.

———. *Radical Love: An Introduction to Queer Theology.* New York: Seabury Books, 2011.

Comstock, Gary David, and Susan E. Henking, eds. *Que(e)rying Religion: A Critical Anthology.* New York: Continuum, 1999.

Córdova Quero, Hugo. "Risky Affairs: Marcella Althaus-Reid Indecently Queering Juan Luis Segundo's Hermeneutic Circle Propositions." In

Dancing Theology in Fetish Boots: Essays in Honour of Marcella Althaus-Reid, edited by Lisa Isherwood and Mark D. Jordan, 207-18. London: SCM Press, 2010.

Countryman, L. William, and M. R. Ritley. *Gifted by Otherness: Gay and Lesbian Christians in the Church.* Harrisburg, PA: Morehouse, 2001.

De La Tore, Miguel A. *Out of the Shadows, Into the Light: Christianity and Homosexuality.* St. Louis: Chalice Press, 2009.

Guest, Deryn, Robert Goss, Mona West, and Thomas Bohache, eds. *The Queer Bible Commentary.* London: SCM Press, 2006.

Hanks, Tom. *The Subversive Gospel: A New Testament Commentary of Liberation.* Cleveland, OH: Pilgrim Press, 2000.

Nickoloff, James B. "Sexuality: A Queer Omission in U.S. Latino/a Theology." *Journal of Hispanic/Latino Theology* 10.3 (2003): 31-51.

Tanis, Justin. *Trans-gendered: Theology, Ministry and Communities of Faith.* Cleveland, OH: Pilgrim Press, 2003.

Tigert, Leanne McCall, and Maren C. Tirabassi, eds. *Transgendering Faith: Identity, Sexuality & Spirituality.* Cleveland, OH: Pilgrim Press, 2004.

12

Liberative Theologies of Disability

Sharon Betcher

In a world ever evolving, bodies interact with and modify themselves in relation to their environments. The body is not so much closed in (and therefore "whole") as it is an open, interdependent, and dynamically responsive organism. The body will be born, given evolutionary and genetic conditions, with differential variations; it can also be conditioned by disturbances within the ecological biomes that nest the human self. The body's performance can be torn open by social encounters, ranging from war to accidents to conditions of labor. The body, then, remains porous to the outside world, with an openness that is never completely under our control. Variation is therefore a condition of becoming. To put it differently, disability—as Irving Zola first put it—is a universal human condition. Any human is, contrary to modern strivings for "wholeness," only temporarily able-bodied. A liberative theology of disability consequently thinks about life in terms of a world of becoming and emergence. This challenges certain teachings regarding "the order of creation" and, in Christian theology, "The Fall," which treats disability as paradigmatic of sin and brokenness.

Basic Tenets

That the human community culls out "disability," that purportedly evidentiary physical or psychic vulnerability in the extreme, which is then turned into a reason for social exclusion, tells us how uncomfortable cultures can be with these basic scenes of biological variability and ecological dependence. Anomalous bodies, "the disabled" in other words, appear only over against cultures' psychic and social (followed by architectural and technological) investments in how the body "should" appear. "Diss-ing" a body, even summarily naming out another as "disabled," constitutes a form of racism, a social-class exclusion from the West's "cult/ure of public appearance," configured as somatic wholeness.

Western modernity, the dual age of scientific and colonial discovery, polished the optics of disability—hence, of the normal and the civilized over against the deficient and degenerate. Yet disability may be one of the longest-standing configurations of human-on-human marginalization, since disability names the exclusionary perimeter of what a culture interprets to be constitutive of the human. From Aristotle to modernity, the "degenerative," with which disability remains definitively limned, factored also into how we thought about racial, gendered, and sexual differences. Aristotle, in *Generation of Animals*, contending that "The female is, as it were, a deformed male," established the male as the generic human. He also arranged somatic diversity into a hierarchy of value by relying on this value-dismissing sense of what was degenerative and therefore invalid. Comparably, during the Western Enlightenment and its simultaneous development of philosophical humanism and economic colonialism, the West celebrated its civility in establishing the generic representation of humanity, "the man of reason," over against the degenerate types, racial others, the working class, women, and persons with disabilities [hereafter "**pwds**"], who purportedly weakened the civic body.

Pwds: An acronym often used by people with disabilities and advocacy organizations to refer to persons with disabilities.

Even after the last five decades of liberative movements, disability remains outside a sociocultural *cordon sanitaire*. While the differences of race, gender, and sex have entered into the positive consideration of human difference, the category "disability," which historically informed the constructions of race, sex, and gender, remains in circulation, negatively projected upon corporeal variables. This undoubtedly has to do with reading all pwds' human variations as essentially negative, as deficiency veering into degeneracy. Disability names that venue where human communities attempt to situate a boundary between civilized life and bare life, life that is considered not worth living.

The modern West empirically received and evaluated differential variations in the human community into but two categories of the normal and abnormal, or the able and the "invalid," based particularly on visual perceptions. What constitutes "normal" is not so much true to nature as it is a statement of the values that generate and are generated by a certain way of looking at the world. Perception is always already riddled with affect and interpretation. Perception is

Normal: Westerners are geared toward ranking themselves around notions of norms and averages—in terms of intelligence, weight, income, and health standards, like cholesterol or blood pressure.

informed by how we feel in the presence of one another, and that feeling can occasion the reach for a hard-and-fast principle to mitigate any sense of discomfort; hence we develop notions of wholeness. In classical metaphysics, a sense of the norm of nature and the will of God twined around each other to generate Augustine's suspicion of the "monstrous" bodies within and on the edges of the civilized world at the cusp of the fifth century. Today, this division consolidates the power of science as a dominant discourse. Culture inherently shapes what we value and how we measure human life today, centrally in terms of "the body." Disability can seem a kind of unshakeable, biological fact when we forget the role of culture in the development of what counts as human biology and medicine.

Whether greeting pwds as a monstrosity or, contrarily, a marvel of inspiration, such postures demonstrate a way of holding us at a distance. Once identified as non-normative, persons become magnets for not only cultural anxieties but cultural ambitions. **Normates**' anxious attention to "impairment" or dread of monstrosity can overrun pwds with the dream of miraculous remediation, whether religious faith healing or technology. This, of course, is the crux of the issue: can normates come to terms with pwds not as "invalids" but as members of the human race without fix or cure? Most pwds after all yearn not for cure but for societal change. Can pwds be allowed to speak of the value of their life experience? Allowed to negotiate their own interface with adaptive technologies without prescriptive stereotypes like "wholeness"?

Normates: Pwds speak of persons who, by virtue of their economic status and controlled morphology, assume the culturally authoritative power of normalcy as "normates."

Normalcy, disabilities theorist Lennard Davis explains, is less the truth of human nature than it is a sensibility of a certain kind of society. Along with the development of statistical mathematics in the eighteenth and nineteenth centuries came the notion of the average person. The notion of the norm implies consideration of the majority population. But given a select population that is then averaged, no person might fit the norm. Nonetheless, this construction of the norm, used in industrialization and public health, led to utopian ideas of, in the words of the French statistician Adolphe Quetelet, "the perfectibility of the human species" such that "defects and monstrosities disappear more and more from the body." "Disability" appears all the more starkly over against this constructed expectation of the norm, which also then aggravates the mentality of rehabilitation. Decolonizing theorist Ashis Nandy, critiquing the practices of the British Empire in India, likewise insisted that normalcy—practiced on colonial subjects as much as on persons

Body differences are not inherently a hardship, a pity, or a tragedy; the morphological and neurological givens are just that, the conditions of our liveliness. Rather, socially constructed barriers and visions of life based on refusing to value pwds, in looking at us as if we were deficient, constitute the conditions from which pwds seek liberation. Most persons with stigmatic impairments report being both completely surveillanced (that is, always stared at) and totally anonymous (that is, unknown or reduced to being but "that condition"). "The stare" creates a patrolled perimeter whereby persons shut down any desire to know pwds as human, as neighbor, as interesting and smart. Persons are not, after all, so much indifferent to disability as repulsed by it.

Given that "disability" arises in how we feel in the presence of other bodies, the liberative movement of pwds engages aesthetics, gut feelings in others' presence that inform the optics of how one looks at the world. Feelings generate the stigma of difference, and oppression uses aesthetic judgments to exact its violence. Revulsion, disgust, fear of pain, and the fear of the contagion of affiliation with one deemed "less" continue to inform the exclusion marked "the disabled." Consequently, evaluations of "low quality of life" for pwds exceed anything self-reported by pwds and consistently overrun our own testimony. Dread of the plasticity of flesh, then, makes consideration of value as human beings and to human culture virtually unthinkable. (Because humans are social creatures, this affect can, it must be noted, saturate pwds' own self-assessment.) Comparable, then, to the way in which Nelson Mandela insisted that liberation of South Africans depended upon the liberation of Afrikaners from fear, a liberative theology of disability depends upon training normates to practice freedom from reactivity, to move through disgust and aversion without turning aside.

with disabilities in the metropole—constitutes something of a cultural pathology. The fixation on order and boundary can be obsessive, puritanical, and therefore expelling. A commitment to normalcy can in this way, Nandy asserted, hide the violence of the powerful. Further, normalcy acts as a hegemonic force by which persons identify with the powerful; it can be then a form of internal colonization.

Monster or Marvel, Tiny Tim or Transformer: Crips are often caught up in storylines culture, including science, that tells about hope, possibility, or the overcoming of obstacles. Conversely, think also of how the disabled body has been used in literature to shade the moral character of an actor, for example, the pirate with a hook hand as representative of evil (Captain Hook in J. M. Bairre's *Peter Pan*), or for developing the sympathetic sentiment of the onlooker, for example, Tiny Tim in Charles Dickens's *A Christmas Carol.* The development of *X-Men* in comics may be a relief from the representation of disability as congruent with the lack of moral integrity—for example, Professor Charles Xavier—but it conversely sets an inhuman bar of attainment. Biotechnoscience, taking up where the religious miracle left off, has attempted to prove its transcendent capacities by yoking them to remediation of disability. Persons with disabilities can unwillingly be made to appear as spokespersons for the marvels of technology, or be made to live, formally or informally, on the inspirational speaker's circuit. That may be a better option than begging, but it still treats the pwd as somehow exceptional to what can be lived as a human life. The bodies and lives of pwds, then, are used to tell stories not their own. These representations and story arcs can sweep pwds into their own metabolic energies, as if they are exemplary of pitiable tragedy to be coddled in conspicuous compassion or themselves evidence of an arc of history that moves from tragedy to triumph. A crip may all too easily embrace this triumphant arc, getting

But as far as the marginalization of persons with disabilities creates (through expulsion of the devalued other) another hidden valuation of the crowd, a liberative theology of disability also challenges the sociocultural value placed on ability, efficiency, and productivity—these objectifications and potential enslavements of human flesh. The medical category "disability" was generated in the West during the development of industrialization, and simultaneously with urbanization. Persons could participate in the modern capitalist economy to the extent that they could use their bodies as a natural resource for sale on the market; that created contrarily the exclusion of disability. From a disabilities perspective though, industry reductively values even "normal" bodies submitted to the measure of "labor power." And normalcy now, given deindustrialization, refers to nothing so much as the decorous appetite of the consumer citizen.

Colonialism, which likewise grew up in the age of scientific discovery, borrowed the same optics. Today's economic globalization evidences a similar way of leveraging the precariousness of life into which each is born upon certain bodies. This insinuates a close history not only between colonial subjectivity and disability, owing to war and economic and social disruptions, but also to contemporary neocolonial practices such as the dispersion of ecological pollutants and the economics of globalization, which occasion population swathes of disablement. The globalization of the economy and technology at the hands of the global financial elite means that "disability" remains, as it has been during Western industrialization and urbanization, a means of sorting usable from waste-able lives.

Liberative Theology in Action: Is "Disability" Another Name for "Social Suffering" or a Way to Forget the Political Circumstances Where Bodies Take Place?

Indra Sinha's novel *Animal's People* (2007) includes a lightly veiled account of the world's worst chemical disaster, the 1984 explosion at the Union Carbide pesticide plant in Bhopal. The explosion itself killed thousands, but survivors, having ingested the toxic fumes and residual chemicals, have been left physically impaired; hence the story of "Animal." In Sinha's narrative, Animal endures the corkscrewing of his spine by walking on all fours. His name comes from the way onlookers greet him as "animal," not human.

Here disability results from the practice of global capital moving operations where worker safety and environmental protections are limited or nil, thus displacing the precariousness of life off-site of the privileged or protected classes. In situations like this, as also in migrant farming, fracking zones, First Nations reserves, and geographic zones where class and poverty keep voices of resistance suppressed in the name of economic development, scholars from the Global South encourage us to speak in terms of "social suffering," warning that "disability," given the West's definition of this as an individual medical condition, actually precludes appropriate sociopolitical analysis. Disability in the West appears to be a minority subject position; but in the Global South, disablement appears within a swath of social suffering, among persons identified for economic uplift.

The idea of disability as personal tragedy needing repair can be used by neocolonial powers, whether church or state, for championing their humanitarianism, whether a child

caught up in notions of the supercrip who overcomes all adversity. Most pwds would prefer, however, to be just another human keeping company with you.

The stare: Our eyes can, when looking upon another, behold or withdraw, can punish or welcome. For pwds, "the stare" names a particular way in which we get caught on the normate's eyeball. While curiosity can simply be roused by what we didn't expect to see, the stare names a way in which that curiosity take shapes as compulsive fixation, even dynamic struggle. Through the eyes, the starer demands that pwds lower their eyes or turn away. In other words, the starer demands that the pwd yield his/her personhood. The stare ramps up an ordinary way of taking in information from our world by using the eyes aggressively to interrogate the other's being. The West has privileged the ocular as the road to truth (hence, "seeing is believing") and lives with a visual overdetermination of our intersubjective world.

During modernity, this aesthetic sense of encyclopedic order preferred gardens with linear rows and cities set upon a grid. The development of clinical medicine brought such expectations to bear upon the body. Disability consequently appears to be disorder, a visitation of chaos—hence, the compulsion to rehabilitate pwds. The stare can be re-enforced by these cultural assumptions that the visual is a clear indicator of the good, the desirable, the beautiful. The question "What happened to you?" is similarly related to the onlooker's assumption about the orderliness of life and wholesomeness of the human body's becoming. That same assumption can be turned into pity—consigning, through a glance, this condition of our liveliness and loveliness to the "tragic."

Nancy Mairs's quote: "Keep your chin up," we say (signifying courage) "and your eyes open" (alertness); "stand on your own two feet" (independence) "and tall" (pride); "look straight in the eye" (honesty) . . . By contrast, physical debility connotes vice, as in "sit on your

injured during the U.S.-Afghanistan conflict fitted with prostheses or various such missional programs. Christian mission is, however, often motivated by using just such individual cases to affect the distribution of compassion. Consider the countless photos of disabled bodies circulated in magazines or television ads by groups emphasizing global mission.

Christian mission, from the early sixth-century missions to the colonial era, has, in fact, been mapped by directing itself to the needy others lying on its borders. "Disability," in other words, became a geopolitical map for Christian politics of rescue, moving from the benevolent superior to the pitiable other, a geosocial map that continues to shape the practice of compassion in Christian community. Given that 80 percent of all pwds live in the Global South, how might this analysis of disability as *social* suffering impact Christian global mission campaigns?

While a liberative theology of disability does appreciate the difference between bodies, it simultaneously critiques cultural definitions of what it means to be human, not only the way normalcy captures individualism but the way bodies can become but "labor power" or simply the citizen consumer. Christian anthropology does not reduce a body to what it can do in the name of productivity, but it appreciates the neighbor for who she or he is as an other. We can now begin to glimpse but one way disability theology can be a valuable experience for the human community: what has been called disability may serve as a critical epistemological location from which contrarily to view the capture and captivation of the body by sociocultural forces.

That the insights of **crips** (the term "crip," not "crippled," assumes the integration of this interface of flesh and world, not worrying its ramifications into a permanent, decisive trauma, but living mindfully with and through its perturbations) might be valuable to the human community is certainly evidenced within Christian Scriptures, where spiritual authority was yoked with experiences of what we would today identify as disability: stuttering Moses, limping Jacob, and Paul "made perfect in weakness" (2 Cor. 12:9). Pwds' awareness that we are not in control of even our own lives can be a key for renovating Western cultural convictions about human subjectivity, learning thereby to release the arrogance of rational mastery so as to take up our lives as participants in a vulnerable, ecological communion. After all, only where the human community has severed its core sense of subjectivity from disability could the human be thought of as an agent in control. In this way, pwds see ourselves as a people with valuable reflections on what it is to be human, as artists and philosophers, as persons, having reclaimed ourselves from sites of rehabilitation into self-styling artists of life.

ass" (laziness); "take it lying down" (weakness); "listen with half an ear" (inattention); and get left "without a leg to stand on" (unsound argument). The way in which the body occupies space and the quality of the space it occupies correlate with the condition of the soul: it is better to be admired as "high-minded" than "looked down on" . . . , to be "free as a bird" than "confined to a wheelchair." . . . The fact that the soundness of the body so often serves as a metaphor for its moral health, its deterioration, thus implying moral degeneracy, puts me and my kind in a quandary. How can I possibly be "good"? (*Waist-High in the World*, 1996)

Crip: Some pwds speak of ourselves as "crips," which queers rhetoric meant to humiliate us. Crips refuse to see ourselves as essentially deficient, degenerate, or defective, sensibilities that any use of the term "disability" tends to reenforce. Crips critically challenge the cultural division between ability and disability, insisting upon our capaciousness and valuable contributions to the human community.

Liberative theologies of disability, as this insinuates, critique cultural optics that capture or captivate the body, psychic disaffection with the variability and vulnerability of life (whether resentment of pain in a world of becoming or revulsion in the presence of somatic and neurological variation), and presumptions about nature and body, especially as these become embedded in and circulated through a theology of creation, christological accounts of healing, justice and mission as well as eschatology, our fondest hopes and yearnings. Christians should be aware that these optics that pwds experience more intimately as "the stare" can be hidden from plain sight by lodging them in sensibilities such as the "will of God" or metaphysics, that vision of ultimate reality. When ultimate reality, heaven, or pre-lapsarian Eden is imagined as a realm without pain, tears, suffering (although Christians proclaim a God who has emptied God's self into this world without transcendental reserve and who has intimately shared with us the pain passages of the world), then bodies of pwds are seen as but a visitation of pain. A reminder is in order that earlier stages of Christian theology shaped Western biology and medicine, which assume suffering as inherently a diminution of life, as if pleasure and pain were opposed and we must eradicate pain in order to have a life of meaning.

A liberative theology of disability will remind Christians of a theological anthropology based in our shared identity as people of Spirit and inherently communal, relational, and interdependent. Our vocation as Christians is to hold life in the grow light of our loving, reposeful attention without judgment. The value of life should never then fall but to an individual pragmatic assessment based on economic value. Further, a Christian liberative theology of disability will challenge any sense of greeting morphological variation as deficient, since we all are made in the image of God as social, relational beings, capable of participating in the physics of love. A Christian liberative theology of disability challenges any insinuation that morality is visually obvious in/on the body, as if somatic difference made one morally questionable, whether owing to thinking it "God's will" or suspecting that "one gets what you had coming to you." And finally a liberative theology of disability will consider unjust the willful economic leveraging of the precarious nature of life, leaving certain populations exposed to conditions that disable.

The Basic Need for Liberative Theologies for Persons with Disabilities

Exclusion of persons living with somatic, neurological, and/or psychological variations transpires within society at large as well as within Christian teachings. Most pwds and their intimate families, in fact, find themselves outside religious community, not only because it often proves structurally inaccessible but because spiritual sentiments can be uncomfortably filled with paternalizing assumptions. *Culturally speaking*, a pwd must constantly navigate the discrepancy between onlookers' assumptions regarding our presumed deficit and our own sense of such as a social attitudinal barrier impeding our actual quality of life. While others want to fix or pity us, to rehabilitate or teach us, pwds want simply to get on with life. Unwittingly, onlookers, including medical experts, tend to presume to know what we need and so to speak for us. Consequently, the disability rights movement's rallying cry has been "Nothing about us without us," thereby reclaiming our ability to interpret our own experience.

Pwds are faced not only with discriminatory attitudes and exclusionary human architecture, but with poverty, unemployment, hate crimes, and domestic abuse. The Americans with Disabilities Act (ADA) took effect in 1990, and yet unemployment of pwds remains around 65 percent. Many pwds are self-employed, suggesting that either institutional and/or attitudinal exclusion remains prohibitive. The rate of poverty among pwds is more than three times that of the general population. Pwds with a college education are employed at half the rate their temporally able peers are; and professionals who experience a life-onset disability will not infrequently experience downward mobility, if not outright unemployment. Poverty and disability remain so codetermining that upward of 85 percent of those whom urban studies refer to as "the homeless" will be pwds.

Amidst cosmopolitanism, disgust can be one of the most frequently encountered barriers. Civic "ugly laws," again insinuating that boundary between civilized and other bodies deemed unsightly and therefore indecent, remained legislatively in place until the mid-1970s within North American communities; these prevented pwds from being seen or, especially, eating in public. Sterilization of pwds was carried out as an aspect of the post–World War II eugenics project. The Holocaust itself included not only Jews and gays but pwds. Yet civic revocation of such policies does not necessarily change cultural views of pwds as disgusting and/or ugly, as sexless or better off if so.

Since 80 percent of all disabilities are found outside the West, we must look at the economic, the ecological, and the political scenes that occasion impairment. These range from the human-on-human politics of war, gang or tribal violence, wherein disabling another, whether by machete or landmine or other acts of terrorism, is meant to humiliate the enemy, to the restricted food supplies occasioning diabetes among indigenous peoples, to the lack of appropriate ecological and work-safety protections in economic development zones. Migrant farmers and their children as well as those working in maquiladoras, sweatshops, and chemical production sites are regularly exposed, while simply trying to make a living, to carcinogens as well as herbicides and pesticides causing birth defects. The same holds true for those working in or living in the buffer zones of nuclear power plants (whether Fukushima, Chernobyl, or Hanford), chemical dumps (Love Canal), pulp mills, and nuclear test zones (Solomon Islands).

Theological Exclusions

Disability has appeared in the annals of Christian systematic theology to be the epitome of the "brokenness" of human and terrestrial life. While pwds do not think of ourselves as "broken," we tend to become within theological venues the proof of that systematic contention of "The Fall," the evidence of a morally and therefore ontologically corrupt world. Christians can then *mistakenly* try to comfort pwds by confessing that "we are all broken."

Metaphysical explanation of the "brokenness" of pwds, which always already depreciates our livelihood, can also become more narrowly focused, as normates look for moral causation for disablement in the immediacy of one's relations, as if disability were obviously punishment for sin, if not of the individual then of the generations. Or as if disability were, apropos of Augustine's interpretation of Jesus and his disciples' encounter with blindness (John 9), material debris awaiting another demonstration of God's power, since surely, at least in Augustine's mind, the resurrection promises our remediation to a fixed norm of nature.

Comparably, disability construed as "suffering" may open out the question "Why is there suffering?" That question itself diverts energy from appreciative acceptance of pwds into rational speculation. Within normate refusal to admit that the passages of an evolving world and the differing *teloi* of systems occasion general suffering lies human resentment at the conditions of becoming, resentment against life within the presence of pwds or, comparably, hidden when we are excluded. What theology in this classical, systematic vein has not been able to honor is the lives of pwds as consistent with the creative dynamics of flesh, as the expressive face of nature.

The so-called miracle tradition of the Christian gospels assumes as a textual hermeneutic the optics of modern Western medicine, that life for a pwd is nothing but pain, and that the body must be made whole in order to enjoy "quality of life." Western modernity, itself motivated by trying to reclaim the Earth as Eden, fomented a great divide between pleasure and pain, leaving Western culture consequently pain avoidant, even though pain informs moral sensibilities. Because we learned to dismiss pain as informing us about the world and because pwds were considered to be sunk in pain, pwds could not ever have an authoritative role in biblical text or in Christian teaching, preaching, or mission. Modern Christians could not imagine Jesus as one who might himself have been despised owing to his nonclassical beauty (Isaiah 53) or as one among the tableau of "cripped" spiritual authorities, extending from Jacob to Paul. Pwds were rather seen as identical to the paralytic carried on a stretcher and lowered through a roof to be laid before a wholesome Jesus for healing.

The constructed nature of this modern angle of vision, despite its claim to "realism," may come into greater focus as postcolonial literature (like Salman Rushdie's *Midnight's Children*) narratively employs the crip as protagonist so as to tell the story of life from the underside of empire. Comparably, disability figures in the gospels may speak more forthrightly from the underside of the Roman Empire: empires, as North American First Nations people likewise assert, can be bad for your health, even as empires use healing as an excuse for colonial trespass. Persons from the underside of empire may well be able to honor Jesus himself as crip, unlike modern Western biblical scholars, who look to him as "vital, pure and busy healer" of the miserable broken lot of humanity (per von Harnack). Further, the Gospels may not be as interested in medical cures as liberal Christianity, in concert with modern Western medicine, rehabilitation, and civility, has assumed. Maybe, as with contemporary postcolonial novels, those born under Roman imperial presence protested the economic capture and social captivation of life by volleying images of the vulnerable body (namely, the slaves' body as made deaf, blind, or lame in order to prevent flight to freedom), making a show of themselves so as to protest the hidden presumption of the disposability of bodies not counted worthy of life.

Enacting ethics with the model of Jesus as healer, religious paternalism presumes to know that crip morphology constitutes a deficit, and to act on behalf of the "needy." Here, pwds become but objects for normates' spiritual practice, for their demonstration of **conspicuous compassion**. Spiritual practice can feel good, because it borrows this morphological mapping of the superior over the presumed needy. The tendency of Western medicine as well as Christian theology is to rehabilitate the other or, failing that, offer pity, charity, or inclusion under the dictates of "the normal," again, a compulsion yoked to this culture's strong sense of natural order and its fear of chaos. From the perspective of pwds, tolerant inclusion, like hoping for miracles, attempts but to overlook our difference: given that our bodies are the condition of our liveliness, pwds are not necessarily interested in making our difference disappear. Pwds find our liberation when others, having worked through their own resentments and disgust, engage us as ourselves always already human and of value.

Conspicuous compassion: The optics of wholeness and the cultural presumption of normalcy can inform the spiritual practice of compassion to such an extent that the act of compassion actually performs or creates the boundary of exclusion. That is, it theatrically generates the dividing line between the presumed normal and those deemed "the poor, sick, and needy." Consequently, the performance of giving accrues as spiritual prestige or class status for the giver.

Main Themes and Methodologies

The centrality of the body to liberative theologies becomes more troubling when we turn toward liberative theologies of disablement. Our modern sense of the body as wholesome, agentially capable, youthful, and ever productive appears to critical scholars of disabilities as but an idealization, a hallucination. While feminist thought invoked "the body" so as to ground reason and cognition, because of the visual overdetermination of what counts as normal and modernity's preference for the individual, disability continues to appear as if it were a naturalized presocial given. Within a more interdependent social community the bodies of pwds would not, for example, appear to have "special needs." The same would be true if cities, transportation systems, buildings, and desks were constructed around consideration of universal access. A liberative theology of disability will therefore both challenge the religiocultural imaginary, as feminist Mary Daly did in relation to the purported maleness of God, and critique the injustice of social, cultural, and political exclusion of pwds.

Leading Scholars and Figures

Soon after the passage of the landmark legislation known as the Americans with Disabilities Act (ADA) of 1990, Nancy Eiesland proposed the first liberative theology of disability with the publication of her *The Disabled God* (Abingdon, 1994). In this early text, "disability" remains closest to the commonsense idea: disability is something that one has when one's body or mind does not work in tune with the ideal, biological template of the human body. Eiesland consequently proposed a disability theology on the model of a minority political identity, which assumed pwds need to be liberated from prejudice and unjust social structures, such as workplace exclusion, into human acceptance. In this very important stage, liberative action proceeds by way of cultivating self-acceptance, dignity, and pride as well as generating solidarity among those who have been "diss'd."

Eiesland reminded persons that the resurrected Jesus appeared to his disciples as identifiable by his wounds, making pwds no less than of the same nature as God. Eiesland's theology remembers Jesus as one who shares the experience of pain and rejection, who is recognizable as scarred by life with the world. That Christic image may not be so distinct from the image of the "suffering slave-servant" (Isaiah 53) informing the Gospels' early representation of Jesus or, today, of Dalit theology, the theology of India's Untouchables. Eiesland's most radical offering may be her vision of God in a sip-puff wheelchair, an image of divine vulnerability as affectively challenging as Mary Daly's refusal of God as male patriarch. This appreciation of vulnerability with and to the world occasions a rethinking of who can be admitted for ordination into Christian ministry. Disability was often used as a justified exclusion for ministerial candidacy insomuch as wholeness, meaning an intact and normate body, was considered representative of God.

Taking up the work of a liberative theology for persons with disabilities by assuming the social construction of reality, thereby challenging culture's construction of **ableism**, wholeness, and "the natural body," have been Deborah Creamer, Thomas Reynolds, and myself, Sharon Betcher. In her *Disability and Christian Theology* (2009), Creamer, while not ignoring pwds as a minority identity, proposed "the limits model" to redress the false distinction between capacity and incapacity. All persons enjoy capaciousness, and all persons also experience limits. Creamer's attention to this shared sense of limitations, given all of us at points in our day enjoy assistive technologies, from glasses to medications to elevators and curb cuts accommodating briefcases and strollers as much as wheelchairs, puts disability on a continuum of human experience. Limitation is a completely unremarkable aspect of what it means to be human.

Ableism: Ableism, like sexism and racism, names attitudes, beliefs, and practices that foster discrimination. Ableist presumptions tend implicitly to rest on a sense of the normal or an assumption about the species typical—as if a body were necessarily energetic, vital, and whole. Ableism assumes the experience of disability to be a deficit and therefore makes normalizing assumptions and/or riddles speech with exclusionary assumptions—as, for example, when describing something as a "lame" idea or, now in religious terms, speaking of others as "deaf" to the Word of God.

"Disability" is not a shared experience, but a shared oppression. The experience of what culture marginalizes as "disability" is incredibly singular and particular. None of us as pwds have, phenomenologically speaking, the same experience of the world. This also influences how we write and think as liberative theologians and scholars of disability. Even as the following distinctions still overly homogenize our experiences, being aware of some of these perspectival divergences can be helpful in reading and engaging pwds. The situation giving rise to a particular variation of the flesh, whether congenital or life-onset, is one of the key differences among us. If one is born with a particular body, a pwd may not resonate with notions of "atypical" functioning. In that situation, what others view as morphological diversity is simply the condition of one's liveliness. It is not necessarily experienced as "loss" or "tragic." Those with stigmatic impairments will have a different relationship with cultural institutions than those with hidden illnesses such as chronic fatigue or depression. Neurodiverse engagements with culture, as lived by Temple Grandin for example, will provide different views on the world than those pwds with mobility or morphological variations. And "the able-disabled" will bring forward distinct issues from those who are considered profoundly disabled. Deaf culture does even not think in terms of impairment, seeing itself as a unique and distinct culture.

How shall we speak inclusively? Language itself can be one way in which habits of consciousness and attitudes are shaped and transmitted. The "disabled" or "handicapped," like terms of specificity, for example, "the blind" or "the deaf," sink personhood inside a singular somatic or mental characteristic, making that the whole truth of a life. Such terms are projected disqualifications that subsume one's entire person. Today we speak in "people-first" terms, such as "persons with disabilities." Admittedly cumbersome and still focused on the individual and not the social policy or architectural structures that hinder our lives, the term does, nonetheless, insist upon our shared humanity.

In *Vulnerable Communion* (2008), Reynolds revisits our understanding of the basic nature of being human, focusing upon the vulnerability with which each of us is born. Reynolds challenges persons to amend their sense of the human-rights agenda so as to build into this notion of "rights," protective of the singular individual, relational responsibility. Further, Reynolds brings Christian theological reflection on the communal and interdependent nature of life to bear on liberalism's self-sufficient individual. Wholeness, Reynolds claims, is not a statement about the individual, but the product of a genuinely inclusive community that justly tends one another's vulnerabilities by practicing divine hospitality.

In my own work, *Spirit and the Politics of Disablement* (2007), I look back at culture through critical disabilities studies theory. By looking back at those who stare, I critically challenge Christians' desire to belong to the caste of the "normal," especially insomuch as that tends today to be a class of conspicuous consumers. Here the cultural location of disability becomes a locus from which to free up bodies captivated by cultural idealizations and other such spiritual delusions. Likewise, I critique those venues of theology that have absorbed such assumptions, especially Spirit as the agent of final perfection, of miraculous remediation.

In my recent book, *Spirit and the Obligation of Social Flesh* (2014), I work through affects, like disgust and pain avoidance, that also occasion the individual exclusion of pwds. Such affects, naturalized by majority opinion, create social-class chasms and shape urban geography. Given that, I suggest how Christology might be reconceived as a spiritual practice for carrying one another's pain, and how Christians might meditate with christological iconography so as to cultivate nonreactive love and to work through disgust. In this way, I append to the liberative agenda of redressing architectural barriers to inclusion the issues of normate affect, hoping to lower the barriers of fear and aversion in the practiced life of Christians.

While early work in disability assumed a sense of stigmatic difference, especially around morphology and mobility, and therefore dealt with exclusion remediated by access, Reynolds, along with Molly Haslam and Amos Young, and also Jean Vanier, Hans Reinders, and Stanley Hauerwas, have more directly addressed issues of intellectual impairments. Neurodiversity, autism for example, as well as profound intellectual and compound impairments, proves particularly intransigent to liberative movement, owing to the way Western culture prizes the human as the rational, logical animal. These considerations bring us once more full circle to the question of theological anthropology: What does it mean to be human? Liberative theologies of disability prize interdependent relations, our ability to love as a shelter extended over our mutual vulnerability, the precariousness and porosity with which each of us are born.

Future Trends

As we enter the Anthropocene era, when humanity recognizes itself as the dominant force of nature on planet Earth, our human future may depend on coming to grips with "crip ecology" in two senses. In one sense, outside the imaginary and economics of modernity, life appears mutative, not as orderly as our gardenlike, bucolic picture of nature would have us imagine. In another sense, as dystopian literature already has in mind, any number of us may live with what we today call disabilities. Climate change and epigenetic mutation, owing to plastics and other pollutants, do not stay cordoned in our waste zones but circulate through generations of human flesh. Ecology names an integrated network of humans-in-the-land, such that whatever we've attempted to throw "away" comes back through the bio-organic constitution of human flesh. Migrant farmers often are the first interface with toxic chemicals, but PCBs in fish and nuclear particulate know no boundaries of class or culture.

Given this, there would appear several forward trajectories for liberative theologies of disability: (1) revisiting cosmology as itself chaosmic; (2) changing our aesthetic vision to include the fluctuations of body and flesh over time and place; and (3) realizing that ecological practices that dispel pollutants cycle back as human-on-human injustice, generating swaths of social suffering. Most liberative movements have challenged culture's aesthetic vision. Think of the chant "Black is beautiful" and the "Campaign for Real Beauty," sponsored by Dove and Walmart, which aims to broaden appreciation of women's diverse body types. Morphological and neurological variance too can be lived artfully, not just in the classical sense of the body as, for example, of Paralympic athlete Aimee Mullins but also as seen in Rick Guidotti's "Positive Exposure" campaign.

Disability activism has focused on opening out the field of life to and for somatic and neurological diversities. During this same time, however, "health" has become the assumed measure of the good life in Western culture. In that vein, health can become, unannounced but true, the skinline of a new racism, a subtle dividing line between worthy over against wasteable lives, both in North America and, given economic globalization, transnationally. Economics constantly influences how we view the life of the body today, as employable, as a good consumer of culture, of when and how the body becomes a burden to one's self or others. In such diverse scenarios as reading a fetal ultrasound or living into old age when flesh expresses itself in life-onset disabilities, we are confronted with how to value life, with the fact that health is never a static state. At the same time, these are scenes riddled with the projection of disability as suffering, as experiencing low quality of life, as a turnoff to desire, as the opposite of health. A liberative theology of disability will straddle this divide, critiquing culture's definition of what makes for a good life.

Study Questions

1. **"Who do you say that I am?"** Through the hermeneutic of modern realism, Jesus has appeared as "vital, pure and busy" come to heal the "miserable, disabled wash of humanity" (von Harnack). This image of Jesus follows on a certain discomfort, already evidenced in patristic theology, with a biblical interpolation of Jesus, carried over from Isaiah 53 (the Song of the Suffering Slave), as disfigured. When Jesus, remembered as "vital, pure and busy," is set over against disability, then Jesus becomes the model of healing, whether in Christian mission or in the theaters of science and medicine. What might happen to Christian theology if Jesus were again thought in terms of Isaiah 53 as a cripped figure? This would be, in terms of image, consistent with postcolonial literature—such as the figure of Saleem Sinai in Salman Rushdie's *Midnight's Children*. What would it mean for you to relate to Jesus as cripped, to see this Jesus as *homoousion* or "of the same nature" with God? How might it differently inform Christian mission?
2. **"The blind see, the deaf hear, the lame walk . . ."** (Matt. 11:5; Luke 7:22). Given its place in the Advent liturgy and in hymnody, this headline from the Christian Gospels, a poetic refrain first loosed by the prophet Isaiah, continues to shape Christian expectations. Ask pwds how they

experience this persistent pinning of hope to cure (or is that "erasure of"?) our difference. Now consider that in the world behind the biblical texts slaves were often hobbled, blinded, or had their eardrums punched out in order to keep them from fleeing (see, e.g., the story of King Zedekiah in 2 Kings 25, where the king, like other captives, was intentionally blinded by his captors as he was led into exile). How might that history of human enslavement, itself the decisive history of the Jewish people, generate different meanings related to Christian hope for human bodies?

3. **"Worse than death"** summarizes a view of morphological, neurological, and/or psychic alterity as unlivable, as a repression of life, even, then, as worse than death. This dread of disability, projected onto crips, affects prenatal screening as well as the resourcing of lives differing and judicial mercy extended to those who euthanize children with disabilities. Yet this purported "low quality of life," as presumed by onlookers, even health professionals, is not necessarily the self-reported experience of pwds. Normates' exponentially escalated dread becomes the value basis for exclusion of anomalous bodies, as happened during the Holocaust, as may happen through genetic science and fetal testing, and as may have happened during the triage at Memorial Medical Center in New Orleans during Hurricane Katrina. Given Christianity's own tableau of spiritual authority refined amidst disability (e.g., Jacob, Moses, Paul, Jesus), what thoughts occur to you as a rationale for "conserving disability," as disabilities theorist Rosemarie Garland Thomson puts it? Consider this: Is the body perfectable? Is that a worthy goal?
4. **Representations of disability in popular culture**: Consider the image of Jesus as healer in the film *King of Kings* (1961), which presumes that pwds want to be cured. Notice the similarity of that miraculous remediation of disability to the pivotal turning point set at the heart of the ecological morality lesson of *Avatar* (2009): Jake Sully, referred to as "the meal on wheels" and carried through an overtly imitative christological passage from grave to *pietà* on the lap of the Na'avi woman, Neytiri, is resurrected into wholeness by transmitting his consciousness into the hybrid Na'avi body. Over against that image, consider *The Station Agent*, as played by short person Peter Dinklage, in the movie of this name (2003) as well as the quadriplegic Philippe (played by Franois Cluzet) in *The Intouchables* (2011). What might be considered the structures of oppression as experienced by persons with disabilities among this latter set of movies? And for what, if not medical or miraculous cure, do these persons hope? Considering now only *The Intouchables*, think about what the person with disability (here Philippe) might share with his French-Algerian caregiver, Driss (played by Omar Sy). Why are both considered "untouchable"?

5. Given that all humans are only ever temporarily able-bodied and that with increased longevity all of us can expect to live some phase of our lives as a person with a disability, **identify your own fears** related to living with a mutative, ever-changing body and/or with impairment. How might you, theologically speaking, address that fear?

Suggested Reading

Betcher, Sharon V. *Spirit and the Politics of Disablement*. Minneapolis: Fortress Press, 2007.

Brock, Brian, and John Swinton. *Disability in the Christian Tradition: A Reader*. Grand Rapids: Eerdmans, 2012.

Creamer, Deborah B. *Disability and Christian Theology: Embodied Limits and Constructive Possibilities*. New York: Oxford University Press, 2009.

Eiesland, Nancy L. *The Disabled God: Toward a Liberatory Theology of Disability*. Nashville: Abingdon, 1994.

Moss, Candida R., and Jeremy Schipper, eds. *Disability Studies and Biblical Literature*. New York: Palgrave Macmillan, 2011.

Reynolds, Thomas E. *Vulnerable Communion: A Theology of Disability and Hospitality*. Grand Rapids: Brazos, 2008.

Index